D1594769

Italians in Toronto

MCGILL-QUEEN'S STUDIES IN ETHNIC HISTORY
Donald Harman Akenson, Editor

1 Irish Migrants in the Canadas
A New Approach
Bruce S. Elliott
2 Critical Years in Immigration
Canada and Australia Compared
Freda Hawkins
3 Italians in Toronto
Development of a National Identity, 1875–1935
John E. Zucchi

Italians in Toronto

Development of a National Identity, 1875–1935

JOHN E. ZUCCHI

McGill-Queen's University Press
Kingston and Montreal

ISBN 0-7735-0653-5

Legal deposit fourth quarter 1988
Bibliothèque nationale du Québec

Printed in Canada on acid-free paper

This book has been published with the help of a grant from the Social Science Federation of Canada, using funds provided by the Social Sciences and Humanities Research Council of Canada.

Funding has also been received from Multiculturalism Canada.

Funding has also been received from Multiculturalism Canada.

Funding has also been received from Multiculturalism Canada.

Funding has also been received from Multiculturalism Canada.

Canadian Cataloguing in Publication Data

Zucchi, John E., 1955–
Italians in Toronto
Includes index.
Bibliography: p.
ISBN 0-7735-0653-5
1. Italian Canadians–Ontario–Toronto–History.
I. Title.
FC3097.9.I8Z83 1988 971.3'54100451 C88-090303-1
F1059.5.T68916 1988

To my parents, Jacûm and Nives,
in appreciation

Contents

Maps

Tables

Preface

One of the difficulties with studying Toronto's relatively small Italian community before 1935 is the scattered nature of the sources. No single depository provides the bulk of the materials for writing a history of the group and few newspapers have survived from the early community. I am indebted to many individuals and institutions. The staffs of many archives and libraries were extremely helpful: the Inter-Library Loans Office at J.P. Robarts Research Library, University of Toronto; Archives of the Roman Catholic Archdiocese of Toronto, especially the late Rev. James McGivern; the United Church archives; the Multicultural History Society of Ontario, all in Toronto; the Public Archives of Canada in Ottawa; the Library of Congress in Washington; the New York Public Library Annex; the archives of the Franciscan Province of the Immaculate Conception in New York; and the archives of the Baltimore Province of the Redemptorists, in Brooklyn, New York. In Rome, I am indebted to the staff of the *Centro Studi Emigrazione*, especially to Dr Gianfausto Rosoli, who taught me to be streetwise in Italian archives and libraries; also to the staffs of the *Archivio Storico* at the *Ministero degli Affari Esteri*, and of the *Archivio dello Stato*, and to the *Società Nazionale Dante Alighieri*. I am most grateful to the late Dr Giovanni Battista and Mrs Vera Cragnolini for generously allowing me use of their apartment in Rome; it made my stay in the Eternal City so very pleasant. In many of the small towns which sent immigrants to Toronto (i.e. sending towns), officials were very helpful in allowing access to available registers and documents. The Social Sciences and Humanities Research Council of Canada, the Ontario Ministry of Colleges and Universities, the *Ministero degli Affari Esteri*, the University of Toronto Ethnic and Immigration Studies Programme, and the Associates of the University of Toronto offered me generous support in the forms of fellowships and travel and research grants during the research phase of this project. The Faculty of Graduate Studies and Research at McGill University provided typing services, and Mr J. Critchley was very patient and helpful in keying in numerous revisions in early drafts of the text.

An earlier version of chapter 2 appeared in *Gathering Place: People and Neighbourhoods of Toronto, 1834–1945*, edited by Robert F. Harney (Toronto: Multicultural History Society of Ontario): 121–46. Part of chapter 3 appeared in a different form in *Studi Emigrazione/Etudes Migrations* 77 (1985): 68–79.

My greatest intellectual debt is to Professor Robert F. Harney, who supervised this study in its dissertation form, and whose enthusiasm first drew me to the field of migration history. His advice has been indispensable, as have been the comments and suggestions of Professors J.M.S. Careless, Raymond Breton, R.J. Vecoli, and Donald Akenson.

The staff of McGill-Queen's University Press have been ever cheerful and most helpful and encouraging. Philip Cercone first suggested I publish this book, Joan McGilvray guided me through all the steps, Susanne McAdam supervised the production, and Colleen Gray was indispensable with her copy-editing. Thank God for editors!

My wife and son, Maria Cecilia and Giacomo Benedict, have been extremely patient and generous during the revision stages. I am grateful to them as I am to my parents, to whom this book is dedicated.

Italians in Toronto

Introduction

Toronto has one of the largest Italian populations of any city outside Italy. While the estimated 400 to 500 thousand Torontonians of Italian origin constitute a smaller group than in New York, São Paulo, or Buenos Aires (Argentina), the 160,000 Italian-born immigrants in Toronto match their counterparts in number in those other cities. The vast majority of the city's residents of Italian origin are connected to the great immigration which followed 1948, especially the years 1951 to 1966.[1] Before the Second World War, however, Toronto already had a significant Italian population with three Little Italies, three Catholic parishes, and three Protestant churches or missions, numerous clubs and associations, newspapers, and ethnic city directories. There were at most about 15 to 20 thousand Italians in Toronto in this period – a fraction of today's community.

This book is an internal history of the Italian immigrant community in Toronto from the 1870s to the 1930s, the period we might call the prelude to the great immigration. Although it deals with the early Italian inhabitants of the city, it is not within its scope to present a catalogue of Italian pioneers. In this volume, I allude occasionally to what we normally call the "second generation," that is, the children of the immigrants, but this is not a multigenerational examination of ethnicity. I make use of a number of quantitative sources, but again, this study is not concerned with a demographic breakdown of this immigrant community. "Cliometrics," the study of history based on quantitative sources, has made great strides in recent years, especially in the area of social history. Although this book uses quantitative data, it is based on qualitative sources which are different but certainly not any less revealing than statistical data.

How then might we classify this volume? *Italians in Toronto* is an example of immigration history, or more exactly, migration history. It is especially difficult for Canadians to grasp the meaning of this expression. For almost twenty years now the country has been inundated with such terms as multiculturalism, minority rights, third force, ethnic roots, to the point that they seem almost interchangeable. As one historian has noted in a recent article, when it comes to studies in immigration and ethnicity, it is difficult to differentiate between academic research and policy making, between an historical interest in immigration and its place in society and coming to terms with the postwar wave of immigration and the resulting plethora of diverse, visible, and invisible ethnic groups.[2]

What is migration history? It is a field concerned with the whole question of migration in its historical context. Its interest is primarily the migrant, and it attempts to study the migration experience in its integrity "as a complete sequence of experiences whereby the individual moves from one social identity to another."[3] Although migration history is sensitive to the politics, economics, and social forces of the individual countries with which the migrant under study is associated, it is not constrained by the category of national history; yet, paradoxically, it is sensitive to the problem of ethnic identity. If we are to study the "complete sequence," our focus must be the migrant in his or her old world setting, the commerce of migration which takes the migrant from Point A to Point B, and the new world setting.

In recent years, we have seen a great growth in the literature on ethnic groups in Canada, in history, in the social sciences, and in fiction. These studies have reflected the reality of the polyethnic composition of the population and self-awareness on the part of each immigrant group, their consciousness that they are Canadians and yet distinguishable from other Canadians. The studies also have reflected the investment of millions of dollars, at all levels of government, into the promotion of multiculturalism, that brainchild of the Liberal government of the late 1960s, which grew out of the Royal Commission on Bilingualism and Biculturalism.

Unfortunately, however, the literature on the subject has also been, on the whole, mediocre. Although there have been some excellent studies on various ethnic groups or the concept of ethnicity, most of the work by lay scholars and serious academics has concentrated on individual or collective hagiographies, on policy making, or on studies on prejudice and racism.[4] True, some advances have been made. For example, historians no longer associate Canadian immigration exclusively with the peopling of the west. Although urban historians have become aware of the existence of immigrant groups in the city, they have not delved deeper into the place of the immigrants in the urban centre beyond acknowledging their presence in the urban context, examining generally their settlement patterns, or their relationship to political parties. Labour historians have fared better, especially in the 1980s. Now that the fruitless debate has been abandoned on whether class or ethnicity is the master key to unlock the mysteries of society, labour historians have begun to examine more seriously the complexities of the immigrant experience of the working class.

This study falls into the realm of migration history, but it also deals with the question of ethnicity. In the following chapters I will examine the background to the emigration of Italians to Toronto, their settlement and occupational patterns, ethnic enterprises, religious and institutional history in order to understand how their sense of identity changed with their immigration to Canada and, more specifically, to Toronto. In other words, the immigrants who came from Italy in the late nineteenth and early twentieth centuries strongly identified themselves with their hometowns or home districts. Yet, in Toronto they also came to identify strongly with an "Italian" community. To understand why this was so is the main problem this book addresses.

The theme of hometown or regional loyalties among Italians has satiated the recent literature on Italian immigration both here and in the United States. Yet local loyalty was a real phenomenon among Italians and most Mediterranean peasants. Italian bureaucrats, philanthropists, clerics, or journalists who visited Canadian and American "colonies" at the turn of the century were struck by the hopeless provincialism of their conationals in the North American urban centres. In 1904, for example, Adolfo Rossi, head of the *Commissariato Generale dell'Emigrazione*, an Italian governmental agency responsible for overseeing the condition of emigrants at the time of departure from Italy, those in transit, and those already living abroad, observed that the family ties of the southern Italian "are deep and tenacious; in their hearts they develop an attachment to the fellow townsman along with affection for their family. This is followed by loyalty to friends of relatives, and then to co-provincials. On the outskirts is the stranger, the *indifferente*, the man from whom the southern Italian instinctively shies away. A Genoese, a Lombard, or a Tuscan are as different from a Calabrian or a Salernitan as is a Canadian."[5]

Amy Bernardy, an Italian writer who travelled often to Canada and the United States, was also struck by the bond to the hometown that the immigrant maintained. In *America vissuta* (1912), an account of travels through American Little Italies, Bernardy asked: "What in fact have we in a Little Italy if not a series of villages, even if they are all gathered under only a few village bell-towers? The immigrants cluster around numerous nuclei and are polarized by as many leaders as the sum of the villages, bell-towers, and small churches from which they have come ... This disposition is a fertile creator of nuclear colonies and thwarts every attempt to expand horizons in people, to rouse them, or to change the moral order in their settlement."[6]

Early twentieth-century visitors to American Little Italies understood not only the sentiments of Italian immigrants towards their own regions but, more importantly, the stronger loyalties that tied each immigrant to his own village. They perceived clearly that for the emigrating peasant, the last glimpse of the village bell-tower evoked greater sorrow than the disappearing image of the ports of Naples, Genoa, or Trieste.

Contemporary American social scientists were also interested in studying the loyalties of Italian immigrants in North America. Robert E. Park and Herbert A. Miller, for example, in their well-known *Old World Traits Transplanted* (1921), emphasized the unity and solidarity of the community from Cinisi, Sicily in the East 69th Street and Avenue A district of Manhattan. For Park and Miller, internal jealousies and feuds were not signs of fractionalism but rather a continuation of old world customs, exemplifying the close-knit nature of this community.[7]

In her study *Greenwich Village, 1920–1930*, (1935), Caroline Ware contended that "it was only the experience of being in a foreign land which made many of the immigrants feel themselves to be Italians at all rather than citizens of the particular town or province." In both *Greenwich Village* and elsewhere, Ware viewed old country nationalism as a defense mechanism "against being treated as a 'Wop' – rather than as a positive manifestation of group solidarity." In another article, however, Ware noticed that the attempt to instill American patriotism in the immigrant provided the terms and consciousness of national allegiances and identification. She also observed that successful immigrants entered the general American community and "those leaders who remain within [ethnic] groups are thus often those who can exploit group consciousness for their own ends."[8]

This book examines an immigrant community in Toronto between 1875 and 1935. Although during those years Toronto's Italian immigrants came from a host of towns and villages, a few towns were especially prominent. Each townsgroup created its own socio-economic structure in the city to provide jobs, beds, prospective mates, and a circle of friends for its immigrants. This functional dimension helped maintain the loyalties of the immigrant towards his townspeople. With the help of marriage registers from the Italian Roman Catholic parishes in Toronto, city directories, and other reports in Italian and English, I have tried to reconstruct the inner history of some of the townsgroups and trace their boarding, settlement, and occupational patterns, and their influence on the identity of the individual immigrant. Then, through a study of the Italian and non-Italian clergy and notables, using correspondence, newspapers, business bankruptcy records, mutual aid society reports, consular reports, and other sources, I attempt to explain how, through their urban experience in the new world, most of the townspeople eventually acquired an Italian national identity.

This study recognizes that the immigrant, no matter how parochial, arrived in Toronto with at least some sense of identity with his region or nation. However, in order to develop a sense of belonging to a homeland or a people, a specific factor or series of factors had to precipitate changes in the loyalties of immigrants. The nature of settlement in the new world, occupational structure and enterprise, and religious practices all played key roles in forming an Italian ethnic consciousness among Toronto's Italian immigrants. The formation of an élite of labour agents, bankers, wholesale grocers, mutual aid society officials, and professionals was also instrumental in promoting an Italian identity among these immigrants. Historians of nationalism have advanced many theories on how a national consciousness emerges among the masses. Some elements appear to be common to the phenomenon – the growth of an intelligentsia asserting and using symbols of national feeling; the creation of myths to enhance national pride; the embracing of nationalistic sentiment by the bourgeousie or the élites and other interested groups for their own ends; and the use of monuments, music, and other media as agents of propaganda.[9] As we shall see, all of these elements played a role in the creation of an Italian national consciousness among immigrants from the peninsula in Toronto before the Second World War.

The process of acquiring a sense of nationality, however, should not be viewed as a struggle between national and local allegiances, but rather as one of expanding loyalties. The immigrant's identification with the Italian nation, therefore, can be viewed as an expansion of horizons rather than a forsaking of hometown ties. Yet another way of examining ethnic identity is in the context of two planes of loyalty, to hometown and nation. The immigrant lives consciously on both planes, and in different social situations stresses one or the other loyalty. Robert Harney has borrowed the useful term "chiaroscuro" to describe this approach; local and national loyalties are analogous to the light and dark contrasts in painting.[10] This theme of contrast between the two loyalties permeates each chapter of this book.

Chapter 1 deals with the old world the emigrants left. The perspectives of Italian statesmen and men of letters regarding emigration and its relationship to the country's colonial policy are juxtaposed with the informed "foreign policy" of the villages from which the emigrants departed. Each hometown developed the necessary socioeconomic infrastructures for the migration of its townspeople. The town's early adventurers selected destinations in the new world and training in specific occupations was emphasized to provide prospective emigrants with skills. Because the migrant's livelihood depended so much on the migration traditions of his hometown, he continued to identify with his townspeople upon his arrival in the new world.

The immigrant's settlement experiences also influenced his changing sense of identity. Chapter 2 examines the settlement of Toronto's Italian immigrants both in the three main Little Italies and in other locations. The chapter contrasts the settlement experiences of a number of townsgroups which came to the city through migration chains with the development of larger Little Italies, inhabited not just by chains of townspeople but also by those migrants drawn to the city by Italian labour agencies. In Toronto, the immigrant learned to live simultaneously in two worlds, in his townspeople's and in

Toronto's Italian community. A third world, that of the "Canadians," existed beyond the first two. Although some immigrants eventually assimilated to that world, they will not be the focus of this study.

Occupation and enterprise is the theme of the third chapter. Here the occupational chains of particular villages in Toronto are compared to the work opportunities created by the labour agents or *padroni*. The two structures eventually merged, creating a few "typically Italian" occupations – construction labour, tailoring, laundry work, and fruit vending. As the immigrant's employment became recognized as an Italian occupation by the host society, so did the immigrants come to identify more and more with an Italian community, accepting that the stereotype applied to them as a group, as well as a certain amount of segregation.

Chapter 4 is concerned with the attitudes and premises of Toronto's Catholic church hierarchy and Italian priests regarding the *italianità* (Italianity) of the immigrants. It contrasts their views and expectations with the immigrants' participation in the church, and their persistence in practising hometown forms of worship in Toronto's Italian parishes.

The fifth chapter recognizes that settlement, work, religion, politics, and worship all contributed to the formation of a national identity among immigrants. The chapter, however, focuses on the notables of the colony who strongly influenced the greenhorns to develop a national consciousness. The élite emerged between 1885 and 1914, consolidating the community and developing a market for goods and services. Its members used the terms of patriotism and ethnic solidarity to justify their leadership roles.

Chapter 6 was written as a result of the arguments posed in the previous chapter. It discusses how the Italian fascist consular representatives between 1924 and 1935 capitalized on the work of the élite in developing patriotism and Italian ethnicity, and in doing so captured institutional, political, and social control of the community.

This book focuses on the immigrants, not their children. Although it is analytical, it is also a narrative and covers the period from the midnineteenth century to the outbreak of the Second World War, concentrating on the years from the mid-1890s to the advent of the Great Depression.

Undoubtedly, an Italian ethnic group emerged in Toronto during the years under study. Although individuals or groups slipped into Canadian society, the book emphasizes the assimilation of various townsgroups to an Italian community in Toronto – individuals and groups who would establish institutions and settlements which would both welcome and launch the immigration of the 1950s and lead to the creation of the Italian community in Toronto as we now know it.

CHAPTER ONE

The Old World

Between 1880 and 1915, millions of emigrants left the Italian peninsula. The diaspora and its causes have been discussed at length by numerous historians both inside and outside Italy.[1] In this chapter I shall examine not only a generic Italian diaspora, but the emigration from Italian towns whose emigrants settled in Toronto in large numbers during these years. These towns included Laurenzana and Pisticci (region of Basilicata); Lanciano, Rocca San Giovanni, and Fossacesia (Abruzzi); Boiano, Casacalenda, and Montorio nei Frentani (Molise); Vita, Termini Imerese, and Pachino (Sicily); Monteleone di Puglia and Modugno di Bari (Puglia); Gravere and Meana di Susa (Piedmont); Terracina and Sora (Lazio). In addition, two clusters of towns prominent in Toronto will be studied: one from the region of southern Friuli and the other from the province of Cosenza.

This chapter also examines the prevailing views of Italian men of letters, bureaucrats, and academics regarding Italian emigration, and especially Italian emigration to Canada. Their views are contrasted with the attitudes of the townspeople regarding the diaspora of their hometowns. While Italian government officials believed that Italian peasants should work on a farm colony in Argentina or the Canadian west, the people of each town prepared their own migration chains to specific destinations around the world – in agriculture, or construction, or industrial labour – to meet their short-run needs.

Much of the information on the towns was compiled from a commission of inquiry into the Italian south and Sicily between 1904 and 1908 and from annual statistical records on emigration prepared by the Italian government in the late nineteenth century.

Map 1 Principal Hometowns of Toronto's Italian Immigrants, 1875–1935

The most important of the early "sending" towns was Laurenzana, situated about 150 kilometres south of Rome, 35 kilometres from Potenza, and at 850 metres above sea level. Laurenzana is in the heart of the Italian south, well beyond the town of Eboli which, according to Carlo Levi, was Christ's stopping place – presumably a region so miserable and desolate that even Christ had abandoned its inhabitants.[2] Today, Laurenzana has a population of about 3,500, less than half its total 100 years ago. The picture is characteristic of many towns and villages in Sicily and in the south, northeast, and northwest of Italy. Hundreds of thousands of emigrants left each region for a nearby city, another country, or another continent during the century following Italian unification.

Although each town had a particular causality for its diaspora, Italian statesmen, politicians, reporters, reformers, and, later, historians isolated several factors – rising population levels, lack of industry, unproductive land, scarcity of resources, high taxes, acts of God – often summed up in one word, *miseria*. Laurenzana, for example, was located in a district plagued with a sterile "clayey soil, malarial and terribly uneven, which cannot at all be transformed." The high altitude of the town produced cold winters with up to five months of snow. That is why the earliest migrants were shepherds who participated in the annual winter transhumance to the grazing grounds by the mild Adriatic coast of Puglia. A memo from the municipal secretary in 1902 to an Italian commissioner referred to his home area as "a derelict province" in need of drinking water, fertilizers, subsidies for paupers, and railroads (the nearest railroad to Laurenzana was forty-five kilometres).[3] In addition, Laurenzana was only a few kilometres from Montemurro, the epicentre of a devasting earthquake in 1857 which left its mark on many surrounding towns and villages.

Shipping companies were also to blame for the exodus. A debate among the Italian intelligentsia waged through the late nineteenth and early twentieth centuries over whether peasants left the country spontaneously or whether they were induced by the agents and subagents of the shipping lines.[4] Both sides, however, agreed on one issue – that the peasants were fleeing the countryside for the ports of Naples, Genoa, Trieste, or Palermo. Laurenzana had a population of 7,300 in 1881; within six years it declined to 6,200; by 1901, it had plummeted to 4,300 and by 1908, to 3,000.[5] In 1872 an Italian parliamentarian remarked to the interior minister that "the Italians are leaving," but few people would have predicted that in the ensuing years the exodus would take on such enormous proportions. Between 1881 and 1891 over 135,000 peasants ventured to, among other places, the agricultural colonies of the Argentine *pampas* and the Brazilian *fazendas*, to the sewer, roadway, and building projects of New York City, or to the railroad camps of the American and Canadian wests. In 1906 alone 787,977 emigrants left the peninsula. In 1913 the figure reached an alarming 872,598. Between 1896 and 1915 about

16 million Italians went off elsewhere in search of a better livelihood, either permanently or for a season or two. Only about one-third to one-half of these men and women eventually repatriated.[6]

From the late 1860s the increasing pace of the emigration troubled statesmen and reformers. They wished to bring respectability to the new nation through a program of industrialization where industrial expansion in the north would be funded by the rural areas of the country, which, to a great extent, meant the south. Yet, in the late nineteenth century the peasants were joining the proletariat of foreign countries rather than providing a labour force for the Italian manufacturing sector. The reason was clear: Italy had not prepared an adequate infrastructure to employ its prospective industrial manpower resources. Yet, the government continued to tax the peasants and agricultural day-labourers, the classes with the least disposable cash. Here indeed was proof that the *risorgimento* (Italian rebirth) had failed. Italy, the former (in Metternich's words) "geographical expression," strove to become a nation. Indeed its ultimate ambition was to achieve the status of a Great Power of Europe. Yet thousands of its peasants chose or felt forced to depart annually from their villages. The peasants internalized what they thought were the political lessons of the *risorgimento* and adapted them to their particular circumstances. "They had learned from the experience of the unification of the peninsula that a nation does not exist but rather must be created; and so they left as they used to say 'to create America' [*a fare l'America*, i.e., to make a fortune]."[7]

The public embarrassment of mass migration stirred further debate between the political Right and Left. The former contended that emigration must be contained or reduced, while the latter defended the civil rights of the peasant, which included freedom of movement. This tension led to a series of circulars and laws in 1868, 1873, 1888, and 1901. None of these official statements approached the issue of the peasant's right to emigrate, for emigration had become an economic necessity and a stabilizing force. Although a national disgrace, the exodus provided a "safety valve" or an alternative to protest or class frictions. In Basilicata, emigration was described "as a desperate strike of quiet collective protest." Lawmakers regarded emigration as pathological and they found it expedient to point an accusing finger at and regulate steamship companies and their agents and subagents despite town mayors' guarantees that emigrants would leave even if not "induced" by steamship lines' emigration agents.[8]

New emigration laws alone, of course, did not relieve the tension of the debate. Rather they created further controversy. Much of it centred on the role emigration would play in Italy's plans to form an empire, a "Third Italy." From the 1880s, the age of Prime Minister Crispi, national attention focused on Italy's need to expand beyond its borders. Colonial expansion would enhance national prestige by placing Italy on the same footing as the Great Powers of Europe. The colonies would also prevent national disgrace by providing a demographic alternative to emigration. A corollary of these objectives was that the *italianità* of nationals abroad would be preserved. Yet, especially after Italy's demoralizing defeat at Adowa in 1896, it was apparent that for some time, at least, a "fourth shore" would not be forthcoming. In fact, emigration continued and reached alarming rates between 1896 and 1914.

Instead of peopling her own possessions Italy was *colonizing* Buenos Aires, New York, Philadelphia, Rosario and its surrounding wheat fields, and the coffee plantations of Brazil. In the early 1900s, Antonino di San Giuliano, who would become Italy's foreign minister between 1910 and 1914, described emigration as a "national disgrace." During a visit to the United States, he proclaimed in the "Dantesque hells of 'flame and smoke' " that "while the other great and prolific peoples possess either vast territories or extensive colonies, where their sons can conserve the national language and the ethnic imprint in which language is the preponderant factor, Italy disperses to the benefit of others that precious force and ... will become compared to the others a nation always less important."[9]

According to those who dreamed of Great Power status, if Italy was unable to create her own colonies immediately, then she had to find some means of maintaining world respect by ensuring that her nationals living abroad should not "benefit others." The most sensible solution was to preserve their *italianità*. The politician and man of letters, Pasquale Villari, expressed this goal most eloquently as early as 1896: "Wherever the language of Italy is spoken, we recognize brothers, and wish to tie even more closely those bonds which Nature has created and which man cannot break."[10]

To maintain those bonds, Italian emigrants or Italians living in *terra irredenta* (unredeemed lands) such as Trieste or the Trentino region were to be instructed in their own language and culture. Villari's exhortation was accepted and promoted by others in scholarly journals or the bulletins of various institutes. One writer revelled in the fact that Italians in New York spoke to him "about their fatherland's literature, because they know the works of their Great Men from Dante to Manzoni ... about the monuments, cathedrals, the works of art that illustrate their homeland and make it admirable among peoples! New York has numerous such intellectuals, cultured Italian spirits. Their propaganda in the midst of the American element, will help, without doubt, to create more cordial, affectionate links between the two peoples, and between the two nations." Another emigration specialist voiced his concern that nationality could not be maintained abroad without a proper education in Italy before emigrating. The premises were evident: although the emigrants had found a niche in the American economy, they were still regarded as Italian subjects and were therefore to focus their lives around an Italian national, not a peasant, rural, or inborn American culture.[11]

A program to keep centres of Italian immigration in foreign countries as Italian as possible, however, posed some conceptual problems. First, many of the emigrants from Italy were illiterate and incapable of transmitting national culture. As a result, rather than creating a *Grande Italia* (Great Italy), the foreign ministry realized only a myriad of "Little Italies," literally, a fragmented dream.[12] Second, the political and academic communities became confused about a nomenclature for those neighbourhoods. At least the large Italian agricultural settlements in Argentina or even smaller ones such as Tontitown, Arkansas resembled Italy's aspirations for Eritrea or Libya. "Colony" was not an inappropriate name for such agricultural settlements, although perhaps inaccurate. However, a North American urban Italian neighbourhood – a Little Italy – bore no resemblance to the foreign ministry's plans for her prospective colonies, especially when the inhabitants of those congested districts occupied the lowest rungs of the occupational ladder as outdoor labourers, pedlars, or even more embarrassing, as street musicians or "Dago monkeymen." Nevertheless, these emigrants would not be lost to foreign countries, for they were part of the Great or Larger Italy. Thus the term *colonia* came into use well before the turn of the century to describe urban Little Italies. Until the Second World War, travelling inspectors, reformers, priests, and statesmen writing in various agency bulletins such as *Bollettino dell'emigrazione*, *Rivista di emigrazione*, *Rivista coloniale*, or *L'Italia coloniale*, and even more scholarly journals, referred to *la colonia italiana di* Nuova York, Filadelfia, Buenos Aires, Caracas, Sydney, Cairo, and Toronto. At times even the province of Ontario's Italian population was considered a *colonia*.[13]

The confusion grew even greater when the Italian intellectual community attempted to define the role of immigrant communities in foreign countries *vis-à-vis* Italy's colonial policy. The most powerful group influencing Italy's program of expansion, the Italian Colonial Institute (*L'Istituto Coloniale*), organized annual Conferences for Italians Abroad beginning in 1908. Representatives arrived not only from those communities on which Italy had designs – the Trentino, Trieste, Albania, or Eritrea – but also from the Little Italies of North America. Toronto's Italian community, too, had a representative at the 1910 conference.

In the same way, the *Società Nazionale Dante Alighieri* (Dante Alighieri Society), a cultural organization formed in Rome to preserve *italianità* among Italians in the unredeemed territories, opened branches in many Little Italies throughout the world at the turn of the century and later. Toronto's chapter was inaugurated in 1905.[14] Between the 1890s and the First World War, Little Italies around the globe were enveloped in the Italian imperialist program. Yet their specific roles as well as the official Italian attitude towards those "colonies," was never made explicit. While urban settlements were an embarrassing shibboleth of Italy's failure as a colonial power, those citizens living abroad, if inculcated with the mother culture, could enhance the country's prestige in Europe and overseas. On the one hand, the peasants in those "Dantesque hells" were Italian nationals; on the other, they were hopelessly parochial, identifying only with their respective regions or hometowns. Nevertheless, these settlements were still labelled colonies.

One of the areas some observers found increasingly promising for the future of Italian emigration or colonization was that huge mass which had confederated around the time of Italy's unification. In 1900 Canada indeed seemed a bright light to an overpopulated peninsula intent on expansion. That year, the Canadian prime minister, Wilfrid Laurier, spoke of a new era, "Canada's century." The Liberal government's interior minister, Clifford Sifton, had recently implemented a policy to settle the western prairie provinces with "stalwart peasants in sheepskin coats." The agenda for the 1900s envisioned bountiful grain exports from the west complemented by a strong eastern industrial sector. To ensure that products from both areas moved efficiently, a transcontinental railway had been completed in the 1880s and plans for a second railroad to span the country were almost realized. Even though Clifford Sifton had communicated his determination to keep Italians out of the country because he felt they were unsuitable for agriculture, and even though the superintendent of Immigration wrote in 1908 that "the Department is doing nothing to encourage the emigration [*sic*] of Italians," officials in Rome felt that in due course Canada must accept the nationals of a Great Power.[15]

Besides the occasional letter from early explorers and mercenaries, Italy began receiving relatively detailed reports about Canada from the midnineteenth century. Piedmont (Kingdom of Sardinia) had maintained a consular agency in Montreal well before Confederation or the unification of Italy. A Montreal businessman, Henry Chapman, performed the duties of consular agent from 1861 to 1869 in addition to running his private business. His short reports to superiors in Turin, and later, Florence, discussed imports into Canada, shipping, immigration, and general economic conditions.

Chapman was replaced by Angelo Gianelli in about 1870 in Montreal. In 1872 this Genoese food importer published a detailed thirty-three page political, commercial, economic, and geographical survey of the young country. He devoted a few pages of the report to the Italian colony in Canada, which then numbered about 150; 75 dwelt in Montreal. Gianelli mentioned his own fruit importing firm as one of the colony's important businesses, as well as Catelli's, the country's first pasta enterprise (before 1869, pasta was imported from France).[16]

It was not until the 1880s that Italian statesmen began looking to Canada as a target for their country's peasant emigrants. One report from the Agriculture, Industry and Commerce Ministry noted that "Canada's climate is healthy [*sano*] and the land is fertile and particularly adaptable to the production of grain." In 1881 Egisto Rossi, one of the most astute students of the Italian diaspora, published a book on the *Guidance of Italian Emigrants in Italy and Abroad*. "The country has enough bricklayers, carpenters, iron-workers," warned Rossi, but, "there is always room for good farmers." He gave no indication that most of Canada's Italian immigrants were either navvies on major outdoor construction sites – railways, dams, bridges, canals – or plying their trades or perishable goods on the streets of the country's major towns and cities. Rossi's opinion that western agricultural settlements were most appropriate for Italy's departing peasants were in step with general Italian hopes for the country's emigrants – agricultural colonies, albeit preferably in Italian possessions.[17]

It is not surprising then that political observers, priests, and statesmen in liberal Italy (1900–14) should have developed an interest in the former British colony. Here was a land in need of agricultural settlers where Italians need not disgrace their mother country by living in the cities of Montreal and Toronto. Rather, the peasants could honour the homeland by demonstrating their land-cultivating skills in Canada's breadbasket. Some individuals were opposed to Italian emigration to Canada – for agricultural pursuits or otherwise. One student of emigration, Paolo Emilio De Luca, for example, argued that Canada could not play an important role in Italian emigration because the country was looking for colonists with capital. Alas, because Canada had no Italian colonies, the peasants must learn English. However, De Luca argued that the peasants were illiterate and ignorant and unable to learn English, let alone accumulate capital. One need only recall, he continued, the disastrous attempt by Swiss speculators to establish an Italian agricultural colony in Canada in 1900 and 1901 "which caused infinite misadventures and misery for many of our emigrants."[18]

However, De Luca was one of the rare voices warning against settlement in Canada. Much more vocal were the individuals who promoted the Canadian west to Italians. One of them was Pietro Pisani, a diocesan priest from Vercelli (Piedmont), who had travelled widely in North America, visiting numerous Little Italies. He spent one year in Chicago and organized Toronto's first Roman Catholic Italian National Parish during a short sojourn there in 1908. Pisani, like some other writers, tried to persuade the Italian reading community that Italian emigration must be directed towards agriculture because of the squalor, filth, and overpopulation of a Little Italy. He compared the Little Italies to the worst streets of crowded Naples, with the added nuisance of hundreds of wagons, vendors' tables, buses, and streetcars. Although well-travelled and educated, Pisani betrayed his own parochialism when he complained that in addition to many Italian dialects, immigrants' ears must suffer "the horrible idioms of foreigners, especially the Chinese and Poles, blaspheming in every tongue." Not only was this a harmful ambience for the immigrant, it was also an embarrassment to the mother country, for "in New York they honour us by calling those places Little Italies, almost as if the Beautiful Country [Italy] were nothing better than the amplification of those miseries and that squalor [*miserie e sozzure*]." "Agricultural colonization," according to Pisani, was the solution, especially in the Canadian west and specifically in Manitoba. This was the essence of his two-part article on the Canadian prairies, of a second article on Italian emigration to North America, and a book exploring Canada's prospects for Italian emigration. In the book, published in 1909, Pisani spoke very highly of Toronto's Italian neighbourhood, indicating that conditions were much better among the Italians there than in Montreal or Ottawa. Still he was not persuaded that Italian emigrants belonged anywhere but on a farm in Manitoba.[19]

Other writers concurred with Pisani's views. A notice in *Rivista di emigrazione* in 1914 on the province of Ontario devoted two pages to Italian farmers in St Catharines, Port Robinson, Welland, Sault Ste Marie, Port Arthur, and Fort William. It reminded readers that "our agricultural emigration should not forget that Canada is an agricultural country *par excellence* and her future wealth will depend on the land; therefore one must have the foresight to purchase cultivable lands rather than lots for purposes of speculation."[20]

Observers of Italian emigration basically assumed that Canada offered Italian immigrants the best prospects for agricultural colonization. Some, however, were also confident of Canada's industrial potential and envisioned their countrymen among Canada's urban, industrial workforce, or even working in outdoor construction labour gangs. Perhaps they were encouraged by Canada's exhibit at the 1906 Milan International Trade Fair or by Sir Wilfrid Laurier's comments in Rome that "vous avez une belle race. We require good European arms; this year we need at least fifty thousand immigrants to help build new Canadian railroads."[21]

In 1914 Carlo de Stefani's article on Canada and Italian emigration assumed that his countrymen would do better as farmers. In addition, he noted that muckers would easily find work in mines, railroad, and canal construction, and in street and sewer construction in municipalities. Fruit vendors, bakers, confectioners, maids, cooks, and waiters, not to mention engineers, industrialists, capitalists, and medical doctors would also find work. Other writers also allowed for the possibility of their countrymen working in Canadian industry and construction. The *Rivista di emigrazione* referred favourably to Italian industrial workers in a number of Canadian towns and the *Bollettino dell'emigrazione* published numerous articles before 1914 referring to Italian emigrants' experiences in Canada's urban centres. After 1920 another bulletin, *Emigrazione e lavoro*, occasionally warned Italian emigrants about changes in Canadian immigration laws or labour gluts in certain industries.[22]

By this time, however, Italian bureaucratic opinion had accepted Italian emigration to Canadian cities. In fact, in 1923 the *Commissariato Generale dell'Emigrazione* (a bureau responsible for surveying Italian emigration and the conditions of emigrants in their respective destinations) opened an office in Ottawa which enabled emigrants to by-pass new, stringent Canadian immigration laws. The Royal Italian Emigration Society, through a special agreement with the Canadian Ministry of Labour, provided for the immigration of Italians into Canada for specific projects – in industry, construction, and especially railroads – when the need arose. The Royal Italian Emigration Society became effectively a labour agency. Companies such as Holmes Foundry in Sarnia and Dominion Coal took advantage of the scheme.[23]

Eugenio Bonardelli, an expert on Italian emigration affairs, was one of the early heads of the Royal Italian Emigration Society in Ottawa. Bonardelli, who had written extensively on Italians in North and South America, preferred agricultural settlement but then he also accepted industrial – especially skilled – labour. He perceived that a tacit hand behind Canadian immigration laws discriminated against southern Europeans, and especially Italians, just as an inborn prejudice among Italian statesmen made them look condescendingly on the rural peasant emigrant. Canada's immigration laws of 1910 threatened the future of Italian emigration. One stipulation barred entry to any immigrant belonging to a race presumably unadaptable to the climate or needs of Canada. Since special laws already checked East and South Asian immigration, Bonardelli concluded that the 1910 measures aimed at Europeans, and especially Italian sojourners. Bonardelli also took issue with the new law allowing for the deportation of members of secret associations, and men carrying dangerous weapons, maintaining that the law was a response to the Black Hand and stiletto scare of the period.[24]

Bonardelli correctly observed that while Canada wanted agricultural settlers, it was believed that Italian peasants were not used to extensive agricultural activities nor did they possess the capital to purchase agricultural implements. Both governments, Italy and Canada, were to blame for discouraging Italians from agricultural pursuits in Canada. The *Commissariato Generale dell'Emigrazione* in Rome argued ignorantly, as did Canadian environmentalists, that the Canadian climate was too harsh for Italian peasants. The Italian government offered little aid to overseas countrymen: only two Italian consulate-generals were located in the Dominion, in Montreal and Halifax. On the other hand, the Canadian government was unwilling to train Italian peasants and transform them into extensive agriculturalists. As a result, the peasants met their short-run needs as navvies on railroads and canals, sewers and streets, working six months and returning to their hometowns or the nearest Little Italy with the season's savings for the rest of the year.[25]

Bonardelli felt that the fact that so many Italians had become fruit vendors and owned shops in all major Canadian towns and cities was an optimistic indication that they would not provide only unskilled labour for mines and railroads. The country, however, must eventually relax its requirements and accept more nonagricultural immigrants as it became an agro-industrial economy. Bonardelli envisioned the future of Italian emigration in Canada as lying in that direction.[26]

The millions of villagers who left the Italian peninsula before the First World War, however, had their own sense of direction. Although politicians might blame emigration agents or lack of native industry for the heavy thrust of the diaspora, the peasants had developed their own rationale for emigration. A young man wishing to marry might need to purchase a home and a plot of land; a father might have to provide a dowry for his daughter to avoid the shame of having raised a spinster; another might leave for political reasons, to avoid military service, or even to escape a love affair gone sour; another might emigrate solely for adventure. These men had no idea about government debates over their conditions, about the statesmen's recommendations that they settle on a New Jersey farm rather than in New York City, on a Manitoba homestead rather than in Toronto or Montreal. In short, their motivation for emigration was usually the need for cash to meet long-run objectives. And neither did they have faith in the nationalistic rhetoric of politicians. When

Pasquale Villari asked Italian workers building the Simplon Tunnel between Italy and Switzerland whether they loved their country, they answered, "for us Italy is whoever gives us our bread."[27]

Yet, the unification of Italy, some scholars argue, was largely responsible for compelling the peasants to search for another Italy. The Historic Right (1871–76) attempted to create a national market and an integrated national economy by building and subsidizing railroads, canals, merchant marines, and steel mills. The effects of that program of economic development filtered down to the peasants in the form of higher taxes, including the infamous *macinato* or gristmill tax (abolished by the Left in 1876). To the peasant, the new taxes and the money-lenders were the two most concrete symbols of the new cash economy. The southern and northern peasants suffered the general trend of decreasing prices in the quarter-century beginning with the agricultural crisis of 1874. Steamships, advanced agricultural technology, and access to capital in the United States, England, and Russia made it impossible for Italian agriculture to compete effectively on the world market. To add to this state of affairs, natural disasters afflicted the Italian peasant. In the 1870s and 1880s, Italian vineyards expanded by about 40 percent in order to capture the market lost by the French due to the dreaded vine disease, phylloxera. In the late 1880s the same disease struck the Italian vineyards. By then, France had replanted many vines and had also won a bitter tariff war with Italy – a battle which especially hurt the latter's agricultural sector and rendered useless extensive capital outlays for replacing the diseased vines.[28]

These problems were chronic throughout most of rural Italy and especially in the south, among the towns whose emigrants would venture eventually to Toronto. Interest rates, for example, reached peak levels towards the end of the nineteenth century in the villages surrounding Termini Imerese (northwestern Sicily). A further problem was the lack of credit institutions in such villages as Aliminusa, where peasants easily fell victim to usury. In Alia in 1906, interest rates stood at 10 to 15 percent, very reasonable compared to rates of 50 to 100 percent just a few years earlier. Even back in 1884 in Alcamo, near the town of Vita, capital funds were available for aspiring small proprietors at the high rate of 15 percent.[29]

Most of the emigrating peasants were at best small landholders, but usually day-labourers who would stand in the town piazza every morning hoping to be hired by a land-holder. Their wages were pitifully low. One sojourner from Casacalenda who had just returned from Montreal in 1907 claimed that "before leaving for America, I earned £1.29 a day. [Between 1900 and 1915, one dollar equalled between four and five lire.] I paid £90 a year rent for the home: I simply could not get ahead." What he failed to mention was that even if he was fortunate enough to work six months of the year, he still must feed his family and perhaps pay taxes.[30]

Taxes were burdensome, especially as wages decreased in the late nineteenth century. One goatherd in Termini Imerese complained that taxes on beasts of burden were oppressive: in 1905 he paid £.50 on each goat; two years later the bill came to £1.10 – one-half day's wages. Much more severe was the *focatico* or hearth tax. Domenico Martelli, a peasant from the town of Isernia (Molise) lamented that "the peasant lives uncomfortably because he is oppressed by taxes. My family of six pays a hearth tax for all six members even though four of my brothers live in America, and my father is old." The town of Vita in western Sicily was divided into two opposing factions when these taxes were raised in the 1890s. Some townspeople charged that members of the party in power in the town council were taxed leniently in comparison to members of the opposition party. A petition claimed that the "hearth tax has become the most burdensome and odious tax because it is employed to a great extent for personal ends, for revenge and favouritism." As if that were not enough, town council introduced a heavy burial tax – the equivalent of two to three days' wages – for bodies transported to the cemetery in daylight hours. Ten petitioners, claiming to be "extremely poor," sent a letter to a commission revealing that they had been each charged £5.35 for the burials of their children – the equivalent of two to three days' wages.[31]

Eking out a living became onerous in the 1890s in Sicily and southern Italy, especially when the dreaded phylloxera struck the peninsula in 1891 and southern Sicily in 1893. Not only did small and large landholders lose the capital they had invested in the vines only a decade previously, day-labourers also faced severe unemployment because they were left with grain-seeding and harvesting which required 30 to 35 days of labour during the year, whereas vineyard maintenance and grape harvesting required 100 to 150 days. Not until after the turn of the century did Sicilians begin to restock their vines and by that time the labour shortage caused by emigration had boosted the day-labourers' wages by two or three times the rate of the 1880s.[32] In the meantime, however, vine cultivation and grape harvesting, two of the greatest sources of income, were not a possibility for the day-labourer.

Besides financial and employment hardships, the peasants of the south and Sicily had to contend with disease and epidemics. Malaria thrived in the valleys of Basilicata and Calabria and in the marshes and swamps of Sicily. One village thirty-two kilometres from Palermo was literally wiped off the map – everyone left that malarial stronghold. "Malaria is very widespread," the provincial doctor of Trapani in western Sicily, G.G. Simonciari, informed an investigatory commission. "More or less all the *comuni* are infected ... Mortality due to malaria is second only to tuberculosis." Disease was the final straw for some prospective emigrants but some diseases might very well have been spread by returned migrants. Almost every town in the provinces of Chieti and Campobasso, and in western Sicily, visited by a parliamentary commission between 1904 and 1907, reported that tuberculosis and syphillis had increased significantly in recent years. Many town doctors and officials placed much of the blame for the rising incidences of such disease on the repatriated migrants. An emigration official in the region of Friuli noted the same problem in the province of Udine. Giovanni Cosattini drew a connection between the fact that his province had the highest rate of temporary migration in the country with Udine's dubious distinction in 1896 of recording Italy's highest death rate from syphllis.[33]

Some towns were plagued by a variety of maladies. Dr Francesco Meanceri of the province of Siracusa (southeastern Sicily) reported that twelve of thirty-two *comuni* (townships) in his province "had serious outbreaks of traucoma." Twenty-eight of the townships suffered from malaria in 1900: 500 to 600 deaths were recorded in that province annually at the turn of the century, but by 1907 the figure had dropped to between 400 and 500. Siracusa was also afflicted by a meningitis epidemic in 1904. Most severely affected were six other Sicilian towns including Pachino, Avola, and Floridia – all of these towns sent emigrants to Toronto. Pachino sent an especially large contingent.[34]

Unemployment, economic cycles, infertile land, and disease certainly helped convince peasants to "seek their Italy" elsewhere. Other forces also drew them out of their hometown. Labour agents and steamship lines agents swarmed into villages throughout the peninsula inducing peasants to work at job sites in other parts of Italy or Europe, or to purchase steamship tickets for employment in the Americas. At first, information was disseminated by travelling agents and through the mail by steamship agencies to town councils. In 1884 and 1885, for example, seventy-eight *comuni* in the province of Udine, in Friuli, received steamship schedules from the Colajanni steamship agency in Genoa. Twenty townships received booklets and other literature from agents and subagents, including one of the earliest towns in the region to send migrants to Toronto, San Giorgio della Richinvelda.

In the province of Cosenza (Calabria), the township secretary of San Vincenzo la Costa (another early sending town to Toronto) received advertising literature from steamship companies. By 1887 agents and subagents were to be found everywhere. Twenty-one agents were operating in Udine in 1887; eighteen subagents were also trying to attract prospective emigrants. Twenty-three towns in Cosenza were serviced by agents or subagents including San Fili and San Vincenzo la Costa, both eventually sending many emigrants to Toronto. The prefect noted that all the agents in Cosenza worked for the Italian shipping cartels, *Società di Navigazione Generale* or *La Veloce*, and that they did not use pressure tactics with the emigrants except in some towns such as San Vincenzo la Costa. An agent was also found in another significant Toronto sending town, Boiano, and in five surrounding towns. Laurenzana, also had a subagency in 1887 as did twelve nearby villages. A perusal of the annual review of Italian emigration, *Statistica della emigrazione italiana*, reveals agents or subagents in scores of towns in each Italian province.[35]

Though acting in his own interests, the emigration agent proved propitious to the peasant. Perhaps more than any single person, the agent drew the peasant into the "modern" world by giving him the choice of remaining in his village or improving his lot by working outside his traditional pale. By doing so he made the peasant aware of alternative ways of meeting his traditional objectives regarding family, inheritance, or accumulation of land. The new possibility of choice introduced by the agent, who acted as an intermediary between capital and labour, brought the peasant squarely into "modern" society. Deference to the former landholding nobility or priest diminished. The new patron was not respected for his religious office or landholdings but rather for his role as a middleman between the peasant and a steamship passage, and ultimately a season's employment and cash.

The decision to leave was made sweeter for the peasant by tales of the profits to be reaped in "America" – a term that became a euphemism for El Dorado. The peasant was not always a helpless simpleton to be exploited by emigration agents; nor was he an idealist seeking freedom from economic or political oppression. He had an inkling of the economic advantages of working on the Canadian transcontinental railroad or the Toronto Street Railway gang for a year rather than waiting in vain in the hometown piazza for work that might never come.

The government commissions that travelled through the south at the turn of the century are replete with interviews of *americani*, the returnees, who compared their old and new world wages. In the village of Gibellina, not far from Vita, in western Sicily, a day-labourer in 1905 could earn £2.5 a day and sometimes up to £5 in the summer, whereas one peasant in the town reported receiving £5 to £6 daily in Louisiana, and £3.75 a day during the winter, a time of unemployment in his hometown. The town of Cefalù, in northwestern Sicily, near Termini Imerese, itself a significant source of Toronto's Italian immigration, had a range of wage levels in 1905 for the different functions of the day-labourer. Vine work commanded £2.10 to £2.50 a day; seeding £1.50; hoeing and harvesting, £1.24. In addition, the labourer received wine, usually one-fifth of a litre a day. A peasant from that town who had been to "America" for one and a half years reported earning up to £11.25 daily there. He managed to return with £1,000 in savings – more than he could have *earned* in three and probably four years in his hometown! A day-labourer in Caccamo, a village under the jurisdiction of Termini, earned £1.90 a day plus food (bread, food to eat with the bread – usually cheese – olives, and bad wine) or else £3 a day *alla scarsa* (without food). During the harvest his wages rose to £2.25 to £2.50 a day plus food. Before he emigrated a few years previously he earned £.80 with food or £1.70 *alla scarsa*. This labourer emigrated to New York where he worked in the construction of subway tunnels, eight hours a day for £7.50.[36]

In nearby Aliminusa (also under the jurisdiction of Termini), labourers averaged £1 a day with food or £2 *alla scarsa* for nine to ten hours a day in the winter and up to sixteen hours a day in the summer, including one and a half hours rest time. Two *borgesi* (small landholders) who returned from "America" in 1904 and 1907 reported earning £7.50 a day; they planned to return there once the 1907–08 recession ended. A peasant in Vasto (Abruzzi) in 1908 told a commission of inquiry that he had spent three years in America earning the equivalent of £8.79 a day: "There were 5 or 6 of us townsmen; we ate together and lived in one small bedroom. We worked 10 hours a day, on streetcar tracks ... With £2.50 one ate, drank beer, and slept. Once or twice a week we ate meat. One saved more than £5.0 a day." In other words, these peasants *saved* almost three times what they would have *earned* in Vasto. One interviewee from Camporeale, district of Alcamo near Vita, western Sicily, related an almost identical budget breakdown to the commission.[37]

Women's salaries were also much higher in America. According to a report from Bari (Puglia), female sewers, finishers, and seamstresses from the towns surrounding Bari earned the equivalent of £7.5 to £15 a day across the Atlantic compared to the £4 to £5 daily they would have earned in their home province.[38]

The departing peasant, then, had a fair idea about opportunities in, and limitations of, "America." He knew where his townspeople migrated, and that they saved two to three times what he managed to put aside in his hometown. He also understood that there were periods such as 1893–96, 1903, and 1907–8 when one did not go to America because of economic crises. The peasant also realized that emigration would provide a second or third chance when other alternatives had failed. Previous options might have included cash crops. In Termini, for example, one-sixth of the cultivable land was devoted to sumach, a plant used to tan fine leathers. Over one-third of the land was devoted to olive trees. In Susa, peasants picked chestnuts from over 2,800 trees in the 1880s for export to France where they were used in the production of *marrons glacés*. A peasant in Meana or Gravere near Susa in 1910 realized sooner or later that working in a tannery in Acton or Bracebridge, Ontario or as a chef or waiter in Toronto was more remunerative than collecting chestnuts or fruit for export to France. Similarly, a peasant from Termini or Vita understood that a few years on the Toronto Street Railway construction gangs provided a much more substantial income than cultivating sumach or growing olives, while licorice factory employees in the towns surrounding Cosenza would find it more advantageous to work on the railroad tracks of Illinois or Ontario or in a

Toronto tailoring shop. Emigration agents or family or village chain migration offered these alternatives.[39]

It was easy for the peasant to speak of alternatives, but until the late nineteenth century the actual departure was always difficult. More accurately, emigration was particularly onerous for the earlier migrants from each town or extended family – especially the psychological effecting of breaking with a traditional way of life.[40] By the turn of the century, however, most towns in the peninsula had internalized emigration into their way of life. Emigration guaranteed a cash flow which in turn ensured the preservation and enhancement of the values of the peasant's little universe, among them, a home, cultivable land to provide for a future family, and a dowry. Indeed, in many areas, emigration became the only means of perpetuating these values, and a young man who remained at home in the early spring while others left for their annual sojourns would be viewed as a deviant. In 1907, in the village of Alia, one agricultural day-labourer claimed that one normally worked only four months of the year in the village. The previous year he had found only three months' employment because of an unusual amount of rainfall. The only option in his village was to pick and sell wild lettuce from the fields and forests.

Eventually, the peasants of Alia would have the same choice as their counterparts in nearby Montemaggiore Belsito. There, when the peasants "have no work they gather greens; and when they can no longer live they emigrate to America." One peasant in Casacalenda declared in 1908 that in his town "the business fortunes of the few who emigrated to America were an encouragement to others, so much so that emigration reached alarming proportions, and thus peasants, artisans, and finally proprietors of all ages took the road to America where they ameliorated their economic condition ... As a consequence ... one sees only widows, children and older people, unable to work the land ..." One of the men left behind in the diaspora from nearby Boiano, Salvatore Ferrazzo, expressed the regret that "like me, all those who have not been to America – about 2/3 of the town – live very badly." In some areas almost all family members emigrated. In the towns surrounding Bari many young women went off each season to other towns in the region as olive pickers, wool-carders, or weavers, or to the needle trades in New York City to earn a dowry. Many towns around the city of Potenza (Basilicata) lost from 30 to 47 percent of their populations between

1881 and 1901. Laurenzana lost 40 percent. In the words of one observer writing in 1903, "the population today is literally reduced to the weakest and least productive: older people, the infirm, women, children." Emigration from Pisticci was so rampant that "a great extension of fertile fields remains entirely uncultivated because of a labour shortage." Clearly by 1908 emigration was not a sign of deviance or breaking with a traditional lifestyle but an accepted part of Italian peasant life.[41]

Each town developed its own migration tradition, usually part of a broader tradition of its district, which included the surrounding cluster of towns. Steamship and labour agents and subagents, specific migration occupations and destinations, the fellow townsman who kept a boardinghouse in the target city, the age of the migrant at his first departure were all part of the town's migration lore. Emigrants from a particular town might end up in a host of destinations but usually the streams were directed towards two or three targets. For the towns which sent representatives to Toronto before World War Two, the Ontario capital was only one of a number of arrival points and usually the least significant.

There were exceptions, of course. Emigrants from some towns had no specific destinations. Rather, they fell into the category of *girovaghi* or wanderers – pedlars, street musicians, performers, and the like. The knife-grinders of the Val Rendena in the province of Trento (Trentino-Alto Adige) had plied their trade through five continents by the time they reached Toronto around 1900. So had the plaster statuary makers and vendors from Lucca (Tuscany) who appeared in Toronto in the midninteenth century. The street musicians from a cluster of towns surrounding Potenza – especially Viggiano and Laurenzana – had played on the streets of all major cities in North and South America, Australia, the Transvaal, China, and even Alaska before arriving in Canada. The fruit pedlars and merchants of Termini Imerese, although not truly wanderers, were dispersed throughout the North American continent. Beginning in New Orleans in the 1860s, the *termitani* developed networks in most major cities on the continent and in many minor ones. The Chicago colony was the largest and the townsgroup in Toronto was, in fact, very much a derivative of the former. In 1925 Termini's immigrants owned about one-quarter of Toronto's fruit stores and constituted one of the most significant groups of *paesani* (fellow townsmen) in the city's Italian population. Yet, between 1901 and 1921, Toronto received only about 5 percent of Termini's annual emigration.[42]

Other sending towns which contributed to Toronto's population had fewer traditional migration targets. In the Cosenza area, for example, in 1887, 46 permanent emigrants had departed from Aprigliano (pop. 4,071) for Rio de Janeiro, Brazil and Constantine, Algeria. Fifty-four permanent emigrants had left Castiglione Cosentino (pop. 1,447) by that year; most of them had gone to New York and Chicago. Another nearby town which eventually sent many emigrants to Toronto was San Vincenzo la Costa (pop. 2,125). In 1887, 61 permanent emigrants from that town lived in Brazil and Argentina and in the American midwest, working on railroad construction projects. In the northeast of Italy near Susa, Gravere (pop. 1,366) sent migrants to Lyon and Marseilles as weavers, agricultural labourers, and leadworkers in 1881. One generation later the town population had dropped to 974 with 400 temporary migrants and many permanent emigrants (one-half were women) working in France, Germany, and America as waiters and labourers. When the *graveresi* began their movement to Toronto in the early twentieth century, they worked mainly as waiters, chefs, and short-order cooks in the city's hotels and clubs.[43]

Boiano's emigrants, who at the turn of the century would begin their pre-eminent role as jobbers and pedlars in Toronto's banana trade, came to that city after having established themselves in São Paulo, Buenos Aires, New York, and Duluth. Of a total population of 5,708, 170 *boianesi* were already living abroad in 1887. Before emigrating to Toronto in 1903, Liberato Chiovitti travelled from Boiano to Waverly, New York, where his uncle, a labour agent in the town, found him a job with the Lehigh Valley Railroad. At about the same time, Louis Jannetta arrived from the mining town of Hibbing, Minnesota. Fossacesia, a town in the province of Chieti (Abruzzi), sent its early migrants to Buenos Aires and Greece.

Pisticci's early emigrants in the 1880s were bricklayers, ironworkers, carpenters, tailors, and barbers in Buenos Aires, but by 1900 the major streams of outdoor labourers were flowing towards the eastern seaboard of the United States and to Toronto, the destination of many of Pisticci's barbers. By the 1920s, Codroipo, in Friuli, would become a significant source of building tradesmen and brickmakers for Toronto. In the nineteenth century the town's migrants were leaving for South America as agricultural colonists or for Germany and Austria as brickmakers, bricklayers, carpenters, and miners. The annual trek to *le germanie* (Germany and Austria-Hungary) had become the most important work tradition of Friulan builders by the late nineteenth century. Boys were trained in specific trades and thus prepared to emigrate at a later age. Modugno di Bari's (pop. 12,464) 1,000 emigrants in 1920 were mostly outdoor labourers in "America," in Chicago and Toronto. In the same period the diaspora of Pachino, in eastern Sicily, was directed at three cities – Caracas, Toronto, and Lawrence, Massachusetts. Zompicchia, in the district of Codroipo in Friuli, sent townsmen to the brickyards of Bavaria and Toronto, to the gold mines of Alaska, the coal docks of Vancouver, and the docks of San Francisco. One of Zompicchia's migrants, through a network of townsmen, tried his hand at each of these centres before the First World War, finally settling in Toronto.[44]

Vita, situated near Trapani in southwestern Sicily, was a small town of about 5,000 in the late nineteenth century. Like the rest of the region, the town's vines suffered the devasting phylloxera disease in the 1890s. As a result, the peasants left to work in the vineyards of Tunisia. When Tunisia's vines fell victim to the disease, the *vitesi* and other coprovincials directed their emigration towards America. New York became one of their primary targets, and later, Toronto, where the townspeople operated numerous fruit stores. However, many *vitesi* remained in Tunisia and Morocco. Emigration from the Sicilian town diminished as its vines were replaced in the early 1900s, but increased rapidly just before the First World War. The families in Vita probably followed the same patterns of families in nearby Marsala which also sent some emigrants to Toronto. Two or three members from each household would emigrate to America and send back funds to restock the vines. The mayor of Marsala estimated in 1897 that on an average day, £5,000 arrived in the hometown from abroad – the annual wages of fifteen to twenty labourers in the village.[45]

Many Italian townspeople chose Toronto as one of a number of possible destinations in "America." As far as the national politicians and the intelligentsia were concerned, a few principal reasons determined the peasant's decision to emigrate or choose a particular point of arrival. In reality, however, the reasons for emigrating were as varied as the number of peasants that abandoned the peninsula.

Indeed they were the sum total of a myriad of decisions and choices by millions of peasants from thousands of different towns and villages. Only a few citizens of Italy's political, industrial, and commercial capitals would have recognized the names of small cities such as Oswego, Winnipeg, Rochester, or Toronto. The peasants of the small sending towns, however, had developed their own cosmopolitanism. Toronto was a household word in the sumach fields of Termini Imerese, the fruit orchards of Gravere and Meana di Susa, and in the pastures of Boiano. While the Italian nation attempted to assert itself by conquering new territories and creating colonies, the townspeople provided for their families, enhanced their village status, and secured their succession by developing their own settlements in North American urban centres. The *paesano* in the Dantesque hells of the new world was not lost to his hometown but was merely sojourning in his hometown's "colony" abroad. Thus, unknown to most of Toronto's citizens, the city developed small but closely knit colonies of townspeople from Laurenzana and Pisticci, Gravere and Meana di Susa, Casacalenda and Boiano, Monteleone di Puglia, Ghivizzano (Tuscany), Codroipo, Terracina, San Sisto and San Vincenzo la Costa (Calabria), Termini Imerese, Vita, and Pachino, and many other Italian hometowns before the Second World War.

CHAPTER TWO

Settlement

The peasants who emigrated to Toronto from many villages and towns in Italy left their country not as Italian nationals but as people of their hometowns. While the unification of the peninsula and the subsequent period of consolidation instilled some sense of national consciousness into the Italian peasantry, the emigrant's primary affections and loyalties were directed at their *paesani* or fellow townspeople. These allegiances were not totally sentimental, for a townsgroup (or hometown group) met specific economic needs as well. The peasant ultimately looked to his townspeople to provide him with capital and information for emigrating from his hometown to Toronto. The chain from the town might depend on the goodwill of a group of townspeople in Toronto, or even on a labour agent from the hometown operating in the Ontario capital. On the other hand, a labour agent in Toronto or Montreal who obtained labourers from many Italian towns might be responsible for helping the sojourner to move to Toronto. Even in that case, however, the emigrant relied on his townspeople to get in touch with the network of agencies and subagencies which eventually would lead to a job and cash.

In Toronto each townsgroup developed its own community. This did not necessarily mean that each group lived on the same street or even in the same neighbourhood. At the same time, the process of settlement influenced the development of an Italian community in Toronto and of distinctively Italian neighbourhoods. This chapter examines the development of both types of communities in Toronto between 1875 and 1935, and, more specifically, the physical, distinguishing features of each community. Marriage registers of the three Italian Catholic parishes in Toronto and city directories were most helpful in reconstructing the communities of each townsgroup and the Italian community as a whole. With these two sources it was possible to trace the principal boardinghouses for each significant Italian hometown group in the city.

One useful way of examining the formation of a Little Italy and understanding what constitutes the residential area that bears that title is to examine the features which attract its inhabitants. In *The Image of the City*, Kevin Lynch argues that in order to come to terms with the confusion of the urban world, a citizen develops his own mental maps of what he considers the important locations or "nodal points" in the city.[1] These nodal points heighten the individual's sense of the morphography of his habitat. Later in this chapter a study of the nodal or focal points of some of the townsgroups in Toronto and of the city's "Italian" immigrants between 1885 and 1935 will indicate the nature of a Little Italy and some of the reasons behind its evolution. This approach will give some sense of the early settlement of each hometown group and of how the community as a whole affected the old world local and national loyalties of the immigrants.

Three forces should be singled out in studying the genesis of a Little Italy: (1) the precursors, the itinerant vendors and tradesmen, who established an Italian presence in the city. These included fruiterers from the province of Genoa (Liguria), plaster statue makers from the province of Lucca (Tuscany), and street musicians from the provinces of Genoa and Potenza (Basilicata); (2) the *padrone* system, that is the network of labour agents who brought many immigrants from diverse Italian towns and villages to North American industry, railroad, and other outdoor construction projects; and (3) chain migration, the mechanism by which the members of respective villages were ensured a job and lodging when they reached their destination in the new world. Each of these avenues was functional in helping the prospective immigrant move out of his hometown and into a North American city. By relying on a *padrone* or a fellow townsman for his venture, the immigrant placed himself in a new series of relationships. The act of emigration created immediate needs – steamship tickets, work, a boardinghouse, traditional foods, newspapers, a letter box, deposit accounts, and knowledge of the methods of transmission of savings overseas to the hometown. The way the *padrone* provided for the immigrants' needs shaped to a great extent the nature and physical structure of a Little Italy.

Midnineteenth-century Italian immigration to Toronto can be divided into two groups: early men of letters and soldiers of fortune until the 1850s, and northern Italian craftsmen and pedlars until the 1880s. Among the early Italians in the city were the Roman-born British imperial officer, Philip De Grassi and, in the mid-1820s, James Forneri, a Piedmontese professor of Modern Languages at the University of Toronto.[2] Northern Italian – mostly Genoese – craftsmen, pedlars, and service tradesmen followed them. The earliest among them was Francesco Rossi, Toronto's first confectioner and ice-cream maker who had been in the city from at least the early 1830s, at first on King Street near Bay Street, and later on Queen Street. By 1860, seventeen Italians lived in the city, including a baker, three organists, a painter, a street organist, a plaster of paris manufacturer, a grocer, a shoemaker, a boardinghouse manager, a picture-frame manufacturer, and a bird-cage maker. Some of these craftsmen were Genoese and lived on the northern end of Chestnut Street in what would eventually become Toronto's first Little Italy in the Ward.[3]

By the 1870s more Italian immigrant tradesmen had arrived in the city – a butcher on Spadina Avenue and Dundas Street, barbers at King and Yonge streets and on York Street; the Canessa brothers, Nicholas and Peter, Genoese brushmakers on Portland Street and on Yonge Street, and a plaster statuary artist on Stanley Street. A wire-worker, pedlar, and two butchers had also settled in the emerging Italian neighbourhood, as well as a Genoese street musician turned mirror manufacturer. The early Italians in the city, like other midnineteenth-century Italians, had plied the occupations learned in their hometowns around the world until they found a significant clientele in Toronto. Some of Toronto's midnineteenth-century Italian immigrants came to the city after spending a few years in London, Liverpool, Manchester, or New York. Some remained in Toronto, while others journeyed elsewhere in search of other opportunities. These predecessors of the Italian colony in Toronto did not comprise a recognizable Italian neighbourhood.

The early settlement of Toronto following the arrival of the Genoese was very much determined by labour agents in the city and elsewhere who acted as middlemen between Canadian capital and Italian immigrant labour. At least from the early 1880s Toronto was host to the *padroni* and their clientele of stonecutters, unskilled outdoor labourers, and railway navvies. The significant labour agents in Montreal, Albert Dini and Francesco Cordasco, who provided navvies for the Canadian Pacific Railway (CPR), viewed Toronto as an annex to their operations – Dini's brothers managed an auxiliary office on York Street. Nevertheless, the shape of Toronto's early Italian neighbourhood was still very much a product of their agencies and of the transient labourer's sojourning way of life. Boardinghouses along Elizabeth Street or Centre Avenue were filled in the winter with many navvies returned from their outdoor worksites. In 1897, a young *Daily Mail and Empire* staff writer, later prime minister, William Lyon Mackenzie King observed that "as a rule, a good percentage of them [Italian immigrants] are absent from the city during some months in the year," working on railroads near Hull, Muskoka, and Niagara Falls, on the Peterborough canals, or the Ottawa and New York railroad bridge near Brockville.[4]

When Italians began coming to Toronto in the last half of the nineteenth century, the Ontario capital was undergoing spectacular growth. With excellent transportation links and as capital of the province, Toronto rapidly became a leading commercial, financial, and small manufacturing centre. Small labour-intensive craft shops were giving way to more concentrated enterprises, although many small craft shops continued to operate during this period of transition.

As the city developed an industrial base and absorbed a growing population, it was segregated into a number of zones. Much of the large industry – breweries, distilleries, and some metal manufactories – located in the southeast end of the city, especially on the lakefront and just west of the downtown commercial district, along Niagara or Portland Streets. Late in the century meatpacking firms were established in the West Toronto Junction and on Niagara Street. As well, some large factories appeared in the suburbs. The Toronto Carpet Mfg. Co., for example, opened in Parkdale in the west end in 1899, and Canada Foundry (later Canadian General Electric) completed construction of its massive premises at Dufferin Street and Davenport Avenue in 1905. The warehouse area and markets were located along Front and Colborne streets, and by the late nineteenth century the commercial district had extended from Front Street to King Street and was edging northward. Most residential neighbourhoods were located between Gerrard and Bloor streets and some upper- and middleclass suburbs developed in Yorkville and Forest Hill, just north of the city. The Toronto Railway Com-

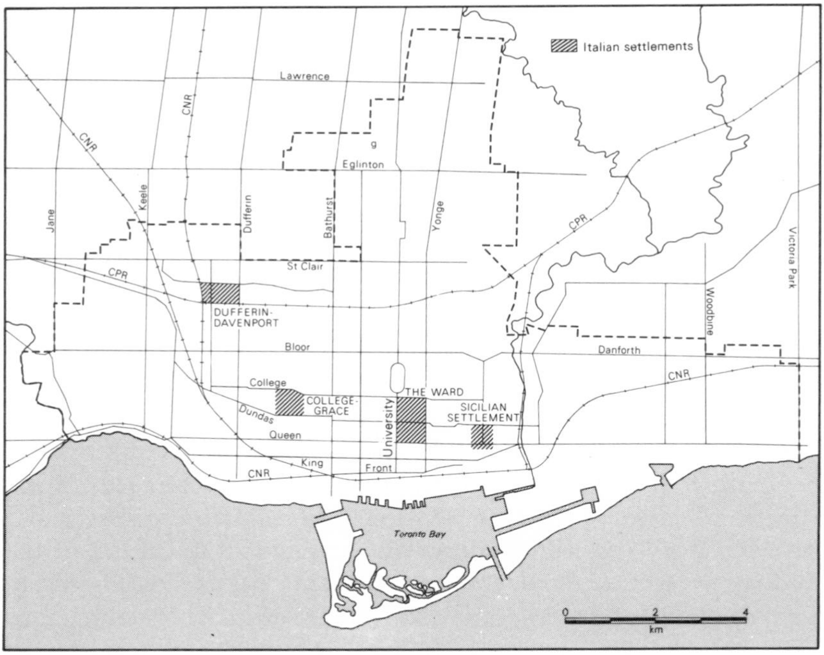

Map 2 Italian Settlements in Toronto Before 1940

pany, founded in 1891, gave the upper classes easy access to their suburban homes. Many of the working-class immigrants from Britain and continental Europe lived below Gerrard Street well into the twentieth century, near the industrial areas of the east end – in Cabbagetown and in the city's prime immigrant receiving quarters, the Ward.[5]

The Ward, bounded by Queen Street West, University Avenue, College and Yonge streets, was a convenient location for the city's early immigrants (see map 3). Located in the southern end of the St John's Ward, in the late nineteenth century this "Alsatia and St Giles of Toronto" was the largest and most populated residential zone south of Gerrard Street. From the midnineteenth century until the 1930s that neighbourhood housed successive waves of immigrants from the British Isles, continental Europe, the United States, and rural Ontario. From the early Scots, Scotch-Irish, and English, white and black Americans, to the later Germans, Polish and Rumanian Jews, Italians, Norwegians, Poles, and Ukrainians, most residents of the Ward were either artisans, small merchants, or were involved in the service trades. The Ward lay on a path directly north of the arrival points of the immigrants – the Great Western Station at the foot of Yonge Street and Union Station, at the Esplanade and Simcoe Street. The boardinghouses, operated by labour agents and grocers of various nationalities, formed a continuous trail along York Street from the railroad stations to the Ward. By the 1910s, well over half of the area consisted of East European Jews, while Italians made up over 10 percent of the inhabitants.[6]

Although the neighbourhood was teeming with activity and the composition of its population was exotic, it also betrayed the ills of overcrowding. In 1897, Mackenzie King reported in one of his early assignments, "Foreigners Who Live in Toronto," that among Italians in the Ward, "two or three families in one house is not uncommon when times are hard." King added that although "in grouping so closely together they have maintained the reputation enjoyed by their countrymen in American cities ... they are free from the terrible overcrowding which is evident in the Italian quarters of Chicago and New York."[7] The overcrowding in the slum district caused by the return of migrant outdoor labourers from the Toronto hinterland during the winter season, coupled with the shabby conditions of the houses, created a fertile field for urban reformers of the progressive period.

Reformers tended to see the Ward on two levels: writers juxtaposed the dark underside of Ward life with an explicit description of the quaint features of the neighbourhood. In 1909 Augustus Bridle described the Ward as a "shoptown, the most cosmopolitan part of Toronto," but in the same paragraph he alluded to the "phonograph blaring at the corner ... to the shuffling, gabbling crowds and the flaring little shops." This two-tiered perception also applied to Italians in the "Ward." Emily Weaver, in a *Globe* article, noted the Italians' "hot southern blood and the too-ready knives of some immigrants," but she immediately added that "in the past, they [Italians] remind us, Italians – Columbus and the Cabots – have done great things for Canada." There was yet hope for these short, swarthy labourers who could not quite fit into the reformers' image of "sunny Italy" and its high culture.[8]

Despite the progressives' litany of shortcomings of the Ward and its inhabitants, immigrants – primarily Jews and Italians – remained in the neighbourhood in large numbers well beyond the first mass

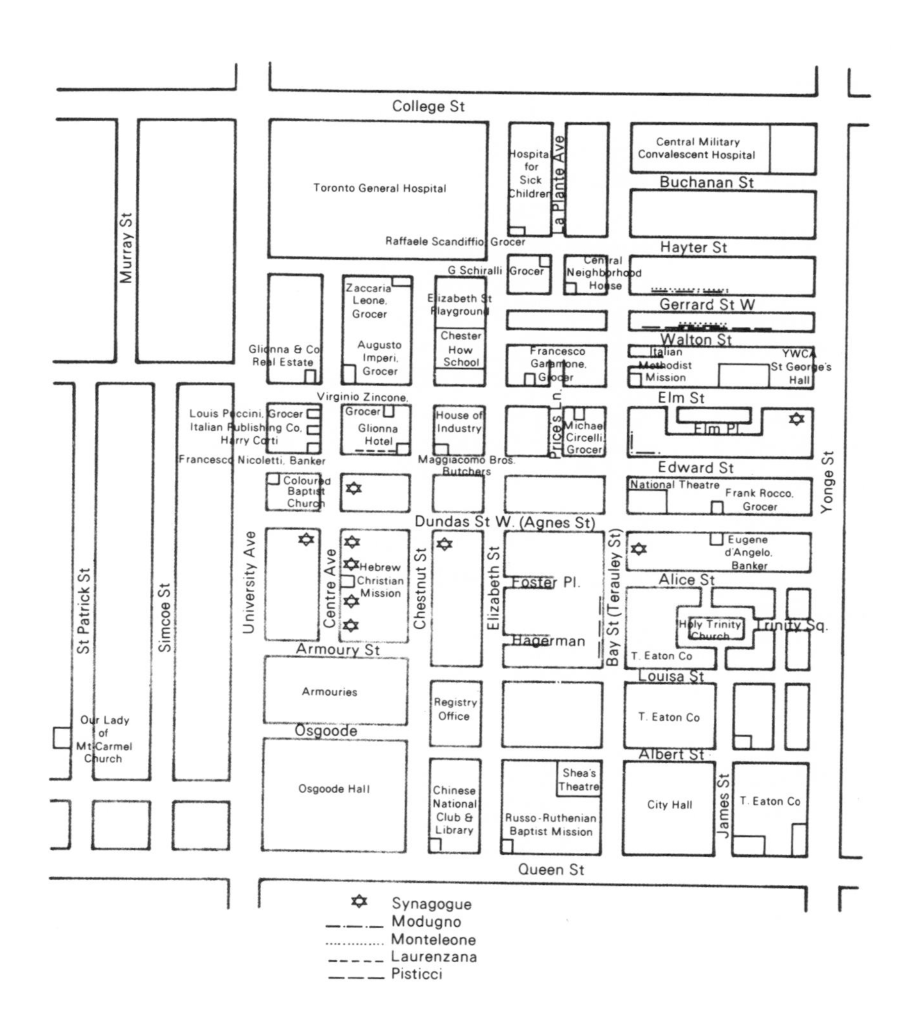

Map 3 Italian Settlement, The Ward, 1915

expropriation in 1908 for the construction of the Toronto General Hospital. The central location of the Ward made it attractive to the early immigrant. In a 1906 article on the Ward, "Evolution of the Slum," *The Toronto Daily News* argued that "every room which is situated near the centres of employment is eagerly competed for, and the landlord is sure of tenants no matter how wretched the rooms may be."[9]

The Italian population in Toronto's first Little Italy in the Ward was to a great extent settled by single, male sojourners from many hometowns whose work and lodgings were provided by labour agents. Toronto's two other Little Italies were also very much the product of the *padrone* system. However, in both of these settlements, less important *padroni* brought most of the early Italians from their own villages. Street and railroad construction attracted the early residents to those new settlements. Mansfield Avenue, originally Cowan Avenue, near College and Grace streets (see map 4), was a receiving centre for many of the destitute Irish in the 1870s and 1880s. The Italians eventually replaced many of the Irish, who had settled in that western part of Toronto. Almost all of the early Italian immigrants who took up residence in the area were from the towns surrounding the city of Cosenza in Calabria, particularly from San Vincenzo la Costa and San Sisto. The earliest Italian on Mansfield Avenue was Salvatore Turano, a grocer from San Sisto, who was most likely the earliest *padrone* and boardinghouse keeper in the area.[10]

Meanwhile, further north and west, along Dufferin Street near Davenport Avenue (see map 5), a new Italian neighbourhood emerged in the 1890s. At its western fringe was the junction of the Northern Railway and the Ontario and Quebec District line of the CPR formed the eastern boundary of the West Toronto Junction. Railroad and construction labourers, who worked at railway maintenance, sewer installation projects, and the macadamization of dirt roads, were the earliest migrants to these areas. In 1905, Canadian General Electric started production at its new Canada Foundry plant at Lansdowne and Davenport avenues. The surrounding land was owned by Canadian General Electric and, because workers moved into nearby homes, the entire area resembled a self-contained company town. After bitter walkouts at the plant in 1903–5, many Italian moulders, especially from Terracina (Lazio), settled there and replaced many of the strikers who moved to the United States.[11]

The annual winter influx of labourers before the First World War influenced the quality of life as well as the physical structures of the three Italian neighbourhoods, but especially of the Ward because it was the prime receiving centre for Italian sojourners in Toronto. The discrepancy between official census population figures and unofficial estimates gives some idea of the enormous impact of the transient

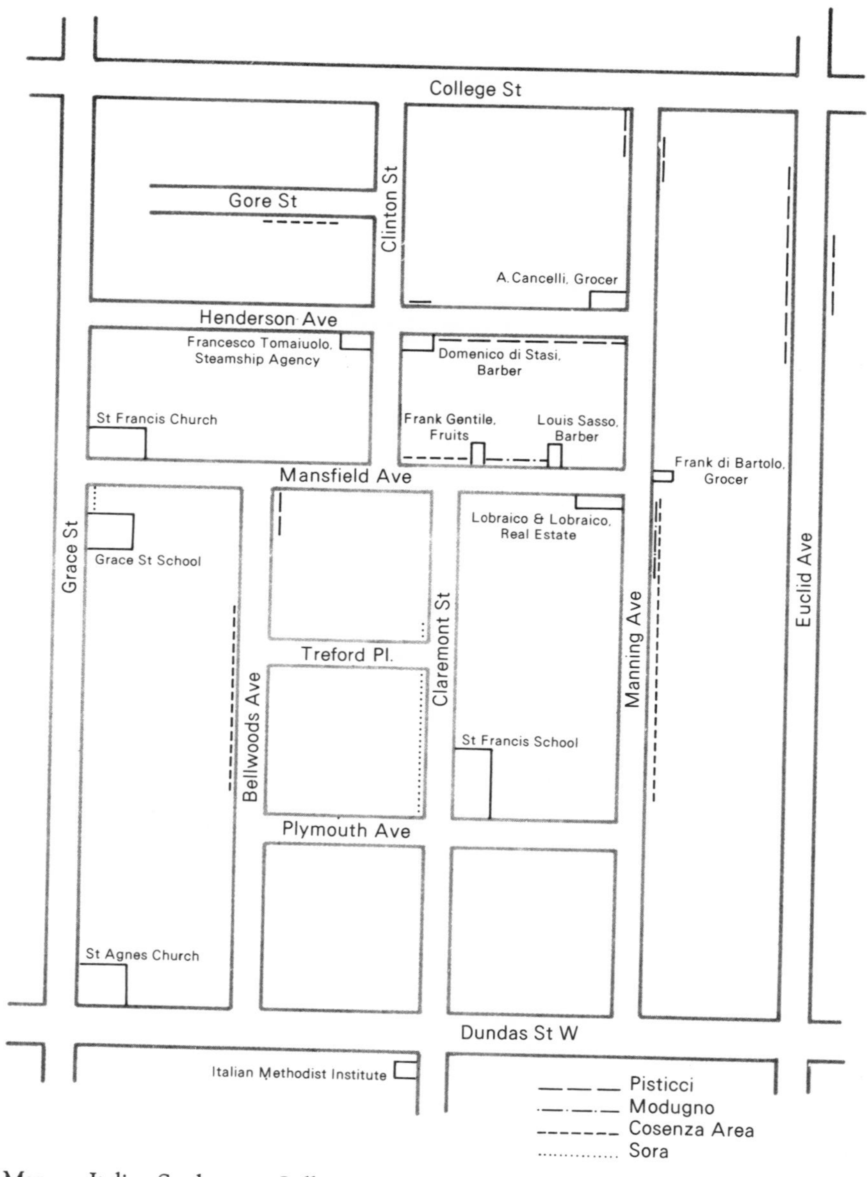

Map 4 Italian Settlement, College-Grace District, 1915

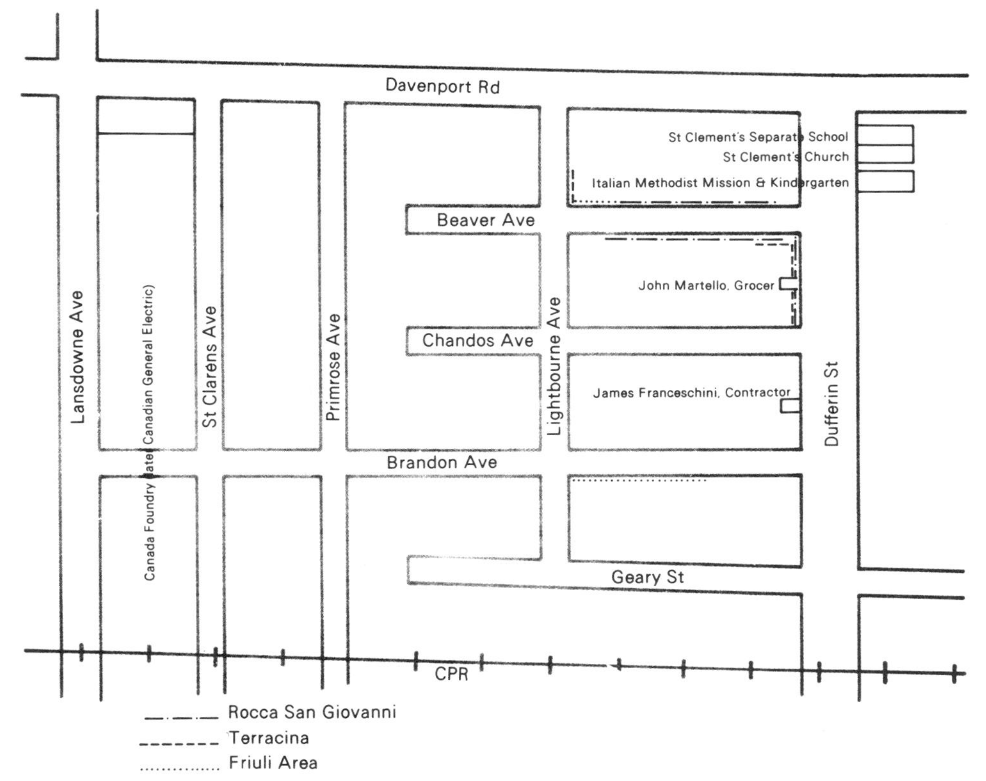

Map 5 Italian Settlement, Dufferin-Davenport District, 1915

sector on the Italian population. One travelling emigration inspector from Rome estimated the city's Italian population in 1902 at 4,000, only one-quarter of whom were permanent. In 1913, another inspector from the same organization estimated that 5,000 of Toronto's 14,000 Italians were sojourners.

In 1911, the census recorded 1,475 Italian males and only 609 Italian females within the federal electoral district of Toronto Centre, where the majority of the city's Italian population resided. Even in 1906 with the Italian population at about 5,000, *The Globe* "stated on good authority that the overcrowding this winter is chiefly among the Jews. Between 2,000 and 3,000 Italians have gone home to Italy for the winter, and in this way the Italian element is not so strong in

Table 1
Population of Italians in Toronto, 1891–1941

Year	*Population: Italians in Toronto*	*Toronto's Population*[v]
1891	570[a]	181,215
1897	750[b]	
1900	2,000[c]	
1901	1,156[d]	208,040
1902	4,000 (1,000 permanent and 3,000 sojourners)[e]	
1904	5,000[f]	
1908	6,000[g]	
1909	6,000[h]	
1910	7,000[i]	
1911	4,873[j]	376,538
1913	10,000[k]	
1913	14,000 (9,000 permanent and 5,000 sojourners)[l]	
1915	12,000 (6,000 permanent and 6,000 sojourners)[m]	
1917	10,000[n]	
1921	8,934[o]	521,893
1931	15,507[p]	631,207
1931	8,000[q]	
1932	10,000[r]	
1934	10,000–12,000[s]	
1934	10,000[t]	
1941	17,887[u]	667,457

Sources: [a] *Census of Canada*, 1891; figures are for "racial origin of population" of Greater Toronto.
[b] King, "Foreigners in Toronto."
[c] Church of England Mission, *First Annual Report*.
[d] *Census of Canada*, 1901.
[e] E. Rossi, "Delle condizioni italiana," 9.
[f] Methodist Association, *Italians*.
[g] Pisani, *Il Canada presente*, 38.
[h] Woodsworth, *Strangers*, 134.
[i] Weaver, "Italians in Toronto," 2.
[j] Census of Canada, 1911.
[k] Oranova to Boselli, 7 July 1913, *SDA*
[l] "Notiziario: Informazioni sulle condizioni," 74.
[m] Moroni, "Provincia dell'Ontario," 75.
[n] James Robertson Memorial Committee, *Non-English Speaking Canadians*, 26.
[o] *Census of Canada*, 1921.
[p] *Census of Canada*, 1931.
[q] Ridolfi, *I friulani*, 119.
[r] Napolitano, *Troppo grano*, 19.
[s] Crowley to Parziale, 6 Oct. 1934, Parziale Papers, AFPIC.
[t] *Toronto Star*, 6 Jan. 1934, 5.
[u] *Census of Canada*, 1941.
[v] Toronto's population figures are from the *Census of Canada* for the respective years.

the overcrowded districts as it might have been." The population was fluid – many of the immigrants were single males sojourning in the city for a number of years or winter seasons before returning to their hometowns in Italy, or moving on to another Little Italy on the continent.[12]

It is difficult to provide accurate figures on the city's Italian population before the Second World War. One of the problems with arriving at more accurate figures is the presence of that fluid sector known as sojourners. At the outbreak of the First World War, for example, almost one-half of the population was transient. However, if we cull most of the sources, which ranged from the official census to visitors' published estimates based on hearsay within the Italian colony, we can assume a permanent Italian population of about 9,000 just before the First World War. The population of Italian origin in 1935 was about 16,000. Table 1 lists official and unofficial estimates of the Italian population in Toronto, 1891–1941.

Not all the Italian residents in Toronto, of course, were single males. Some of the earlier settlers either arrived with their wives or eventually sent to the hometown for their betrothed. By the 1880s most of the *laurenzanesi* who had arrived during the previous twenty years were living not as single boarders but in family units. The same was true of many of the immigrants from San Sisto and some of the immigrants from Termini Imerese (Sicily). The influx of male labourers created many opportunities for these families in the Ward to rent out a room or two to migrants. Lodging and boarding influenced living conditions, the family economy, and family privacy. In 1897, Mackenzie King reported that "during the winter season there have been as many as forty or fifty Italians living in a single house on Chestnut Street." In 1910 another writer for *The Globe* observed that Italian women in Toronto cared for their families or even shops, "and often for ten or a dozen or even twenty boarders in addition."[13]

Almost every household in the Ward, and later, in the other two Little Italies put up at least one boarder at some point before the First World War. When James Mavor, a political economist at the University of Toronto, directed a budget study of forty-five poor families in Toronto in 1904–7, he examined seven Italian households in the Ward. One was composed of a family of five plus two boarders (labourers); another family of three housed eleven boarders in a seven-room house. One eleven-room house on Chestnut Street contained two families of two members each plus ten boarders. A family of eight and four boarders lived in a four-room house on Christopher Street (the site of the present-day Sick Children's Hospital), while a seven-member family lived with four boarders in slightly more spacious surroundings on Centre Avenue.[14]

The practice of placing sojourners in one's home affected social conditions and relations among the city's Italian immigrants as well as the family economy. The lodgers were a source of income to the family willing to let its rooms – two dollars a week per boarder at the turn of the century.[15] Renting rooms gave the housewife an additional incentive to work at home. The *padrone* became a patron not only of the sojourners but also of many of the families which kept lodgers as an additional source of income. The five or six most important *padroni* each managed at least one large boardinghouse but they could not accommodate the hundreds of workers they hired annually and turned to family-run boardinghouses, thus focusing the attention of a majority of the Italian population of the city on the *padroni*.

Because the interests of most temporary and permanent immigrants in the city were so intently centred on this small group, the newcomers from many towns in the peninsula became aware of their common circumstances and dependence on the labour agents. In the aftermath of the Messina earthquake in December 1908, some Sicilians and Calabrians consulted the consular agent, Victor Gianelli, for information regarding next-of-kin in Italy. However, to achieve results, "a meeting of Italians was held in the office of Dini Bros., York Street, where a cable message addressed to the mayors of the five different cities of Calabria and Messina asking ... for information was sent off."[16] In moments of crisis or need such as the Messina earthquake, Italians turned to their *padroni* for aid or direction. This shared experience of dependence was translated by the immigrants into a shared identity and helped prepare the basis for the development of a Toronto-Italian identity.

From the 1870s until the Second World War, many, perhaps most Italian immigrants, came to Toronto through migration chains from their respective hometowns or with the help of a labour agent from the hometown living in Toronto. Others were brought to the city under the auspices of one of the important Italian *padroni* in Toronto, either directly or after having sojourned in other work camps or Little Italies on the continent. Once in Toronto they continued to identify with their townspeople living in the city. These *paesani*, however, also had allegiances to the mother country, and upon their arrival in North America they felt some affinity to other immigrants from the peninsula, as opposed to other British or eastern European immigrants. If nothing else, the simple condition of living outside their hometown disposed them to associate with other Italians in the city.

Between 1875 and 1935 immigrants from the various Italian hometowns came to identify with an Italian immigrant population and to a great extent, as we have indicated, the *padrone* system was responsible for that. The important *padroni* in Toronto from the 1880s and earlier did not recruit workers from a single Italian hometown; usually they depended on a North American network of labour agents to supply them with navvies when the need arose. At the turn of the century, Albert Dini and Francesco Cordasco in Montreal received their men from agents in Boston, Portland (Maine), Philadelphia, and New York. James Palma of Toronto acquired his labourers from Buffalo and Chicago and other American cities in the late 1880s. Others came from Pittsburgh. Rocco Perretta, a labour agent from Laurenzana (Basilicata) living in Utica, also sent workers to Toronto.[17] The labourers came from a myriad of villages and hometowns in Italy but were all thrust into the same economic process controlled by middlemen. Navvies from different towns worked together during the open season on job sites, ate meals in common, joined in protest against their employers, showed respect or deference to the same *padroni*. The sojourning experience gave many of the *paesani* their first glimpse of "other" Italians.

Upon their return to Toronto in the winter, the sojourners lived and worked with other immigrants from different hometowns who had arrived in the city through the migration chains of their respective hometowns or through *padroni*. More important, the annual winter re-entry created the first truly Italian physical focal points of the emerging community: the boardinghouses owned by labour agents – those of James Palma on Elizabeth Street in the 1880s; the Glionna Hotel on Chestnut and Edward streets, built in 1885 by Francesco Glionna; Michael Basso's grocery store on Chestnut Street in the 1880s and 1890s; Albert Dini's agency on York Street after 1900; Francesco Nicoletti's, Giuseppe Izzo's, or the Trentadue brothers' agencies, all on the corners at Centre Avenue and Elm Street, between 1900 and 1915. That street crossing remained the commercial centre of Toronto's Italian community until the early 1930s. Glionna's hotel was also the first saloon for Italian sojourners in Toronto. Salvatore Turano's grocery store on Mansfield Avenue was the earliest boardinghouse and agency in the College Street and Grace Street Little Italy. Before 1910, John Martello, a grocer from Lanciano (Abruzzi), ran a boardinghouse on Dufferin Street near Davenport Avenue for moulders and labourers from his hometown who worked at Canada Foundry.

These large boardinghouses owned by labour agents and/or grocers, and the large labour agencies, such as Glionna's saloon, were the first outward signs of a Little Italy and the only physical structures of Toronto's Italian community until after the turn of the century. These functional "nodal" points became the visible focal points of the Italian community for the sojourners who wintered in Toronto, the permanent Italian residents of the city and "outsiders." As important components of the immigrant's mental map of Toronto, to a great extent they influenced the newcomers from the various hometowns of the peninsula to develop an Italian immigrant identity in the city.[18]

The patterns of settlement of the permanent residents of Toronto's Italian population, however, were a function not only of the *padrone* system, but also of the migration chains from specific villages. Some of the chains in fact depended on minor labour agents such as John Martello of Lanciano or Salvatore Turano of San Sisto, who functioned as *padroni* only for their townspeople. To be sure, a permanent Little Italy was always built up around labour agencies and boardinghouses. Nevertheless, a close analysis of the street in an Italian neighbourhood reveals that one's decision to settle in a particular location was not based only on economics or convenience – cultural factors were also involved. Indeed the three were often intertwined.

The immigrants who had left the towns of rural Italy under the auspices of their town's migration chains chose specific destinations in the new world.[19] In Toronto and in other Little Italies in North America, the chain provided the new arrivals with temporary lodgings, a job, and an immediate community. It arranged for other needs by introducing the townsman to particular shops, professionals, mutual aid societies, perhaps even a larger circle of acceptable friends. In other words, the migration chain formed by the *paesani* of a particular town to any destination was an intricate socioeconomic system. Because the chain was functional it caused the migrant to continue identifying with his townspeople or with immigrants from the cluster of towns surrounding his hometown long after he had arrived in a North American city. In order to understand how each hometown chain provided for the settlement of its townsgroup members it is essential to know the most prominent townsgroups and their respective populations in Toronto.

The size of the townsgroups ranged from a dozen to a few hundred people, but virtually no estimates by contemporaries have survived. The Glionna family, the largest among the *laurenzanesi*, claimed over 80 members in 1908; by that time at least another 15 families belonged to that townsgroup. One immigrant from San Vincenzo la Costa estimated that in 1920 "a few hundred" immigrants from the Cosenza area (Calabria – the towns of San Sisto, San Vincenzo la Costa, Cerisano, Montalto Uffugo) lived in Toronto. A travelling priest from Friuli, Luigi Ridolfi, recorded 500 immigrants from the Friuli region during his first visit to Toronto in 1931. Estimates of the size of particular townsgroups, however, are rare.[20]

One method of gauging the population of some of the townsgroups or of provincial or regional groups from Italy in Toronto is to examine the marriage records from the Italian parishes in conjunction with estimates of the Italian population in Toronto for the mid-1920s. The marriage registers at Our Lady of Mount Carmel, St Agnes, and St Clement parishes usually included the hometown name of each marriage partner. In all, 1,838 men and women who married at one of the three parishes between 1905 and 1935 had their hometown in Italy listed in the "place of baptism" column. Table 2 records the numbers of immigrants from the most representative regions and provinces in the marriage registers of the three Italian parishes.

Sicily, Abruzzi, Puglia, and Calabria were the home regions of most of Toronto's Italian immigrants – over 50 percent between the four of them. Trapani and Palermo (Sicily), Foggia (Puglia), Cosenza (Calabria), and Isernia (Molise) were the most prominent provinces of origin. A few of the townsgroups claimed a very high proportion of the city's Italian population. Table 3 shows that the Sicilian towns of Termini Imerese (province of Palermo), Vita (Trapani), and Pachino (Syracuse) accounted for over 15 percent of the city's entire Italian population, while Pisticci (Basilicata), Modugno di Bari, and Monteleone di Puglia (Puglia) claimed over 10 percent.

By correlating the proportional representation of each region, province, and town listed in the marriage registers from 1908 to 1935

Table 2
Italians in Toronto, 1908–35

Region	*Province*	*Population Sample From Marriage Registers*	%
Sicily			
	Palermo	113	
	Trapani	140	
	Syracuse	86	
	Messina	18	
	other	26	
Total		383	20.8
Puglia			
	Foggia	124	
	Bari	78	
	Lecce	5	
Total		207	11.3
Abruzzi			
	Teramo	78	
	Chieti	88	
	Aquila	38	
	Pescara	3	
Total		207	11.3
Calabria			
	Cosenza	123	
	Reggio di Calabria	61	
	Catanzaro	21	
Total		205	11.2
Lazio			
	Roma	60	
	Latina	21	
	Frosinone	55	
Total		136	7.4
Basilicata			
	Matera	71	
	Potenza	43	
Total		114	6.2

Table 2 (continued)

Region / *Province*	*Population Sample From Marriage Registers*	*%*
Molise		
Isernia	111	
Total	111	6.0
Campania		
Caserta	68	
Benevento	8	
Avellino	18	
Salerno	18	
Total	112	6.1
Friuli	96	
Total	96	5.2
Venetia		
Treviso	32	
Venezia	7	
other	3	
Total	42	2.3
Marche		
Pesaro	21	
Macerata	7	
Ascoli Piceno	33	
Ancona	6	
Total	67	3.6
Piedmont		
Torino	40	
Allesandria	7	
Asti	1	
Total	48	2.6
Tuscany		
Lucca	27	
Total	27	1.5
Other Regions and Provinces	83	4.5
Total	1,838	100.0

Sources: Marriage Registers, Our Lady of Mount Carmel (1908–35), St Agnes (1913–35), St Clement (1916–35) Roman Catholic Parishes, ARCAT.

Table 3
Prominent Italian Townsgroups in Toronto, 1908–35

Town/Province	*No. Married in 3 Italian Parishes, 1908–1935*	*% of Entries in Marriage Registers**
Vita, Trapani	121	6.6
Termini Imerese, Palermo	97	5.3
Pachino, Syracuse	86	4.7
Pisticci, Matera	69	3.8
Modugno di Bari, Bari	69	3.8
Monteleone di Puglia, Foggia	55	3.0
Boiano, Campobasso	39	2.1
San Sisto, Cosenza	33	1.8
Total	569	31.1

Sources: Our Lady of Mount Carmel (1908–35), St Agnes (1913–35), St Clement (1916–35) Roman Catholic Parishes, ARCAT.

* for which hometown can be traced.

with estimates of the Italian population of the city between 1917 and 1934 [see table 1], a rough estimate of the population of each subcommunity in the mid to late 1920s can be formulated.

There are of course biases in the sample of the population taken from the marriage registers. A small minority of Toronto's Italian community belonged to non-Catholic religious organizations. Some immigrants probably returned to their hometowns in Italy to get married, while others who took non-Italian brides married in Toronto's non-Italian parishes. Because the first Italian parish opened in 1908, townsgroups which had arrived earlier and married earlier would be under-represented in this sample. Most *laurenzanesi* for example, married at St Michael's Cathedral or at St Paul's Church before Mount Carmel opened in 1908. Many Genoese immigrants and townspeople from San Sisto and Termini Imerese were married in the cathedral, St Paul's, or St Mary's before 1908.

The marriage registers, on the other hand, are a good indicator of Italian immigrant population figures for the mid to late 1920s. In the registers, many marriage partners indicated that their parents lived in Toronto so we can assume they had a commitment to the city. The marriage registers therefore provide a fair sample of Toronto's entire Italian population in the period 1925–30. The figures in tables 4 and 5 provide an estimate of the population of Italian regional groups in Toronto, and of specific hometown groups during this period.

Table 4
Estimated Population of Italian Regional Groups in Toronto, 1925–30

Region	*Population*
Sicily	3,800
Abruzzi	2,000
Calabria	2,000
Puglia	2,000
Lazio	1,350
Basilicata	1,200
Campania	1,100
Molise	1,100
Friuli	500
Piedmont	500
Marche	350
Venetia	250
Tuscany	250

As indicated earlier, the Italian sojourners who worked for the more significant *padroni* in the city created mental maps of Toronto according to functional nodal points. Each group of townspeople also charted its own map with its particular points of convergence. Young men arriving from the village needed a boardinghouse. Bachelors who sent home for their betrothed had to place them in reputable lodgings, apart from male boarders and preferably with a widow, before the marriage. The pioneers of the town's chain to Toronto had to be consulted occasionally, either out of deference or because of authentic needs. The homes of the pioneers and the boardinghouses became the central features of each townsman's mental map and it was around these nuclei that each community of *paesani* settled.

Between 1875 and 1930 each townsgroup established itself on particular streets within one or two of the three Little Italies in Toronto and even outside these neighbourhoods.[21] The first recognizable group of townspeople in the city was the street musicians from Laurenzana. Giovanni Glionna and his brothers in 1874 pioneered the chain to Toronto. Glionna had been charged in New Haven, Connecticut with importing four child street musicians into New York for mendicant purposes and soon after the charge he moved to Toronto. His brothers and other fellow townsmen who had lived in the same tenements with him on Crosby Street in Manhattan fol-

Table 5
Estimated Population of Italian Hometown Groups in Toronto, 1925–30

Hometown	*Population*
Termini Imerese	750
Vita	650
Pachino	475
Pisticci	400
Modugno	400
Monteleone di Puglia	300
Boiano	200
San Sisto	200

lowed him. Originally they lodged in, or rented, houses on Chestnut Street, where the Genoese had settled earlier. Eventually they settled at Chestnut and Edward streets. In the early 1880s the Glionnas, who by then had made a small fortune, completed the construction of eleven brick buildings on the northwest corner of Chestnut and Edward streets, including the Glionna Hotel. The corner remained the centre of the city's *laurenzanese* community until the First World War when Francesco Glionna, the "patriarch" of the townsgroup, died. In 1917, with the introduction of prohibition, the hotel closed its doors.[22]

The early immigrants from the village of San Sisto, the town of San Vincenzo la Costa, Montalto Uffugo, Cerisano, and other towns surrounding Cosenza were fruit traders who opened shops along Queen Street West. In the 1890s, Salvatore Turano, who married a *laurenzanese*, moved to Mansfield Avenue where he invested in a grocery store. It was most likely a boardinghouse and labour agency for his townsmen working on road and street railway construction, for within a few years, many Italians, but especially immigrants from near Cosenza, had moved to the neighbourhood. At the turn of the century, the townsgroups from the towns surrounding Cosenza had two focal points: one was Mansfield Avenue where the early fruit traders from San Sisto lived, the other, Vincenzo Muto's home on D'Arcy Street, later College Street. Most prominent among the members of this group were Salvatore Turano and Raffaele Bartello, both owners of stores on Mansfield Avenue. At 92 D'Arcy Street just west of the Ward, Vincenzo Muto from Cerisano kept many lodgers from his town, most of them tailors in his tailoring shop.

Muto moved the business to College Street near Grace Street around 1910 and some of his employees lived above the shop.

In the 1920s two more addresses became important as boarding-houses for bachelors from Cosenza – Carmine Spizziri's home at 30 Mansfield Avenue, and Pasquale Molinaro's house at 19 Gore Street. Molinaro's address became a centre for the Cosenza group in the 1920s when he began a long association with the New York-based *Progresso Italo-Americano* as its part-time Toronto correspondent. Like a number of other *san sistesi*, Molinaro worked as a motorman for the Toronto Transit Commission. By the early 1930s, the towns-groups from Cosenza had settled primarily in the College and Grace streets Little Italy and especially on Bellwoods Avenue, between Plymouth and Mansfield avenues; on the east side of Clinton Street; on Mansfield Avenue, north side; on Gore Street, south side; and on the east side of Manning Avenue. A handful of families lived in or just outside the Ward. A small but significant group also settled in the Dufferin Street and Davenport Little Italy.

The townspeople from Monteleone di Puglia concentrated on York Street in the 1890s but by the turn of the century had settled in what would remain the centre of the *monteleonese* colony until the 1930s – Walton Street and Elm Street in the Ward. Bootblacking was the most prevalent occupation among these immigrants from the Puglia region. From the first decade of the century the shoeshiners of Monteleone opened parlour after parlour in the business district of downtown Toronto. Some also became barbers, while still others moved into the laundry business. From before the First World War, sojourning bachelors from this town had a choice of living with relatives on a *monteleonese* street, or in one of the large boarding-houses run by their townsmen. At 72 Gerrard Street West, between Elizabeth and Terauley (now Bay) streets, Frank Casullo and Mike Volpe, shoe polishers, ran a boardinghouse, probably for employees of their parlours on Queen Street West and Victoria Street. In the immediate postwar period, Louis Colangelo, a labourer, operated a boardinghouse at 32 Walton Street. The two most important homes, however, were those of two grocers (and probably *padroni*) in the Ward, Michael Circelli and Antonio Volpe. Circelli, at 71 Elm Street, housed migrants from Monteleone and Modugno di Bari; both towns were in Puglia, but relatively distant from each other. By 1920, a *modugnese*, Onofrio Giovanielli purchased the grocery business. Betrothed women who had just arrived in the city were usually sent to Antonio Volpe's boardinghouse at 64 Edward Street unless a relative had a spare room to offer.

During the 1920s the townspeople of Monteleone di Puglia gradually began moving out of the Ward but they did not settle in either of the other two Little Italies. Some moved to the Dufferin Street and Eglinton Avenue district, especially on Gilbert Street. Mortimer Avenue and Nealon Avenue were the two most popular streets for Monteleone's emigrants well into the 1950s.

Many of the immigrants from Modugno di Bari, like the *monteleonesi*, were involved not only in the barbering and shoeshining trades, but also in other occupations – in small and large industry and construction. The *colonia modugnese* continued to centre in the Ward until the 1950s, if for no other reason than Mount Carmel Church, the Italian National Parish, which housed the statue of San Rocco. They shared the statue with the *monteleonesi* for their treasured annual feast-day processions. From soon after the turn of the century, the townsgroup from Modugno di Bari lived near the townspeople from Monteleone di Puglia on Gerrard, Walton, and Hayter streets in the Ward. There was also a small pocket on Centre Avenue just north of Elm Street. Before 1915, immigrants from Modugno di Bari had begun settling in the College and Grace streets neighbourhood: along Manning Avenue, especially on the east side; along the north side of Henderson Avenue; on Gore Street; and on Clinton Street just north of Henderson Avenue. Others lived in the east end in the Danforth and Donlands avenues and Danforth and Pape avenues districts (Ravina Crescent, Stacy Street), and further south, especially on Booth Street (near Queen Street and Carlaw Avenue) and Bright Street (near Queen Street and Broadview Avenue).

Most of the large boardinghouses for *modugnesi* remained in the Ward until the 1920s. One of the early important lodging houses for this group belonged to a musician from Laurenzana, Egidio Donofrio, at 62 Elm Street. Donofrio's daughter, in fact, married the patriarch of the *modugnese* colony in Toronto, Nicola Majorana, who lived at 218 Chestnut Street. As noted earlier, Salvatore Turano, one of the leaders of the immigrants from San Sisto had also married a *laurenzanese*. By marrying into Toronto's pioneering townsgroups, these individuals, who were leaders of their respective hometown groups, reflected the reality that townsgroups were not isolated from each other, but, in fact, interacted among themselves. In the 1920s some homes in the other smaller *modugnese* settlements could put up the occasional boarder. Sal and Maria Vitale near Queen Street and Broadview Avenue or Teodoro Zambri near Coxwell and the Danforth, rented out their rooms to a few bachelors.

The immigrants from Boiano (Molise) lived predominantly in the second Little Italy at College and Grace streets, although some settled in the West Toronto Junction; others lived in apartments over their stores on Adelaide Street West. Most of the immigrants from Boiano were involved in the city's banana trade as pedlars, retailers, or wholesalers. A large basement attracted these small entrepreneurs, for banana bunches were ripened on hooks attached to ceiling joists. The most concentrated settlement of the wholesalers, jobbers, and pedlars was Markham Street, between College and Dundas streets – about ten families lived there in the 1920s and 1930s. The central home among the *boianesi* was 105 Markham Street, for many bachelors roomed there before their marriages. Originally the home belonged to the Scinocco brothers, Mark and Michael, banana pedlars; after the First World War, it was sold to Antonio Jannetta, a prominent fruiterer who had moved to Toronto from Hibbing, Minnesota.

The early skilled labourers from Friuli's towns and villages originally lodged in some of the large boardinghouses in or just outside the Ward. A small settlement also opened up in the Coxwell Avenue and Greenwood Avenue area in about 1905. The latter residents were employees of the Toronto Brick Company, and all came from Zompicchia. Friulan brickmakers also settled alongside brick companies in Port Credit, Mimico, and Cooksville. Their residences at the latter resembled a shantytown of tar sheds.

Just before the Second World War the *friulani* began moving out of the Ward. Luigi Del Negro, a bricklayer, ran a large boardinghouse, probably for his own employees, at 591 Dufferin Street, near Dundas Street. By the early 1920s, a mosaic, marble, and tile contractor, John Gasparini, had purchased the home. The site remained Toronto's most concentrated residence of tile setters until the mid-1920s. In the meantime, many *friulani* moved into what would become the centre of their community until the 1960s: the area bounded by Dufferin Street, Davenport Avenue, Wallace Avenue, and the West Toronto Junction.

By the 1930s the Italian population of the Dufferin and Davenport district was composed almost exclusively of skilled and unskilled construction labourers. Streets in the area were filled with boardinghouses owned by *friulani* and immigrants from the towns surrounding Chieti (Abruzzi) – Lanciano, Fossacesia, and Rocca San Giovanni – and from Terracina. Boardinghouses for immigrants from Chieti and Terracina were located on Dufferin Street just south of Davenport Road. Chieti's immigrants concentrated heavily on Beaver Avenue as well as on the corner of Manning and Henderson avenues in the College and Grace streets Little Italy. At first, immigrants from Friuli settled on Symington Avenue and later spread northwest to Wiltshire Avenue and northeast to Chandos Avenue. During the 1930s, the move northward continued as the *friulani* built new homes on Hartley Avenue and other streets in the Keele Street and Eglinton Avenue area in Fairbank.

The barbers and labourers of Pisticci lived in the Ward from the 1890s, on Walton Street between Terauley and Yonge streets, and on Terauley just above Queen Street. Some of the more established barbers moved up to Robert and Major streets during the 1930s. The main area of settlement for the townspeople, however, was the College and Grace streets neighbourhood, especially Henderson Street and Manning Avenue, and Euclid Avenue below College Street. About one-quarter of this townsgroup was dispersed throughout the residential areas east and west of the downtown commercial district. In the 1920s, a number of *pisticcesi* homeowners on Henderson or Clinton streets let rooms to fellow townsmen. Down in the Ward, before the First World War, George Abate, a *laurenzanese* at 65 Elm Street kept many boarders from Pisticci. Two of those boarders married the daughters of immigrants from Laurenzana.

Most Sicilians did not reside in the common areas of Italian settlement in Toronto. Their dispersal throughout the city, necessitated by the nature of their occupations – primarily fruit trading – will be discussed elsewhere. New immigrants from the towns of Vita and Termini Imerese in western Sicily generally boarded with their kin, but each townsgroup depended upon at least one major boardinghouse run by a widow. From just before the First World War, Agata Lamantia, a widow from Termini, put up both men and women in the apartment above her store at 103, and later 894, Queen Street East. Mrs Lamantia's husband died soon after the family's arrival in Toronto. Among the *vitesi* (or as they called themselves, *u vitalori*), the homes of Peter Catania (1018 Queen Street West), Vito Leo (1608

Queen Street West), and Sam Leo (311 Danforth Avenue) were important addresses for single men and women who required lodging. Francesca Simone's home at 18 St Paul Street (in the Queen Street East and Sackville Avenue neighbourhood) was the largest boardinghouse for this townsgroup. Many immigrants from Pachino in eastern Sicily also boarded at her home since other *pachinesi* lived in that neighbourhood. During the war a number of brides-to-be lived at Mrs Simone's house but she usually kept bachelors in the 1920s – six men in two shifts.

The immigrants from Pachino in the Queen and Sackville district were mostly involved in the fruit trade or heavy industry in the east end. Almost the entire population of that group lived east of Yonge Street outside any of the city's Little Italies. Many of them also lived on farms contiguous to those of the *termitani* and *vitesi* in West Hill – on Midland Avenue between Eglinton and Lawrence avenues where they operated market gardens.[23]

Each Italian townsgroup in Toronto, therefore, developed its own particular map with specific focal points within the city. One townsgroup did not dominate any of the streets in the three Little Italies, and no townsgroup lived entirely on one street. The key residential areas or streets of the *paesani* – the boardinghouse for sojourners and betrothed, the homes of the prominent men of the community – were all components of those mental maps, and the products of the chain migration of the townspeople from their homes in Italy to Toronto. The chain itself, the respect one paid to the notables of the town, and the network of boardinghouses, however, were functional and not only sentimental, and thus, to a great extent, they perpetuated the loyalties of the immigrant to his townspeople in the city. Allegiance to townspeople therefore was maintained by the pragmatic or expedient aspects of group cohesion. Loyalty did not mean simple fellow feeling, for it also embraced obligation and debt to intermediaries between the immigrant and his lodgings, job, or future wife. The more a greenhorn was "processed" through a boardinghouse, a job, and perhaps small enterprise by his *paesani*, the more likely were his loyalties to orbit around his townsgroup.

One way of gauging the loyalties of the townspeople is to study their marriage patterns. As some scholars have hypothesized, a high rate of endogamy among immigrants from the same hometown would seem to suggest a very cohesive townsgroup. Similarly, extensive endogamy between immigrants from the same province or re-

Table 6
Endogamy Rates by Parish for All Marriages in which the Hometown of at Least One Partner Appears in the Register, 1908–35

Parish	*Endogamous (town)*	*%*	*Total Marriages*
Mount Carmel	158	22.9	690
St Agnes	78	17.5	447
St Clements	1	1.7	58
Totals	237	19.8	1,195

Sources: Marriage Registers, Our Lady of Mount Carmel (1908e35), St Agnes (1913–35), St Clement (1916–35) Roman Catholic parishes, ARCAT.

gion would seem to indicate a cohesive provincial or regional group.[24]

Of 1,195 marriages between 1908 and 1935 – and these include marriages in which the hometown of at least one partner was recorded by the officiating priest – only 237, or 19.8 percent were endogamous (see table 6). The endogamy rates for the larger townsgroups in the city were not particularly high either.

This data by itself, however, sheds little light on the loyalties of the immigrants for a number of reasons. First, one-third of the Italians in the marriage registers were born outside Italy, and in most cases we do not know the hometown of their parents. Of 1,551 marriages at the three parishes between 1908 and 1935 involving 3,102 partners, we have a hometown listing for only 1,838 partners. About 75 percent of the remaining 1,266 husbands or wives were children of Italian immigrants but were born outside Italy. The remaining 25 percent either were not Italian or their birthplaces were illegible.

The statistics in tables 6 and 7 do not include the children of fellow townsmen under the category of "Endogamous by Town" because it would be impossible to determine the hometown for all second-generation partners. Because the immigrants from Termini Imerese were so numerous, I was able to infer from the names of the marriage partners' parents whether or not second-generation Italians (i.e., children of Italian immigrants, born outside Italy) were from Termini Imerese. Of 109 marriages involving immigrants from Termini or their children, 61 marriages were endogamous to the townsgroup. If we were able to exclude the children of the *termitani* (born outside Termini) from the sample, only 25 endogamous marriages would be tabulated. In fact, in 9 of the 61 endogamous marriages, the bride and bridegroom were both children of *termitani* but born

Table 7
Endogamy Rates for Particular Hometowns, and Their Intermarriage Rates with Home Provinces, Regions, and Country, 1908–35

Town	*Total Marriages*	*Town*	*%*	*Province*	*%*	*Region*	*%*	*Italy*	*%*
Modugno di Bari	46	14	30.4	16	34.8	19	41.3	39	84.8
Monteleone di Puglia	30	22	73.3	24	80.0	27	90.0	29	96.7
Boiano	21	11	52.4	14	66.7	14	66.7	19	90.5
Pisticci	49	22	44.9	22	44.9	29	59.2	48	98.0
Terracina	7	7	100.0						100.0
Fossacesia	17	4	23.5	5	29.4	6	35.3	17	100.0
Sora	26	9	34.6	11	42.3	11	42.3	25	96.2
Apricena	12	3	25.0	3	25.0	5	41.7	11	91.7
San Sisto	21	8	38.1	11	52.4	11	52.4	19	90.5
San Vincenzo la Costa	8	2	25.0	5	62.5	5	62.5	7	87.5
Montalto Uffugo	9	2	22.2	6	66.7	6	66.7	9	100.0
Totals	246	104	42.3	117	47.6	133	54.1	223	90.7

Sources: Marriage Registers, Our Lady of Mount Carmel (1908–35), St Agnes (1913–35), St Clement (1916–35) Roman Catholic parishes, ARCAT.

outside the hometown. A similar knowledge of other townsgroups would certainly reveal high rates of townsgroup endogamy.

A second problem with marshalling data from the marriage registers to estimate endogamy rates is the assumption that peasants in Italy married only people from their hometowns. In the old world village, endogamy did not by itself infer loyalty to the hometown; what *did* infer loyalty regarding marriage was either marrying within the townsgroup *or* into a group outside the town approved by one's townsgroup. In many districts in the old world, one's sphere of action was not limited to the hometown but also to the surrounding towns. For example, because the villages surrounding Susa (Piedmont) – Gravere, Meana, Montepantera, and Venaus – were all involved in the fruit export trade with France, there was much contact among these villages and intermarriage between different villages. As a result, immigrants from various towns in the Susa district also intermarried in Toronto. Of the sixteen men from Susa married in Toronto's Italian parishes between 1908 and 1935 (they came from four villages), seven married women from their respective hometowns. However, eight of the remaining nine bridegrooms married brides from other towns in the Susa district.

This was true of immigrants from the Friuli region, and from the towns surrounding Cerisano in Cosenza – San Sisto, San Vincenzo la

Costa, and Montalto Uffugo. Only a handful of men from Friuli married women from their hometowns; between 1908 and 1935, however, fifty-two of sixty-six men, or 79 percent of *friulani* men in the Italian parish marriage registers, married wives from Friuli. Fifty-eight of sixty-six men, or 88 percent, married women from Friuli or from the contiguous province of Treviso (Venetia).

During the same period, fifteen of forty-three immigrants from San Sisto, San Vincenzo la Costa, Cerisano, and Montalto Uffugo married immigrants from their respective hometowns. However, twenty-six of forty-three, or 61 percent married women from their respective hometowns or from towns in the district of Cerisano. Three immigrants from Pisticci married immigrants from Beralda, the first town east of Pisticci. Similarly, two immigrants from Monteleone di Puglia married immigrants from Accadia, a town just east of Monteleone. Possibly, marriage partners from nearby towns were actually children of *paesani*. For example, the transcripts at the back of the birth registers of early twentieth-century Pisticci indicate that the children of many townspeople were born in Montalbano Ionico, immediately to the southwest of Pisticci, probably because the family had migrated there temporarily for seasonal work. In fact one *pisticcese* in Toronto married an immigrant born in Montalbano Ionico.[25]

Furthermore, a careful examination of the marriage registers reveals that immigrants did not marry people only from towns approved by townspeople in Italy; they also developed new marriage alliances with other townsgroups in the new world. Perhaps because of the dearth of available mates from the hometown, some townsgroups in Toronto sanctioned the new alliances. Some hometown groups formed marriage alliances more readily with particular townsgroups than with others. For example, four men and women from Pisticci married people from Laurenzana, four *modugnesi* took partners from Monteleone di Puglia, and three other immigrants from Modugno di Bari married people from Pisticci. The Sicilians from Vita, Termini Imerese, and Pachino (all from different provinces) intermarried almost to the exclusion of other Italians. It seems that some townsgroups felt an affinity to other townsgroups because of shared experiences in Toronto – either boarding in the same houses, working, or participating in the same enterprises. The early sojourners from Modugno di Bari or Monteleone di Puglia, for example, lived on the same streets and in many cases in the same boardinghouses in the Ward, especially at 71 Elm Street. Furthermore many immigrants from each town were involved in similar trades – shoeshining and barbering.

As table 8 suggests, the immigrants from these Sicilian towns identified strongly with their island. However, regionalism was not the only reason for the high rate of endogamy among immigrants from Pachino, Termini Imerese, and Vita. The three townsgroups shared similar employment and enterprises and lived on the same streets. All three of the groups were involved in fruit and vegetable peddling, retailing, and market gardening. In West Hill, gardeners from all three towns owned contiguous farms. Many immigrants from Pachino and Vita lived on the same streets in the Queen and Sackville neighbourhood. As a result, many marriages were contracted between the three townsgroups. Only two marriages occurred between *pachinesi* and non-Sicilians. In both cases, the outside spouse was from San Sisto, a townsgroup which claimed many of the city's early fruit traders. Two immigrants from Vita married non-Sicilian spouses from Boiano, another town which sent to Toronto many of its early banana pedlars, and later, wholesalers. Marrying outside the townsgroup, therefore, did not indicate disloyalty towards one's *paesani*. Rather the townsgroup itself approved marriage alliances with groups it felt had shared their important experiences in the migration process. When marriage partners could not be found within the hometown group in Toronto, or in the hometown, the townsgroup itself looked to other townsgroups. It was through the townsgroup that the immigrant began to identify with an Italian community in the city.

An Italian community emerged in Toronto from at least the early 1880s – not just the three physical Italian neighbourhoods which would emerge in the 1890s nor the sum of the distinctive hometown groups. Rather, an Italian community based on the sentiments of immigrants from Italy, on the belief that they belonged to a collectivity of people with a shared background and shared interests. Four factors strongly influenced the emergence of an Italian community and its institutions. First, although the immigrants from Italy had arrived in Toronto as people of their villages, they also shared a fellow feeling for their old world countrymen, especially since they lived in a foreign environment. Second, shared experiences encouraged the immigrants to identify with each other. Informal bonds developed between Italians in many situations – on the street, at a

Table 8
Endogamy and Exogamy among Immigrants from Termini Imerese, Vita, and Pachino, Sicily, 1908–35

Town Origins of One Partner	Church Where Married:	*Origins of Other Partner:* *Termini Imerese*	%	*Vita*	%	*Pachino*	%	*Same Prov.*[a] *as Partner*	%	*Sicily*[b]	%	*Other*	%	*Totals*
Termini Imerese	Mt Carmel	45		5		8		7		10		9		84
	St Agnes	16		—		—		—		2		4		22
	Total	61	57.5	5	4.7	8	7.5	7	6.6	12	11.3	13	12.3	106
Vita	Mt Carmel	5		26		6		5		6		12		60
	St Agnes	—		14		2		—		—		5		21
	Total	5	6.2	40	49.3	8	9.9	5	6.2	6	7.4	17	21.0	81
Pachino	Mt Carmel	8		6		14		7		2		3		40
	St Agnes	—		2		2		—		2		3		9
	Total	8	16.3	8	16.3	16	32.7	7	14.3	4	8.2	6	12.2	49
	Total													215

Total marriages endogamous by town = 117 (54.4%)
Total marriages endogamous by province = 157 (73.9%)
Total marriages endogamous by region (Sicily) = 179 (83.3%)

Sources: Marriage Registers, Our Lady of Mount Carmel (1908–35), St Agnes (1913–35), St Clement (1916–35) Roman Catholic parishes, ARCAT.

Notes: [a] where only one partner is from Vita, Termini, or Pachino
[b] where partners are from different provinces and only one partner is from either Vita, Termini, or Pachino

church, on the job, or in enterprise. In the 1880s, for example, fruit pedlars in Toronto were primarily from small towns surrounding Lucca (Tuscany) and Genoa, and from Laurenzana and San Sisto. These men met at the crack of dawn as they loaded their carts in the market railyards on the Esplanade. Third, the growth of the Italian population of the city encouraged the development of a community. Institutional organization among Italians was more viable in 1901 when the population reached 4,000 than in 1891 when it numbered only a few hundred. Fourth, the rate of growth also influenced the development of a Toronto-Italian community. Between 1897 and 1901 the population more than quadrupled from under 1,000 to about 4,000. After the recession of 1907–8, the population rose dramatically from about 5,000 in 1908 to about 14,000 in 1913. This rapid growth consolidated the older members of the community who felt that they had shared experiences in the city: they had formed their own clubs, pioneered the Italian community of Toronto, and believed that the greenhorns must approach them with deference. Many of the young men from Modugno di Bari and the province of Lucca (Tuscany) who had arrived during the ten years preceding the First World War, felt that they were barred from holding offices in the older organizations, and in 1916 these men organized the *Circolo Colombo*, a sociorecreational club affiliated with Mount Carmel Parish.

In fact it was during periods of rapid immigration that many of the institutions and clubs of the colony were formed. The first Italian mutual aid society, the Umberto Primo, was initiated in 1888 by immigrants from Laurenzana and a few Genoese. During the large migration at the turn of the century, two more important mutual aid societies were organized, the Vittorio Emanuele III and the *Circolo Operai dell'Ontario* (Italian Workingmen's Circle of Ontario), in 1902 and 1903 respectively. Many members of these two societies were from the region of Calabria. In 1907, with the backing of the Conservative party, many of the city's wealthy Italians, especially those from Lucca, San Sisto, and Cerisano formed the Italian National Club, an elegant sociorecreational centre on D'Arcy Street. Meanwhile, the Socialists established a branch of the Italian Socialist party. The Sicilians maintained a distance from the community. Rather than join the three main mutual aid societies, they formed their own Grand Lodge in 1909, but only one of their societies, the Trinacria, survived, and was reorganized in 1913. By the First World

War, the institutional bases of an Italian community in Toronto had long been established.[26]

The institutional development of the community was paralleled by the growth of visible Italian focal points in each of the three Little Italies. By 1916 all three neighbourhoods boasted a Catholic church and a Methodist meeting-place. Centre Avenue and Elm Street became the commercial centre of the entire colony. Louis Puccini, Francesco Nicoletti, Virginio Zincone, Angelo Petti, and others operated their foodstuffs importing businesses in conjunction with their banking services and steamship agencies. Smaller grocery stores served specific townsgroups: Joseph Polito catered to the immigrants from Termini. Mrs Farano, on Elm Street, geared her store to the *modugnesi* of the colony, while Michael Circelli's clients were mostly fellow *monteleonesi*.

Some professionals and entrepreneurs – often it was difficult to distinguish the two – began posting their signs in the Ward also. A university-educated immigrant from Bologna, Harry Corti, operated the Italian Publishing Company on Centre Avenue near Elm Street. Starting in 1907, the firm published the *Tribuna Canadiana*, Toronto's third and most successful Italian newspaper. The Conservative party backed that venture. One year later, a publicist and a travelling author and lecturer published a few monthly issues of a national Canadian-Italian magazine, *La Rivista Canadiana*, which lasted only two years.[27] Small pasta manufactories, Italian cigar-making shops, real estate agencies, and a law office also operated in the Ward.

The College and Grace streets neighbourhood saw its first steamship agency in 1916: Francesco Tomaiuolo's on Clinton Avenue. Angelo Lobraico, son of a *laurenzanese*, soon moved to the area and opened a real estate agency on Manning Avenue. A few small grocery stores dotted the neighbourhood including Dominic Di Stasi's, which catered to the many *pisticcesi* in the district. On north Dufferin Street, the churches and Methodist kindergarten were the most important focal points. Growing in importance was the home of James Franceschini, also the headquarters of Dufferin Construction Company, which emerged as the largest Italian contracting firm in Toronto before the Second World War.

Each Little Italy developed a sense of neighbourhood. A *friulano* on Beaver Street in the north Dufferin area might deposit his paycheque at Nicoletti's Bank in the Ward, and might even look for a bride in the small *friulano* community in Port Credit. However, he also felt a sense of loyalty towards Italians in his own neighbourhood. In 1924, when the Fratellanza (Brotherhood) Mutual Benefit Society was formed, virtually all its members were, and remained, skilled labourers from Chieti and Friuli and lived in the Dufferin and Davenport district. Although they came from different regions, the two groups had the common bonds of occupation and residence. Indeed, very few Italian immigrants moved from one of the three Italian neighbourhoods to another. Prejudices developed towards each Little Italy. The Ward was considered a slum by the other two neighbourhoods. The Ward residents found the College-Grace district rough. Meanwhile, those two neighbourhoods viewed the north Dufferin Little Italy as downright dangerous.[28]

Between 1885 and 1915 Toronto's Italian immigrants identified with a number of groups – their townspeople, their neighbourhood, and ultimately with the city's Italian community. They operated on two levels, what Robert Harney has called the "chiaroscuro" of old world local and national loyalties.[29] By the First World War, the migrants from the peninsula had expanded their attachments to townsmen and associated with an Italian population in Toronto. The new horizons originally had opened up in the home village where prospective migrants first heard about their nation. They expanded during the early settlement and work experiences of the sojourner, and as we shall see, continued to expand under the guidance of the emerging community's élite. The chiaroscuro image, however, would remain with the migrant throughout the prewar years. In certain circumstances he would mute his allegiances to hometown and speak patriotically of Italy. In others, he would repudiate membership in an Italian club because his townsgroup had less power than another townsgroup within the association. Unlike the day he first arrived in the city, however, the immigrant who had settled even temporarily in a Little Italy could understand that while his little universe, his idea of Italy, might revolve around his *paese*, a larger body of Italians dwelt in Toronto and he *could* identify with them.

Evangelical work among Italian immigrant children, Italian Methodist Mission, ca. 1910. (United Church Archives [UCA])

Sewing class for Italian immigrant mothers, Italian Methodist Mission, ca. 1910. (UCA)

Louis Puccini in front of his Italian Cash Grocery on Elm Street in the Ward, 1920s. (Multicultural History Society of Ontario [MHSO])

Elizabeth Street Playground, 1913, a popular hangout for Italian and Jewish immigrant children in the Ward. (City of Toronto Archives [CTA])

Dufferin Street looking north from Beaver Avenue at the third Little Italy. On the right is St Mary of the Angels Church, formerly St Clement's, begun in 1915 and completed in 1934. (CTA)

Rear of Elizabeth Street behind the old City Hall, the Ward, 1912. (CTA)

Constructing the main sewer, Barton Street, 1912. Many Italians worked in street and sewer construction for the city and private contractors. (CTA)

Construction at the CPR's West Toronto Station at Dundas Street and Royce Avenue, May 1925. The contractor was Dufferin Construction Co, owned at the time by James Franceschini. Even though he was an important contributor to the Liberal party coffers, he was interned in 1940 when Italy declared war on Britain. (CTA)

Venetian navvies working on the Canadian Northern Railway line at Kamloops, BC, 1911. Italian navvies on the Canadian railways were recruited from Toronto among other places. (MHSO Collection, Archives of Ontario)

Pedlar's cart in the Ward. (UCA)

Laying curve track on Lappin Avenue and Dufferin Street at the city's third Little Italy, August 1915. (CTA)

Street railway construction in Toronto, 1912. (CTA)

CHAPTER THREE

Work and Enterprise

In recent years labour and immigration historians in North America have directed their research to immigrant labour, often involved in mining, capital projects, or urban industry. Encouraged by, among others, Frank Thistlethwaite, Rudolph J. Vecoli, and Herbert Gutman, historians have delved into the workers' premigration traditions to understand their adjustment to the new world urban economy. There are limitations, however, to the approaches of most Canadian and American historians, for they are steeped in a North American-centred perspective: in other words they emphasize understanding the development of an American or Canadian working class within the particular economy and society of the continent. Most American students of labour or immigration direct their attention to skilled and unskilled labour in capital projects or to semi-skilled labour in urban industry. It is unfortunate that the approaches of Robert Foerster in his 1919 classic, *The Italian Emigration of Our Times*, or of Frank Thistlethwaite, in his 1960 address on European migration in the nineteenth and twentieth centuries, have not been considered seriously. Both studies concentrated on the migration of skill rather than a people, and viewed the development of an American labour market as closely intertwined with the development of particular skills "for export" in European villages.[1]

In turn of the century Toronto, few continental European immigrants worked in industry. This was especially true of Italians who worked as unskilled construction labourers, in service trades, and skilled building or manufacturing trades. Those in manufacturing trades often worked as artisans in crafts already falling prey to the industrial order. In all the categories it is not always easy to distinguish between occupation and enterprise. Many of the immigrants with a skilled trade or proficiency in a service occupation set out on their own, or shifted back and forth from wage labour to self-employment, depending upon opportunity. Others worked for or with relatives or fellow townsmen, and although on the one hand they would come strictly under the heading of wage labour, cultural traditions forged a special bond between employer and employee to the extent that the latter shared in the development of the enterprise and participated wholeheartedly in its progress. Indeed, many employees eventually would strike out on their own.

This chapter examines occupations and enterprise in Toronto's Italian community to show the resilience of old world occupational traditions and how they responded to information about work opportunities in North America. The chapter also analyzes some of the images of Toronto's Italian workers constructed by visiting officials from Italy and by native Canadian hosts. Toronto's mainstream society developed its own stereotypes about the skills and occupations of Italian immigrants: an Italian was expected to be an organ grinder, a fruit trader, a navvy, a street labourer, or, by the 1930s, a garment worker. Such factors as the economy, skills imported by the migrants, and stereotyping (performing the trade one was expected to perform), led Italians into a few sectors in the Toronto economy. In other words, Italian-Torontonian work traditions had evolved by the 1930s. This chapter does not examine the employment structure of the second generation, but rather is concerned primarily with the work traditions either imported by the various hometown groups or acquired by them in Toronto.

As indicated earlier, when an immigrant arrived from his hometown, he identified with his townspeople. This was not only a sentimental tie because the townsgroup was also a functional socio-economic unit. It provided lodgings for the newcomer and, as we shall see in this chapter, it also provided employment, training, and at times even a market for new entrepreneurs. After the First World War, both the immigrants who had arrived before 1915, and many of their children, did not depend on the hometown group to provide work or training. This loosened their ties to their townspeople; but as these same immigrants and their children moved into occupations which in Toronto were considered "typically Italian" – occupations in the needle trades, construction, or laundries – they worked with other Italians and came to identify increasingly with the city's Italian community.

Early twentieth-century official visitors and travelling journalists from Italy presented a distorted view of Italians in Toronto as successful men of commerce. This perspective stemmed from confusion over where Toronto's Italian community, and indeed, all North American Italian immigrant communities, fit in Italy's colonial structure. The colonies were to serve primarily as the basis of a mercantilist economy, as a market for the mother country's goods and foodstuffs. They were to be a sign of Italy's rise to world prestige and power. As indicated in Chapter 1, because Italian political economists, politicians, and men of letters perceived Italian urban, and especially rural, settlements abroad as colonies, New York City's Italian immigrant population, agriculturists of the Argentine *pampas*, as well as the two dozen families in Lorette, Manitoba were all perceived as part of the larger Italian imperial structure. Italian visitors to North American Italian urban settlements would have preferred to write about their countrymen's success in agriculture. Because that was not possible, they resorted to describing the entrepreneurial success of urban immigrants, usually in agriculture-related activities – fruit trading, macaroni producing, or market gardening.

It was in that spirit that a visitor from Italy in 1907 viewed the occupational structure and entrepreneurial activity of Toronto's Italian immigrants. Father Pietro Pisani of Vercelli (Piedmont) was sent to Toronto at the request of the city's Catholic archbishop to study the spiritual needs of the Italian immigrant community. Pisani was considered an expert in the field and had already visited many Italian-American urban and agricultural settlements for the same reasons. The young cleric committed his observations to paper upon his return to Italy the following year, publishing a book and an article on Canada and its prospects for Italian emigration.

In his comments on work and enterprise, Pisani portrayed the immigrants as Italian nationals striving to honour the mother country through initiative and ingenuity: "There is an Italian bakery in Toronto that can furnish bread for the entire Italian colony, with a capacity of over 4,000 loaves a day. The owner also owns at St. Catharine's not too far from Toronto, a huge macaroni factory which produces 200 cases a day, not enough to meet the demand of his clientele: so that even this all-Italian industry has a promising future in Ontario. Toronto has its good Italian orchestras, if I recall, which employ a certain number of musicians."[2]

Pisani also described the Sicilian fruit trade: "Almost all the fruit and vegetable trade is exercised by Italians, mostly from Termini Imerese and Valledolmo. They have pretty shops on the busiest streets, like Queen Street, Yonge Street, King Street, where often they end up in groups, almost one on top of the other, forming almost completely Italian nuclei." The priest went on to praise the "good numbers of barbers, plaster figurine makers, colonial' shopkeepers [*negozianti coloniali*, i.e., ethnic shopkeepers], importers of foodstuffs." He was particularly impressed by one Italian company which "has a turnover of approximately three million lire [about $600 thousand] annually." The company, which was probably Charles Ciceri's, "imports from Italy olive oil, pasta, rice, wines, citrus fruits, and preserved foods, which it wholesales across Canada, and thus promotes our products."[3]

When a travelling inspector, Girolamo Moroni, of the Commissariato Generale dell'Emigrazione, visited the city and other Ontario towns seven years later, he also painted a bright picture of Italian enterprise in Toronto: "Our people possess four wholesaling businesses, 200 small groceries, a pasta factory, restaurants, tailoring shops, butcher shops, bakeries, barber shops and retail outlets for sweets, fruits and vegetables. There is only one professional, a doctor."[4]

Another inspector reporting on Italians in Ontario in 1927 inflated the image of Ontario "colonies" even more than his predecessor. Regarding commerce and enterprise among Italians, this observer made brief general comments about the immigrants in the province as a whole instead of examining any specific locality: "Generally the Italians of Ontario are merchants, artisans or labourers: merchants are for the most part South Italian, who dedicate themselves above all to the important trade in fruit and vegetables, so much so that it is considered in Canada an Italian specialty *par excellence*."[5] The report gave no estimate of the ratios of merchant to artisan to labourer.

The travelling inspectors and visitors from Italy depicted a rosy scenario of entrepreneurial success rather than an authentic occupational profile of the community. Two of them, however, listed what they perceived to be the principal immigrant trades of "our people" in Toronto. A notice in a 1913 issue of *Bollettino dell'emigrazione* explained that "the majority of Italians are peasants who work as labourers, however, working 9 to 11 hours a day with average earnings of $1.75 to $2.25." Two years later, in the same journal, Girolamo Moroni reported that most Italians were tailors, barbers, shoe repairmen and shoemakers, orchestra musicians, waiters, carpenters, shoeshiners, etc. At least two of the officials were able to look beyond the examples of the few successful individuals of the community and recognize the vast majority of skilled and unskilled labourers and petty entrepreneurs.[6]

While Italian observers developed a stereotype of the successful Italian immigrant businessman honouring the mother country abroad, Canadian religious ministers and social reformers standardized their image of the bovine yet occasionally boisterous navvy. One writer, Margaret Bell, described a scene of Italian street labourers in the city in 1913: "The picks swing up, then down, then up again. Each swing is accompanied by some utterance, an unintelligible uttering or snatch of song. And you think of the Italian operas and the greatest singers of them."[7]

Bell romanticized the Italian labourer but the superintendent of Immigration in Ottawa, W.D. Scott, understood the practical advantages of this immigrant when he asserted that "the Italian is a good navvy. He obeys the orders of the boss. He is not anxious to go on strike." Scott's image of the Italian as not being prone to strikes was questionable although he was not unjustified in indicating the Italian's proclivity for navvy work. W.G. Smith concluded that the southern Italian selected unskilled outdoor labour because the factory system had developed only in northern Italy; and besides, the Italian had "remarkable endurance and no little skill." Later J.M. Gibbon advocated an even more unlikely theory: the tradition of Italians as road builders went back to Roman times and "Italian labourers were welcome in Canada, particularly as they could stand the heat of the Canadian summer."[8]

The occupational stereotype was based to a certain extent on fact. However, the stereotype also perpetuated itself and eventually deviated from reality. To be sure, the Italian organ grinder was most prominent in mid to late nineteenth-century America and Europe, and comprised a far greater proportion of the Italian immigrant population in North America at that time than later, but the image of the Italian immigrant as a hurdy-gurdy man persisted well beyond the turn of the century. J.S. Woodsworth began his foray into Italian immigration to Canada in his *Strangers Within Our Gates* (1909) with that very representation: "AN ITALIAN! The figure that flashes before the mind's eye is probably that of an organ-grinder with his monkey. That was the impression we first received, and it is difficult to substitute another." And indeed it was! Four years later Margaret Bell in her semifictional article "Toronto's Melting-Pot," described six of seven hurdy-gurdies "crawling lazily along past the rows of shops, past the jabbering workmen who sit loafing on the steps." Even into the late 1930s, J. Murray Gibbon harped on the pet stereotype of the Italian road builder, virtually ignoring the needleworkers who then made up such a large proportion of Toronto's (and Montreal's) Italian population.[9]

Nevertheless, these and other writers occasionally went beyond the stereotype to refer to Italian-Canadian printers, carpenters, artists, cabinetmakers, or ironworkers. They directed much attention to the fruit and greengrocery merchants who represented "proof of their ingenuity and adaptability."[10] W.G. Smith alluded to what he called the Italian immigrants' "transition from the ranks of mere unskilled labourers, in the form of 'construction gangs', to the business enterprises of the fruit trade in which they have excelled." He called the Italian a master in the "green-grocery" and fruit trades "to which he brought ingenuity, deftness, industry and business sagacity that are most praiseworthy." The business acumen of a bootblack, barber, or hurdy-gurdy for that matter was of no consequence. The fruiterer, however, fit neatly into the North American image of the honest, petty entrepreneur. The occupation brought the navvy "into the class of buyers and sellers" but more important, "contributed to the intensification of domestic life which is fundamental to good citizenship. The Italian with a home is potentially a Canadian." Even though most of Toronto's Italian fruit stores were run by two extremely tightly-knit village groups, Smith believed that their experience in petty entrepreneurship would assimilate them to Canadian life.[11]

Similarly, the Italian fruit trade was a "natural" occupation for the Sicilian. His Genoese predecessors had partially conditioned Torontonians to accept him. More instrumental however, in creating the stereotype was the Sicilian pedlar, or bananaman. A poem in an 1895 issue of the *Canadian Magazine* dwelt on "the Italian Fruit Vendor" in downtown Toronto:

Ice'a cream – sex banana 'vive cent.
Pea nut drhee cent sze class.
Ah Lady! sze Talyman's cheap.
You not tink he vill sell, and he vass.

Thus night after night as I stroll down the street
At his cart on the corner this same man I meet,
At the southwestern corner of Ad'laide and Yonge,
Where the Saxon falls sweet from the soft Latin tongue.[12]

By the 1890s the Sicilian pedlar was a normal part of Toronto's commercial trade. When the fruit pedlar from Termini Imerese made the transition from hawker to fruiterer and greengrocer, he was not only acquiring a new status which his fellow townsmen in Toronto expected him to reach – he should become a fruit dealer eventually, wherever he settled – he also was taking on an occupation which fit one of the stereotypes of Italian immigrants Torontonians had developed.

The happy coincidence of the stereotype of an immigrant performing the specialized trade of his village spilled into other spheres. Bootblacking was dominated by the city's Greek immigrants before 1910. However, as their Mediterranean cousins from Monteleone di Puglia and Modugno di Bari (Puglia) became more and more prominent in this business, shoeshining came to be seen as a fitting service trade for the Italian immigrant. Many blacks worked as barbers in mid and late nineteenth-century Toronto, but with the arrival of the earliest Italian barbers in the 1870s, citizens were prepared to accept the many immigrants from Pisticci (Basilicata) and Modugno di Bari who opened barbershops around the city after the turn of the century. A barbershop in the uptown residential areas or the downtown commercial districts became a suitable and acceptable enterprise for the Italian immigrant in post-1900 Toronto.

Stereotyping also played a significant role in keeping Italians out of the industrial sector. By 1900 North Americans recognized Italian immigrants for their pre-industrial work skills or their sheer endurance at hard labour. The writings of W.G. Smith or J.M. Gibbon and others certainly perpetuated this view in Canada. Torontonians therefore were conditioned to accept Italians as appropriate pick and shovel men, as road, sewer, and streetcar labourers. After all, they had comprised a large proportion of the navvies on Canada's transcontinental railway, not to mention many other rail lines on the continent. Many of Toronto's 1,400 street railway labourers in 1907 were Italian.[13]

Until the First World War almost all Toronto's Italian immigrants were employed as labourers in street and building construction, or as tradesmen, carrying out the occupation most common among fellow townsmen in the city. The large industrial firms of the metropolis hired very few Italians. Part of the reason lay in the relative youth of Toronto's industrial life: the city's transition to the industrial age can be dated only to the 1850–1890 period.[14] Moreover, until 1915, the bulk of the labour force comprised Canadian-born, or English, Scottish, Welsh, or Irish immigrants – groups who dominated the population of the city, not just because of their numbers but also due to their knowledge of English, longer period of residence, and perhaps, their own ethnic "chains."

After the turn of the century some companies such as Kemp Manufacturing (metal manufacturing, later General Steel Wares), Massey-Harris (farm implements), Canadian Shipbuilding Company, and Canada Foundry – the latter two had the city's worst industrial safety records – added southern and eastern Europeans to their payrolls. The percentage of foreign, non-British immigrants in Toronto's industrial workforce, however, was much lower than that of Hamilton, Brantford, or Sault Ste Marie, Ontario – cities which had to import many labourers because of their small populations. From 1900 to 1912 the "Annual Report of Inspector of Factories" from the Ontario Department of Labour published a list of workmen injured on industrial worksites in the province. From 1912 to 1915 it listed only fatalities. Merely six Italian workmen and a few other Europeans died or were injured in Toronto between 1900 and 1915, whereas a few hundred Armenian, Italian, Ukrainian, and other eastern European industrial workers were injured in other Ontario towns. It seems that few non-British foreigners worked in Toronto factories.

The image of the Italian immigrant in the industrial workforce of the city was not ingrained in the public mind of Toronto in 1900. Circumstances would change, albeit slightly, during the ensuing fifteen years for a number of reasons. First, the city was expanding and during the middle of the century's first decade (and especially after 1918) it experienced a severe housing shortage. In addition, the Boer War and the city fire of 1904 increased demand for finished products and created more jobs for the city's labour force. Requests to allow females to work longer than sixty hours a week came from factory owners, and even non-British foreigners were hired.[15]

The most important factor behind the Italians' entry into Toronto's skilled industrial workforce was the metalworkers' strikes between 1898 and 1905. The second-largest metal firm in the city was Canada Foundry, owned by Canadian General Electric and situated in the Dufferin and Davenport area, on the western border of what became the third Little Italy in the city. In 1905 the mill employed 1,287 men, 342 of whom were moulders. Along with Massey-Harris and Gurney, this foundry acquired "a notoriety for unsurpassed vindictiveness" during the strike wave at the turn of the century. In 1903, 275 moulders went on strike at eleven metal firms in the city and Canada Foundry convinced employers to hold firm on the nine-hour issue. The company attempted to use 60 moulders from Scotland as scabs; 50 of the prospective scabs protested immediately when they discovered the true purpose of their employment. In May 1905, metalworkers struck and locked out Canada Foundry once again when the company tried to impose individual contracts on its employees. The strike lasted until 1906 by which time most strikers had obtained work in the United States. It was, in fact, in about 1905 that Italian moulders – many of them from towns near Pesaro (Marche), from Terracina (Lazio), Fossacesia, Rocca San Giovanni, and Lanciano (Abruzzi) – began appearing in the Dufferin-Davenport area. A 1913 report for the Italian Commissariat of Emigration reported that about 100 Italian immigrants worked for Canada Foundry. It is unclear, however, if they were hired as scabs, or as replacements after the lockout ended for the foundry employees who had left for the United States.[16]

Toronto's Italian immigrants began establishing themselves in a number of other industries before 1915. There is some evidence of their presence as strikebreakers in the boot and shoe manufacturing business before the turn of the century. During the summer 1898 strikes at J.D. King and Co., the city's largest shoe factory, five Italian scabs attacked a Swedish employee in the shop. Two weeks later a fracas broke out among the Italians themselves when a fellow national "tried to persuade an Italian strikebreaker that they would not take the place of the strikers."[17]

In industry, however, Italians moved primarily into the needle trades, laundering, and brickmaking (besides the metal trades, of course). By 1910 three small settlements of brickmakers from the Codroipo district in Friuli developed in the city's east end (Coxwell and Greenwood avenues), and outside Toronto's west end – in Mimico and Port Credit. By that time some of the skilled Italian men and women had joined the textile and knitting mills and tailoring shops of the city. A number of tailors from Cerisano (Calabria) – Vincenzo Muto, Antonio Mandarino, and Giovanni de Rosa in particular – opened their own shops in the city and hired their hometown people as tailors. Some of the larger industries began to hire Italian weavers, threaders, operators, sewers, and pressers in the pre-1915 period. Simpsons and Sons Knitting Mills, for example, employed about twenty-five to thirty Italian immigrants in 1913.[18] The city laundries provided a first job for many new arrivals, especially younger boys and teenage daughters. The Parisian Laundry was probably the greatest laundry employer of Italian immigrants from all parts of the peninsula (and of Greeks) before the First World War. Vail's, New Method, and New System were other laundries which employed many Italians.

As we have noted, Italian visitors and English-Canadian hosts singled out only those Italian immigrant occupations they wanted to see. The former focused upon the occasional example of entrepreneurial success, while the latter concentrated on the stereotype of the Italian in the lower rungs of the occupational ladder. These commentators could not understand the dynamics by which the immigrants chose specific trades, or the information networks which guided them towards work opportunities. One way of understanding the prewar occupational and entrepreneurial patterns of the Italian community in Toronto is to examine the two in the context of hometown work and migration traditions.

Virtually every immigrant who came to the city arrived as part of his hometown's workforce. That workforce was dispersed in an organized way to various locales or "colonies" of that hometown around the world. By studying the work patterns and roles of the traditional trades of several townsgroups in Toronto, we can see that Italian immigrants not only accommodated to Toronto's emerging industrial economy, but also shaped particular features of the city's service and retail sectors.

Chronologically, the first such group of townspeople who deserve special study, because they provide the initial example of the pattern of target migrants in search of economic opportunity, are the fruit and vegetable dealers who arrived in Toronto in the 1860s from the cluster of towns surrounding Genoa. These early Ligurian settlers will be dealt with below with fruit dealers from other towns in the south of Italy and Sicily.

Arriving at about the same time as the Genoese were the plaster statuary vendors from Bagni di Lucca (Tuscany), and especially from the town of Barga. These boys and men, known as *figurinai*, had literally circled the globe peddling or casting statuettes in urban centres. They had plied their trade in London and Paris from at least the late eighteenth century. In 1821, twenty-three of these figurine makers were recorded in Paris alone, where they were often arrested for sedition for casting moulds of political figures. These men and boys usually travelled in groups of about ten under the direction of a contractor or boss, to whom the apprentices and vendors were apprenticed under two- or three-year contracts. In each town or city visited by the band, the contractor kept a supply of plaster and other goods necessary for his trade.[19] The figurine makers carried their own tools and plaster models. In that way the statuettes and medals were produced in each city and not carried from one locale to another.

When the period of apprenticeship ended, the young men set out on their own to test new markets. Some of them crossed the Atlantic Ocean and journeyed to cities and towns in North and South America. Vincent Casci and Harry Castrucci were among the early figurine makers and vendors in Toronto. Like other *lucchesi*, they made the statues from casts they carried with them, and sold them to the general public, although Casci, as a skilled sculptor, also produced statues for a number of churches. Around the turn of the century Massimo Jacopo Magi settled in the Ontario capital and soon opened his own plaster statuary shop. The Florentine Statuary Company on King Street was probably the largest Italian industrial enterprise in the city and employed many *lucchesi* immigrants before 1940.

The statuary vendors from Lucca, like the fruit traders from Genoa, came from a number of towns in their respective provinces. Neither group formed a large colony. Rather many itinerant vendors from both regions stopped in Toronto during their travels through North America in search of opportunity, and some stayed on. A series of sketches of various townsgroups or regional groups and their skills will give a better idea of occupational chains from the villages of Europe and their ability to provide townspeople with opportunities to practise their trade.

Immigrants from Laurenzana (Basilicata) were the most numerous townsgroup to settle in Toronto in the 1870s and 1880s. Their specialized trade contributed to Toronto's emergence as a city that could offer particular forms of urban culture. Although some *laurenzanesi* became fruit pedlars or merchants, the vast majority, until at least 1900, were musicians – harpists, violinists, and clarinetists. Toronto was the last frontier of these former child street musicians who had previously rambled the roads of London, Paris, Geneva, Barcelona, New York, Chicago, Cleveland, Moscow, Havana, and Rio de Janeiro, soliciting pity and coins from passers-by.

The street harpists and violinists from nearby Viggiano in the Basilicata had gone elsewhere to seek a fortune since at least the late eighteenth century. Francesco Pennela, from Viggiano, began travelling throughout Italy into Provence in the late 1830s with his harp. His nephew left his hometown a few years later and after many travels settled for a few years in Lima, Peru, where he also gave music lessons. Their fellow townsman, Vincenzo Miglionico, left Viggiano in 1806 and returned home in 1832 after having played his harp in numerous cities in Europe and the Americas. By the mid- 1850s, 300 *viggianesi* harpists performed on at least four continents, while Laurenzana, although not yet quite as adventurous, was already sending its teenage musicians to Havana and New York City. Elia Pellettieri ventured to the Cuban capital in the late 1840s with two other teenagers from his hometown, playing the violin and harp. He reached Utica in upstate New York in the 1860s where he opened an Italian immigrant saloon and became a labour agent. These and a few thousand other musicians had begun their travels as children indentured by their parents to labour bosses.[20]

In Laurenzana and surrounding towns, parents indentured their children, aged five to fifteen, to labour bosses. It was, in fact, in this trade that the Italian immigrant labour agent was first given the name *padrone*. The *padrone* made many trips to his hometown to recruit children. As a result, hundreds of "Italian slave children" inhabited the Little Italies of Europe and America, in places such as Five

Points, New York, Saffron Hill, London, the Panthéon in Paris. One tenement on Crosby Street in Manhattan was reputed to have put up close to 100 children in 1873. Eighteen *padroni* and 100 children lived in another building near Place Maubert in Paris. After playing their instruments and begging in the streets, the little slaves would hand over their day's earnings to the *padrone* and share their room with their young colleagues, monkeys, and instruments.[21] Many investigations regarding the children were carried out by reformers, reporters, and Italian consular representatives in Paris, London, and New York during the last half of the nineteenth century. By 1874 the United States, Italy, France, and England had passed laws against the trade, although the child street musician problem continued in the latter country almost until 1890.

After the passage of the Italian laws forbidding child street musicians in 1873, the *New York Times* ran a series of articles on the child trade. The *Times* visited the children's tenements, interviewed musicians who had escaped from their *padroni*, reported on the backgrounds of the children and their bosses, and advocated more stringent measures to protect the "slaves". One of the more sensational reports dealt with the arrest of a *padrone* from Laurenzana. Giovanni Glionna had been charged with importing four children from his hometown for mendicant purposes. He escaped to New Haven, Connecticut, where he was arrested in August 1873. One year later, a Giovanni Glionna appeared in Toronto and began the long chain of *laurenzanesi* musicians who came to Toronto from New York. In Manhattan's Little Italy, the Brancieres, Lobraicos, Laurias, and Laraias – all of them musicians – had lived near their *paesani*, the Glionna brothers, Giovanni and Francesco, before following them to Toronto.[22]

Few of the *laurenzanesi* who remained musicians in Toronto played on the streets. Rather, they performed in vaudeville shows or at tea parties of wealthy families. The transition from street musicians to theatre or dinner entertainers was not a great one. These men were not only musicians – above all they were migrants in search of opportunity and were therefore flexible in their skills. In London, the street organists from near Parma entered the catering trade late in the nineteenth century, and in New York, Laurenzana's musicians switched to the bootblack trade in the 1880s and 1890s. Although Giovanni Glionna had left Laurenzana as a young street musician in about 1865, he became a glazier in New York, and then turned to the music trade upon his arrival in Toronto. His brother, Francesco, had also left Laurenzana as a street musician but became a carpenter in New York. In Toronto he worked as a carpenter for an organ-maker before becoming a labour agent and proprietor of Glionna's Hotel.

None of the early *laurenzanesi* in the city was a musical virtuoso. Rocco Pelletieri, who had joined his *paesani* after spending a few years in Alabama and Tennessee, could not even read music – and he was not atypical in that respect. The *laurenzanesi* had learned the basics of their instruments in their hometowns, but they saw to it that their children received better training in New York and Toronto. Vincenzo Glionna, one of the four original brothers in the city, had fifteen children, all of them musicians. Giovanni and Francesco each had at least one son who was a musician, and at least one daughter married to a performer. Therefore, the family, inlaws, indeed the entire townsgroup, provided a pool of musicians who could be contracted out for different entertainments.[23] In advertisements for their orchestra in the 1890s, Vincenzo Glionna and Dominic Marsicano (the latter was from Viggiano) seemed more like agents than orchestra leaders:

> Glionna-Marsicano Orchestra
> also Mandolin Orchestra
> Music Furnished for Conversaziones, Receptions,
> Weddings, Balls, Parties, Concerts, etc.
> Any Number of Musicians Supplied, and New
> Music Furnished if Required.
> Private Lessons on the Mandolin at 27 Elm St.
> Reasonable Terms[24]

The *laurenzanesi* musicians arrived in Toronto at an opportune time. In the late nineteenth century the city was just emerging from its "hogtown" status. The growing middle class directed its conspicuous consumption towards music and entertainment. Musicians in Toronto were at a premium. In fact, the city's first symphony orchestra scheduled only twilight concerts in order to allow its members to play the theatres in the evenings.[25] As musicians, therefore, Laurenzana's migrants found a profitable niche in the city's economy and were able to adapt their skills to Toronto's needs.

Another hometown group in Toronto, with a different occupation, operated on the same principle of settling in a town in which it had a competitive advantage. The knife-grinders of the Val Rendena, near Trento, had journeyed throughout Europe, Eurasia, and North and South America before arriving in Toronto around 1900. With their wheelbarrows, grinding-stone (*argagn*), and a child apprentice to seek out customers, the grinder ventured from town to town. To "maintain a secret commercial life among themselves abroad" they developed their own slang called "El Taron." The first North American settlers landed in New York with their wheelbarrows in 1886, and began a chain from the Val Rendena which scattered hundreds of grinders across the United States by 1900. It was about that time that the Malacarne family and Lorenzo Binelli settled in Toronto pushing their wheelbarrows and grinding-stone around the city's roads, lanes, and alleys. These pioneers were followed by the Bertelli, Giacomin, and Pozza families before 1915. As in all major towns on the continent, the grinders from Val Rendena and surrounding villages dominated this trade in Toronto.[26]

The immigrants from the villages surrounding Susa (Piedmont) – primarily Gravere and Meana, but also Venaus, Novalesa, and Montepantera – commenced their chain to Toronto in 1907, although the first large influx from these towns began after the end of the First World War. The peasants of these villages grew chestnuts, pears, and apples as cash crops in the late nineteenth century, but some also began travelling to southern France – primarily Marseilles – to work in the catering trades. Others worked in various industries in France and even in the metal trades in the city of Susa. At the turn of the century, migrants from that area took up employment in the leather factories in Huntsville, Bracebridge, and Acton, Ontario. It was not long before some of the migrants escaped the foul conditions of the tanneries for employment in nearby Toronto.

In the city, Susa's migrants sought new work opportunities, most of which came up in the catering trades. Battista Ruffino (arrived in Toronto 1907), Francesco Ruffino (1903), and Frederico Claretto (1907) were the pioneers of the town's migration to Toronto. They, along with 2 later immigrants, Costanzo Bolley and Sam Viglione, were chefs at the King Edward and Royal York hotels, National, Rosedale, Ontario, and Granite clubs, and the Adelaide Grille, and Jensen Restaurant. These 5 chefs sponsored most of the 300 men and women from their towns who settled in Toronto between 1910 and 1940, and they trained many of them as fry and short-order cooks.

Indeed about 100 of the 300 migrants ended up as waiters and fry cooks in Toronto's larger hotels and prestigious clubs, and as short-order cooks in many grills.[27]

Like the street musicians and cooks, most of Toronto's Italian bootblacks were from two towns, Monteleone di Puglia and Modugno di Bari. Some Italians were also involved in the trade before 1915, either independently or as part of a barbershop's services. A number of *modugnesi* operated barber shops and hired boys from their villages to polish shoes in Toronto. Eventually, most of these children apprenticed as barbers. Vince Farano, for example, began bootblacking at age ten – his mother constantly invented alibis for her son when the truant officer appeared at the door – and eventually he opened his own barbershop on Elm Street in the Ward.[28] Almost all of the Italian shoeshine parlours – most of which opened after the First World War – were operated by immigrants from Monteleone, and they recruited their bootblacks from amongst their own people.

Bootblacking, of course, was not a difficult trade. An entrepreneur's main objective was to find a good location for a parlour and trustworthy shoeshiners. For the fifteen to twenty parlours owned by Toronto's *monteleonesi* during the 1920s, a labour market was not a problem; they had only to recruit their townspeople in the city or send for new migrants from Monteleone di Puglia. The Sanella's operated one of the earliest shops on Queen Street West near Bathurst Street as did Angelo Racioppa on College Street near Spadina Avenue. By 1925, Joseph Zambri ran a parlour in the King Edward Hotel: he had operated one previously in the Royal York Hotel. His two brothers and Joseph Volpe owned the United Shoe Shine Parlour at 165 University Avenue near Elm Street. Michael Volpe managed three parlours, on Adelaide Street near Yonge Street and on Yonge Street near Front Street. By the late 1920s, Rocco Romagnolo had opened a bootblack shop at 57 King Street, and Frank Casullo had sold his parlour at 459 Yonge Street near Carlton Street to Tony Colangelo. Dominic Cornacchia shined boots on Adelaide Street West near Yonge Street, as did Giovanni Cornacchia at Bloor Street just beyond Runneymede Road. These entrepreneurs opened their shops after apprenticing with a *paesano*. As their businesses expanded, they depended upon their townspeople for a steady pool of employees.

Since the early nineteenth century, the region of Friuli in north-eastern Italy had sent migrants through Europe and Asia who specialized in three occupations – brickmaking, bricklaying (the Italian term *muratori* referred to bricklayers, stonemasons, plasterers, or stucco workers), and the mosaic, marble, tile, and terrazzo trades. Friuli had the country's highest temporary migration rated in late nineteenth- and early twentieth-century Italy.[29] From the early ages of eight or nine until retirement, the *fornaciai* (brick kiln men), *muratori*, and *mosaicisti* (mosaic workers) engaged in the annual nine-month trek to *le germanie*. In 1880, Giovanni Facchin, whose firm had contracted the mosaic work on the floor of the Paris Opera, sent two of his tradesmen to New York to complete the mosaics at one of the Vanderbilt mansions. These two men then organized the Ideal Mosaic Company and sponsored tradesmen from Friuli to join them; in turn, these tradesmen established their own firms in New York and elsewhere. By 1925 at least one hundred cities and towns in North America claimed one or more *friulano* mosaic, marble, tile, and terrazzo companies.[30]

In the late 1890s, a *friulano* family originally from Fanna, the De Spirts, moved from New York City to Buffalo where they opened a mosaic, marble, and terrazzo firm. From Buffalo, employees were sent to various worksites in the American midwest and west – the Cook County Court House in Chicago and the Central Post Office in San Francisco. The De Spirt family also became interested in Toronto. In 1910, the city's marble and terrazzo workers were just emerging from a long period of inactivity and beginning to work on many of Toronto's new large buildings, such as the General Hospital, Royal Bank, and Dominion Bank building, which required marble and terrazzo interiors.[31] In 1912, Albino Pedron was sent to Toronto by the De Spirt family to work at one of its jobsites and to open a branch office from which he could expand into the Canadian market. Pedron seized the opportunity to establish his own business and the De Spirts had to send one of their sons to compete with their former employee and with some of the older Canadian firms which had been hiring *friulani* mosaic, marble, and terrazzo workers, and tile setters. In 1925, Egidio (Gid) De Spirt replaced his brother, and came to dominate the trade among the *friulani* in the city. De Spirt, Pedron, the Gasparini family, and others sponsored the immigration of scores of tradesmen, grinders, and other labourers, many of whom eventually established their own companies or bought older local firms. By the early 1950s the trade was almost entirely in the hands of *friulani*, especially those from the towns of Sequals and Fanna.[32]

Another group of *friulani* who had been in Toronto since about 1905 were the brickmakers from towns in southern Friuli. Many of them had worked at the same trade in Bavaria, as labourers hauling clay, or as firemen in the kilns. The largest employer in the city was the Toronto Brick Company at Coxwell Avenue and Gerrard Street. A small colony of brickmakers from the village of Zompicchia near Codroipo, in Friuli, lived near the brickyard, on Seymour Avenue. These families and young male boarders had little contact with the large *friulano* neighbourhood at Davenport Road and Dufferin Street, except for the occasional visits of Domenico (Meni) Duz, a *friulano* grocer on Symington Avenue who delivered products of his region to customers in Toronto and outlying districts. Small settlements of bricklayers from Friuli and Treviso were also situated near brickyards in New Toronto, Port Credit, and Cooksville.[33]

Bricklayers and builders from Friuli began arriving in the city at about the same time as the brickmakers. The tradesmen were mostly from Codroipo and its surrounding towns, or from San Giorgio della Richinvelda. The three De Zorzi brothers from the latter town were among the earliest bricklayers from their home region in Toronto. They continued their old world migratory occupation soon after reaching the city in about 1903 and later began building and selling homes. Builders were certainly welcome in the city. Toronto politicians had complained about housing shortages from the 1880s, and by 1906 the issue had almost taken on crisis proportions. In addition, much of the city centre was rebuilt after the conflagration of 1904. The *friulani* were even more welcome when veterans returning to the city stimulated the postwar housing boom.[34]

Many of these builders arrived from their hometowns or from other Canadian worksites during the 1920s. As plasterers, bricklayers, carpenters, tile setters, or labourers, they acquired a significant share of the labour market in the construction of new homes in Toronto's expanding suburbs. Some of the bricklayers and plasterers, such as the Brattis, De Zorzis, Morassuttis, and Del Zottos, became housebuilders during this period. Under a system of trust and credit, they subcontracted various components of their projects to other *friulani* tradesmen. For example, Paul Bertoia and Emilio Muzzo, who ran a plastering firm, also built some bungalows for resale during the late 1930s. Rather than approach a bank or mortgage institution for a second mortgage on the bungalows, they struck a verbal contract with other *friulani* builders. They plastered the bungalows constructed by these builders and, in return, the builders took back a second mortgage on Bertoia and Muzzo's buildings and credited their account for twenty-five dollars for each house that the two partners plastered for them. Through this system of subcontracting, *friulani* builders were able to construct many of the homes in the Bathurst Street and Eglinton Avenue, and Mount Pleasant Road and Eglinton Avenue areas of the city.[35]

Although many of the *friulani* who arrived in Toronto before the depression already had a skilled trade, many were trained by other *friulani* in Toronto or other cities on the continent. For example, some of the mosaic stone-cutters for the De Spirts were brought to Buffalo as teenagers from the brickyards of Bavaria. Paul Bertoia travelled from his hometown to the coal mines of Alberta at the age of sixteen. Through *friulani* contacts he worked as a labourer on the Welland Canal, as a tannery employee in Huntsville, a hod-carrier in Windsor, and a travelling terrazzo grinder for a Toronto firm – in Calgary, Saskatoon, Peterborough, and Ottawa – before a *friulano* taught him to plaster and made him a business partner in Toronto. Among the *friulani*, then, regional ties were closely related to work and opportunity. If a young man arrived from Friuli without a skilled trade, through the networks of workers from his home region he could apprentice with a company involved in one of the building trades.[36]

The house-building trades among the city's *friulani* were integrated vertically. A *friulan* housebuilder could hire immigrant bricklayers, carpenters, roofers, plasterers, plumbers, electricians, and tilesetters from among his old world coregionalists. The trades were also integrated horizontally in that *friulani* entrepreneurs in the same building trades cooperated in lending each other labourers or skilled tradesmen or capital, or even joined in partnerships. Trust between partners did not develop on the job alone but also during their encounters at the Fratellanza (Brotherhood) and *Famee Furlane* (Friulan Family) mutual benefit societies' meetings and celebrations. In fact, it was at these encounters that much of the hiring was done by builders and that many business deals were struck between builders and tradesmen.

Horizontal and vertical integration were also typical of the fruit traders among Toronto's Italian immigrants. Before the Second

World War, the city's Italians dominated the fruit retail trade. As in every major Little Italy on the continent, the earliest traders were from the Genoese hinterland. From the 1850s they peddled their fruit in the city and eventually opened their own stores. The Deferraris and Garbarinos, who arrived in the 1880s, were among the most prominent of the early Italian fruiterers in the city. There was also a significant number of fruit traders from other areas in Italy in Toronto in the late nineteenth century, especially from Laurenzana, and San Sisto and its nearby villages in the province of Cosenza. In 1880, Toronto City Council passed a resolution that all hawkers and pedlars be licensed. Few Italians appeared in the licence books in the years immediately following the implementation of the by-law, but by 1886 at least eighteen licensed pedlars in Toronto were from the peninsula: from Ghivizzano (Tuscany), from Genoese villages near Chiavari, from Laurenzana, from near Trento, and from San Sisto. According to an editorial in *The Evening Telegram* in 1888, the city's pedlars had "helped to a large extent in tripling the fruit imports from the United States to this city within a very few years." They had also "taught the public to acquire a taste for certain fruits previously unknown to them, such as bananas and peaches, etc."[37]

By the mid-1890s virtually all Italian pedlars had opened fruit stores along Queen Street West, beginning with Angelo Deferrari in 1886. In the same period, the immigrants from Termini Imerese (Sicily) began their great migration to Toronto. Pietro Lamantia and Salvatore Caruso were among the earliest pedlars and storeowners – they arrived in the late 1880s – of the hometown group who eventually would dominate the fruit retail trade in Toronto. The *termitani* were followed by the banana pedlars from Boiano (Molise), who in about 1900 began operating their own fruit stores. By 1910, the pioneers of the Boiano chain, Antonio and Luigi Jannetta, Frank Scinocco, and Louis Bush, owned four contiguous stalls in St Andrew's Market. Meanwhile, Dominic Montone, their *paesano*, had become a wholesaler, with a stall at the foot of Yonge Street and outlets on Front and York streets.[38] In the four years preceding the First World War, the immigrants from Vita (Sicily) established their presence in the Toronto fruit trade. Vito Genova, Rosario Caradonna, Leonard Catania, and Vito Sanci, among others, began what would become the second-largest Italian hometown group of fruit retailers in the city.

The Italian presence in fruit trading was felt from an early period and grew stronger decade by decade.[39] In 1895, 17 of 104 retail merchants in the "fruit, fish, oyster, and game" trades were Italian, 5 of them from Genoa. Four years later, the number of retailers had increased to only 110, of whom 19 were Italian. However, by 1905, 140 fruit sellers were spreading east, west, and south from the city centre and 64 of them were Italians. By that time the number of *genovesi* fruit traders had taken second place to their *termitani* counterparts. Another leap in the number of store owners brought their total to 208 by 1912. By then, well over one-half of those merchants were Italian (126). In addition, 18 of the remaining 82 retailers were either Jewish or Greek. Forty-three of the Italians were from Termini Imerese, 11 from Vita, and 10 from the villages surrounding Genoa.

A number of factors accounted for the increasing presence of Italians in this sector. First, the city was expanding at a very fast rate. As the population grew, residential fringes of the city pushed out on all three of Toronto's perimeters (the lakefront formed the city's southern border), and existing neighbourhoods grew more dense. As well, the pedlar was being replaced gradually by the fruit store. In that era of population expansion in the city, the number of fruit stores doubled exactly to 208 between 1895 and 1912, and the fruit pedlars of Termini, San Sisto, Genoa, Vita, and elsewhere found a place in this enterprise.

One of the reasons that the Italians and indeed any fruit dealer could open a fruit store in this period was the high turnover rate of proprietors. Between 1895 and 1905, for example, sixty-two of eighty-seven non-Italians left the fruit retail business, while six of seventeen Italians retired or changed occupations. It is difficult to determine the intensity of the competition for fruit stores. The expansion of the Italian share of the market in this period might very well have moulded the habits of many of Toronto's residents to shop at fruit stores rather than to purchase from pedlars, or travel to the St Lawrence or St Andrew markets. This, in turn, must have created new opportunities for the retailers.

The most decisive factors ensuring the Italians' success in the fruit trade, however, were the cooperative spirit within a townsgroup and even between townsgroups, and the experience the fruiterers brought to the trade from previous migrations to other North American cities. The immigrants from Termini Imerese, for example, had worked as market gardeners or fruit sellers at home in Termini and across North America. The same was true of the *genovesi*. Before the fruit traders from Genova, Vita, San Sisto, Pachino and Termini turned to retailing, they were market gardeners on the outskirts of Toronto. A travelling inspector of the Commissariato Generale dell'Emigrazione from Rome noted that "a number of Italians own or rent gardens in Mount Dennis, West Toronto, and Long Branch, earning discreet profits."[40]

From the turn of the century Andrew Deferrari owned a farm at Mount Pleasant and Eglinton Avenues and later opened a fruit store nearby. The largest groups to engage in market gardening, however, were the Sicilians from Termini Imerese, Vita, and Pachino (Sicily). Joe Mannone and other *vitesi* operated gardens and small farms in Mount Dennis, and the Ciras and other *termitani* cultivated vegetables in Mimico. The most popular location was Midland Avenue between Eglinton and Lawrence avenues in Scarborough. A virtual Sicilian farming village flourished there by the 1920s with gardens run by the Fasolinos (later Fassel) and Calderones from Termini, the Mannones and Acquannos from Vita, and the Ciccinellis, Lucianos, Augieres, and Masseris (Mauceri, later Massey) from Pachino.[41] These truck farms supplied much of the produce sold in the fruit and vegetable stores of their townsmen or relatives. Indeed, the Ciras were able to retail their own produce.

The market gardens also help explain why the Sicilians were the first to capitalize on opportunities and open fruit stores in the east and west ends of the city before other competitors. Because they had been stationed in the northern, western, and eastern boundaries of Toronto and had, in addition, peddled fruits and vegetables in these districts, these people developed a keen sense of market needs in outlying areas. Of course the proximity of the gardens to north Yonge, the Beaches, and the city limits at the ends of Bloor Street and Danforth Avenue gave the Sicilians an early advantage over retailers who might look for fresh produce supplies either in downtown Toronto or outlying villages.

The immigrants from Termini Imerese, and to a lesser extent, those from Vita, were among the most remarkable hometown groups among the fruiterers. Indeed the two towns dominated the fruit and vegetable retail trade in Toronto in the 1920s. Termini's emigrants left their hometown as peasants or agricultural day labourers. In Termini, as noted, they worked as market gardeners, olive pickers, or sumach harvesters. With the development of the fruit trade between Sicily and New Orleans during the 1860s, they began the great migration to North America, at first as sugar plantation workers in Louisiana with other Sicilians, and later as fruit traders. From the sugar plantations they moved to New Orleans, and then to Chicago, New York, Pittsburgh, Cleveland, Toronto, Utica, Rochester, Winnipeg, Ottawa, and many other cities and towns on the continent. In Toronto, as on the rest of the continent, most *termitani* worked in the fruit trade, either as pedlars or store merchants. Some also became jobbers and wholesalers.

What is particularly interesting here is the lack of distinction between the urban and rural nature of their work. When they came to Toronto, the peasants from Termini operated within the migration traditions of their hometown, which, in effect, meant finding a niche in the city's fruit trade, where many of these former peasants continued to maintain their town's agricultural tradition – that is, dealing in the fruit trade or market gardening. However, within the North American context, the fruit traders fit squarely in the tradition of urban merchants. It is therefore difficult to make easy distinctions between the rural and urban nature of the Sicilian fruit traders in Toronto and its environs.[42]

The *termitani* were linked by strong bonds of kinship; all members from the hometown had an ascriptive status within the new world context. Decisions pertaining to work, enterprise, residence, marriage, or friendship were not made independently, but only with the approval of at least some of the other fellow townsmen. In 1925, the population of the *termitani* in Toronto stood at about 750. Most of those who were not involved in the fruit trade, or who were fruit pedlars rather than storeowners, lived in one neighbourhood in the east end of Toronto. All the fruit traders lived along Toronto's major thoroughfares above their shops, while the market gardeners lived on the eastern fringes of the city. As noted in the previous chapter, Termini's immigrants had the highest endogamy rate of any other Italian townsgroup in Toronto. In fact, a number of marriages between the *termitani* were between cousins: 30.2 percent married other Sicilians from outside Termini, most of these from fruit-trading families. The term cooperative spirit used to describe enterprise among the Sicilians is perhaps misleading in that it suggests free and easy obedience to the group. One did not make important decisions – such as establishing a fruit store, marrying, buying a house – independently. Rather, one followed the dictates and prescriptions of the townsgroup, which, in effect, meant obeying and respecting those in the townsgroup who had earned respect.

A chart of the spread of the *termitani*'s fruit stores in the city allows us to understand some of the mechanisms which accounted for their pre-eminence in the city's fruit trade. By 1895, the *termitani* were running fruit stores along Queen Street West and East, immediately on either side of Yonge Street. By 1905 they had expanded in both directions. On Queen Street West, five fruit stores dotted the north side to Ossington Avenue and six shops were located on Queen Street East to just past Parliament Street. By the First World War, *termitani* fruit stores along Queen Street East had multiplied to eighteen, and to twenty-three along Queen Street West. Fruit shops had reached almost to Lansdowne Avenue in the west end and Kingswood Road in the east end. They also moved into other streets – there were eight fruit stores along Yonge Street to Birch Avenue; two on Parliament Street near Carlton Street; two on College Street just west of Yonge Street; two on Bloor Street; and one on the Danforth. Rather than grouping in one geographical area, the Sicilians quickly dispersed along the main arteries of the city.

During and after the Great War, the Sicilians and other Italians took advantage of changing conditions. Shipping restrictions prevented the importation of fruit and vegetables, and potential competitors in the fruit trade were drawn away either to the military or to wartime industry.[43] As a result the Italian presence, and especially that of Termini's and Vita's emigrants, increased significantly (see table 9).

From 1914 to 1925, the fruit stores did not spread farther east or west along Queen or Bloor streets, but extended much farther east along Danforth Avenue, almost to Woodbine Avenue. The latter area opened up in 1917 with the completion of the Prince Edward Bridge (the Bloor Viaduct). By 1925 the fruit traders of Termini were operating at least fifty-five fruit stores along Queen Street East and West; fifteen on Bloor Street; nine on the Danforth; eight on Yonge Street; and six on Parliament Street. They had also moved up to St Clair Avenue West and to the West Toronto Junction.

During the Great Depression the Italians' and Sicilians' share of the fruit trade declined as the number of fruiterers, Italian and non-Italian, increased significantly. Of 550 fruit stores in 1935, 295 were owned by Italians, including 102 *termitani* and 46 *vitesi*. A few Chi-

Table 9
Numbers and Percentages of Italian Fruit Stores, Toronto, 1912–25

	1912	%	1925	%	1935	%
No. of Fruit Stores, Toronto	208	100.0	354	100.0	550	100.0
No. of Italian Fruit Stores	126	60.6	242	68.4	295	53.6
No. Owned by *termitani*	43	20.7	83	23.5	102	18.6
No. Owned by *vitesi*	11	5.3	39	11.0	46	8.4

Sources: Marriage Registers, Our Lady of Mount Carmel Parish, 1908–35, ARCAT; Might's Toronto Directory, 1912, 1925.

nese and Greeks entered the market at that time but the Jewish presence increased significantly, from 28 in 1925 to 71, ten years later. Also British and Irish-Canadians jumped from 67 traders in 1925 to 140 in 1935. It is difficult to explain the decline in the Sicilian or Italian share of the market. Competition from other ethnic groups – especially the Jews in Kensington Market – the attraction of second-generation Italians to industry, the lack of capital brought on by the depression were certainly all factors. Also, it was during the depression that many of the Italian, and other fruit stores, began extending credit; few individuals would take the risk of instituting a fruit store under such difficult conditions without a solid capital base.

The sense of mutual obligation and cooperation help explain how the fruit retailers of Termini acquired capital. During the 1920s when that townsgroup had its largest share of the city's fruit trade, it also had a higher credit rating than the rest of the Italian fruit retailing population in Toronto. In 1925 R.G. Dun rated the credit of 108 Italian fruit stores; at least 33 belonged to Termini's emigrants, and 18 to Vita's. The other 57 came from all parts of the peninsula and Sicily (see table 10).[44]

The credit ratings for Termini's immigrants were significantly higher than those of "Other Italians" and much higher than those of Vita's immigrants. The great discrepancy between the two prominent townsgroups, Vita and Termini Imerese, needs to be explained. First, the *vitesi* entered the city's fruit trade much later than the *termitani*. Whereas the latter opened their earliest outlets in the mid-1890s, the *vitesi* did not begin retailing until twenty years later.

Second, credit and mutual aid among the immigrants from Vita were not as well organized as they were among the *termitani*. Although some *vitesi* and *pachinesi* belonged to the Trinacria Mutual

Table 10
R.G. Dun's Credit Ratings of Italian Fruit Stores, Toronto, 1925

Rating	*Termini*	*%*	*Vita*	*%*	*Other Italians*	*%*
Good	7	21.2	2	11.1	8	14.0
Fair	14	42.4	4	22.2	25	43.9
Limited	12	36.4	12	66.7	24	42.1
	33		18		57	

Source: Mercantile Reference Book.

Benefit Society, immigrants from Termini controlled the society. The *vitesi* did not form their own association until 1935.[45] The high credit rating of the *termitani* as well as their business success can be attributed to their experience, their early entry into the trade, but also to their ability to raise capital. The Trinacria society was a mutual aid organization founded in 1908 and incorporated in 1914 – all of its members were Sicilian and virtually all of them from Termini Imerese. It is quite likely that this society played an important capital-raising function for the fruit traders of that townsgroup during the predepression period. Membership until the mid-1920s rarely fell below 140. Throughout the 1910s and into the 1920s, the Trinacria claimed the healthiest bank account of all Italian mutual aid societies in the city. After the First World War, the balance always remained above $2,000 and was usually in the $3,000 range (see table 11).[46] Sick benefit claims and benefits were much lower among the Trinacria society members than among any other mutual aid society in the city suggesting that the *termitani* had an interest in maintaining a large equity (see table 12). Possibly the Trinacria society used its account as collateral for its members' financing needs in the fruit trade. In fact, during the 1920s, the Trinacria society usually earned twice as much interest as the Italo-Canadese Society, even though the liquid assets of the two associations were equal.

The orderly spread of the fruit stores attests to the powerful cooperative spirit of Termini's immigrants. Greenhorns worked either as street labourers, pedlars, or as employees in their townspeople's or relatives' fruit stores until they acquired the capital and skill to operate their own shops. However, opening a fruit store was usually more complex than that. Entrepreneurship and capital accumulation were intimately connected to questions of marriage and inheritance, ascriptive obligations, and an ethos which assigned a

Table 11

Assets and Membership of Trinacria, Vittorio Emanuele, Umberto Primo, Italian Workingmen's Circle, and *La Congregazione della Immacolata Concezione di Maria SS.* Mutual Aid Societies, Toronto, 1915–22

Society	*Trinacria*		*Vittorio Emanuele*		(*Italo-Canadese*)* *Umberto Primo*		*It. Workingmen*		*Cong. della I.C.*	
	$assets	membership	$assets	membership	$assets	membership	$assets	membership	$assets	membership
Year										
1915	1,341	152	92	29	591	26	1,005	75	425	15
1916	1,831	154	68	18	575	25	688	75	320	13
1917	2,004	156	50	20	526	22	629	47	352	14
1918	2,454	148	42	18	415	16	375	47	396	15
1919	2,719	144			843	110			433	16
1920	3,212	134			1,246	110			472	14
1921	3,331	135			1,765	140			497	13
1922	3,665	123			2,082	124			520	12

Source: "Annual Report of the Registrar of Friendly Societies," in "Report of the Inspector of Insurance," *Sessional Papers*, Toronto, 1915–22.

*In 1919, Vittorio Emanuele, Umberto Primo, and Italian Workingmen's Circle amalgamated into the *Società Italo-Canadese*.

Table 12

Membership, Number of Sick Members, Number of Weeks Sick Benefits Claimed, Annually, 1919–35, *Società Trinacria* and *Società Italo-Canadese*

	Società Trinacria				*Società Italo-Canadese*			
year	#members	#sick	#weeks	$benefits*	#members	#sick	#weeks	$benefits*
1919	144	28	103	515	110	7	71	68.60
1920	134	13	26	125	110	26	85	500.00
1921	135	9	21	145	140	23	63	378.00
1922	123	11	34	170	124	24	123	631.70
1923	121	17	57		148	37	108	
1924	135	12	38		129	30	132	
1925	135	14	68		134	44	—	
1926	153	15	95		191	36	108	
1927	178	13	88		277	64	171	
1928	184	26	155		302	86	334	
1929	174	31	94		294	83	341	
1930	165	25	180		256	85	300	

Source: "Annual Report of the Registrar of Friendly Societies," in "Report of the Inspector of Insurance," *Sessional Papers*, Toronto, 1919–30.

*Total amounts of sick benefits are listed only until 1922.

touch of deviance to townspeople who should opt to remain outside the fruit and grocery trade. Because of the shortcomings of city directories and church registers as sources, it is difficult to trace the life cycles and careers of most immigrants from Termini in the fruit business. Nevertheless, even from a small sample one can acquire some sense of the mechanics of establishing fruitstand after fruitstand during the twenty-five years preceding the Great Depression.

In a sample of thirty-two Toronto marriages involving proprietors or future proprietors of fruit stores, only four bridegrooms owned their own shops before their weddings. Five other men married daughters of fruit retailers and eventually acquired control of their respective inlaw's store, usually soon after the marriage. Two bridegrooms inherited their father's store. The others opened their own fruit outlets very soon after marriage, one or two years later. Before marriage, the latter usually boarded and/or worked as clerks or storekeepers at fruit stores in the city. After, they either acquired control of the store where they had apprenticed or set up their own stands nearby. In fact, many of the fruit dealers who established shops in new areas of the city were old-time entrepreneurs who had sold their former downtown shops to newcomers. In this way, the entrepreneurs were responsible for increasing the density of fruit dealers in the older quarters of the city.

Most of the city's Italian fruit stores were passed on from townsman to townsman and few closed permanently until economic pressures, such as the depression, made it absolutely necessary. If a *termitano* dealer had no male heir, or no son interested in pursuing the career of the small retailer, he had the option of finding a suitable son-in-law who indeed would be rewarded with an ample dowry. Michael Cutrara was a twenty-four-year-old fruit pedlar when he married Rose Giuffrè in 1919. Rose was the twenty-year-old daughter of Giuseppe Giuffrè, a fruit dealer at 585 College Street, who recently had passed away. Michael became the new proprietor of the store after the marriage agreement.

On the other hand, it was not necessary to marry a widow's daughter to receive the inheritance. Giuseppe Zuccaro, a twenty-six-year-old labourer living at 262 Queen Street married Cosimo Franzè's nineteen-year-old daughter, Ignazia, in late 1911. Both had been born in Termini. About three years later, Cosimo passed on his fruit store to Giuseppe. His son-in-law had become a surrogate son because he allowed Cosimo to perpetuate his family heritage. More to the point, the fruiterers of Termini arrived in Toronto with developed capitalistic notions but with a pre-industrial frame of mind. Establishing a fruit store was not simply an exercise in free enterprise. The fruit store was considered a property to be preserved, perpetuated, passed on to succeeding generations. This perspective on the establishment as a form of family inheritance ensured that Sicilian- and Calabrian-owned stores had a longer average life span than other fruit shops in the city.[47]

The fruit stores lasted longer as enterprises not only because they were passed on from townsman to townsman, but because they even passed from one townsgroup to another, especially among Sicilians from Termini, Vita, and Pachino (see table 13). Joseph Deferrari, from Ferrada, Genoa, operated a fruit shop at 1358 Queen Street West for over twenty years beginning in the mid-1890s. He sold it to James Rovegno who in turn passed it on to Louis Conti of Termini Imerese in the late 1920s; Conti resold it to a fellow townsman, Leo Cancilla, by 1935. Frank Akrey (Acri) of San Sisto sold his twenty-five-year-old fruit shop to Antonio Battaglia of Termini Imerese in the early 1920s and ten years later Battaglia resold it to his townsman, Joseph Badali. A significant number of *vitesi* sold their shops to *termitani*. In the late 1920s and early 1930s, Vito Simone and the Acquanno brothers of Vita sold their two businesses on the Danforth to the Azzarello brothers and to Joseph Comella. In the same period, Frank Ferlito of Vita sold his concern to Agostino Spalla of Termini. There were at least three other similar cases. Once a fruit store had been established, the Italian, and especially Sicilian fruit merchants, ensured that if an heirless proprietor should retire from his business, the shop would pass on to another Italian, and usually a townsman or Sicilian.

It is difficult to trace the careers of shop proprietors who sold their businesses; city directories are not always complete because some individuals either left the city or died. From a sample of fifteen such store owners from the 1915–1935 period, three could no longer be located in 1935; two died and their children went into other occupations. The remaining ten opened new fruit stores, in all cases farther east, north, or west towards the city limits. This suggests that the established fruiterers were more enterprising and more inclined to enter the new territories of the city than their younger colleagues. The spaces inbetween the city's centre and its limits were then filled by the more recent, young entrepreneurs.

Table 13
Change of Ownership of Fruit Stores, 1895–1935

	No. of Fruit Stores Which Changed Ownership Between Italians			
Location	*No. of Stores*	*Once*	*Twice*	*Thrice*
Danforth Ave	14	3		
Queen St E.	10	2	1	3
Queen St W.	15	3	2	2
Bloor St	21	3	1	
Yonge St	13	3	1	–
Totals	73	14	5	5

Source: Might's Toronto Directory, 1895, 1905, 1915, 1925, 1930, 1935.

Inheritance or the purchase of an existing store dictated the location of new shops for some entrepreneurs. When Mike Calderone married in 1912, he was working at Joseph Graziani's store at 751 Queen Street East. The following year he acquired the shop, while his old boss moved out to the new residential areas along the Danforth. Giuseppe Arrigo did the same when his boss, Antonio Ponzo of Vita, moved out to the Danforth from College Street in about 1920. Others opened stores near their place of apprenticeship. An astute store clerk had a good sense of market conditions, and most likely was well advised by another townsman and proprietor from the area – Mike Cosentino worked at Joseph Cosentino's (not his father) outlet at 556 College Street in the early 1920s. In 1925 he established his own business at 312 College Street.

Beyond these simple factors one cannot explain exactly why certain sites were chosen or the reasons for the choice. Such decisions were rarely made independently. Each townsman had an ascriptive position in the townsgroup, and he had to heed the advice of those who commanded respect and obligations. Possibly a particular series of blocks along Queen Street were reserved for one family and any attempt by another family to interfere in that market would be censured by the townspeople. Among the fruiterers from Termini Imerese living in Cleveland, Ohio, the group control mechanisms were so powerful that many of the townspeople left the city because a veritable Black Hand controlled the fruit trade.[48] A neophyte fruit retailer responded not only to the prescriptions of unwritten laws, but also, for practical purposes, to the censure or approval of his *paesani*, for often he depended upon them for his initial capital. Any loan from a townsman created a new series of obligations including that of conferring with one's patrons and their patrons' patrons on the suitability of establishing a mart at a particular site.

The fruit vendors from Termini Imerese were an extremely tightly knit group. The close bonds of the group affected work and enterprise but they also perpetuated those bonds. Although the *termitani* competed at the same enterprise, they also had mutual obligations: hiring townspeople as store clerks, loaning initial capital to new young entrepreneurs, counselling them, being aware of the territorial market of a fellow townsman, and not interfering in that market. The *termitani* provide the best example of the benefits to enterprise, derived from ethnic and subethnic ties, but the *friulani* construction tradesmen, the grinders from the Val Rendena, the bootblacks from Monteleone, the barbers from Pisticci, the musicians from Laurenzana, or the chefs and waiters from Susa all operated on the same principles. Mutual obligations and the ties of hometown or region provided each group with an apprenticeship system, a labour market, capital, employment, and opportunity enabling it to compete effectively in a particular trade in Toronto's economy.

Not all of the townsgroups, of course, had cultivated one or two skills, or had developed enterprises to provide employment for their *paesani*. Some townsgroups were able to find a niche in Toronto's industries or construction companies. For example, during the 1910s, some *modugnesi* worked at the City Dairy where Giuseppe Tomasicchio, their townsman, was a sales agent for Italians in the city. Many of Rocca San Giovanni's immigrants were employed at Silknit, a clothing company on King Street West, while immigrants from Apricena (Puglia) were employed by Cook Clothing and Tip Top Tailors. These immigrants were active in the Toronto-Italian Local 235 of the Amalgamated Clothing Workers. However, immigrants from many towns found employment in these firms either through their respective townspeople or through other Italian immigrants. During the postwar period, the dynamics of finding employment came to depend less upon hometown ties as townsmen developed relationships with other immigrants from either the peninsula or different countries. Also, in the construction or needle trades, employers developed perceptions of the ideal worker. In these sectors, Italians were often favoured as hard workers who accepted low wages, and who, through family connections, could provide additional labour when necessary.

By the 1920s an Italian-Torontonian occupational structure had emerged. A number of occupations were particularly cultivated by Italians. Fathers or bachelors without immediate family in Toronto concentrated in some trades more than others, as did sons and daughters still living at home. It is difficult to give exact figures about representation in each trade because cross-referencing names and occupations in city directories and assessment roles reveals that unskilled trades were often omitted from the directories. The most represented occupations were construction, needle trades, industrial labour, fruit retailing, and service trades. A second generation male was more likely to work as a skilled labourer in construction and as an industrial labourer than an immigrant. During the 1930s, a son of immigrants usually apprenticed in the construction trades in Toronto. A father was more likely than his son to be an unskilled construction labourer.[49]

Many sons and daughters of immigrants worked at clerical jobs, often in their parents' fruit store. Daughters and wives were more likely than immigrant males or their sons to end up in the needle or laundry trades. Daughters, not mothers, were prominent as secretaries (mothers obviously did not have the language skills). Daughters working in the needle trades or industry were often employed alongside a brother, sister, aunt, uncle, cousin, or parent.

By the 1930s, then, Italian immigrants and their children found work not only in the traditional trades of their hometowns or as unskilled labourers. In construction work they had joined the skilled labour force and had made forays into industry, particularly the needle trades. Sons and daughters became more represented in clerical positions. Although further extensive research on the employment of the second generation needs to be done, it seems that an Italian-Torontonian occupational structure emerged in which husbands, wives without children, sons, and daughters were the breadwinners. Construction, needle, and laundry trades, and, to a certain extent, industrial labour became "natural" occupational areas for an Italian immigrant worker. It became less common for an immigrant and his children to continue working in the migratory trade of his hometown, but it became appropriate to work in trades considered typically Italian.

Italian reservists march in support of the war effort, 2 September 1915. Hundreds went back to their homeland in the months following Italy's entry into the war. (Public Archives of Canada [PAC])

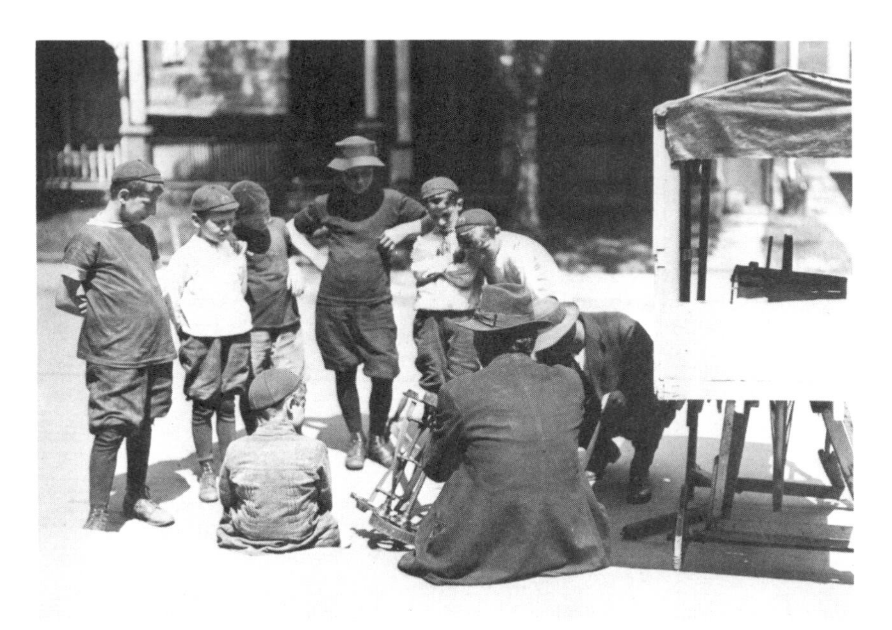

Street knife-grinder, probably from the Val Rendena, Major Street, 1913. (James Collection, CTA)

Italian immigrants from Lucca during the royal visit, 1939. The Florentine Company on King Street was owned by Massimo Jacopo Magi of Bagni di Lucca. (MHSO Collection, Archives of Ontario)

Concertina player, Major Street, 1913. (James Collection, CTA)

Friulan brickmakers at the John Price plant of the Toronto Brick Company in East End Toronto, 1936. (CTA)

Banquet in honour of Emilio Goggio, Italian language professor at the University of Toronto, who was very active in the Toronto Italian community, ca. 1935. (MHSO Collection, Archives of Ontario)

Italian reservists in World War I parade, 1915. (PAC)

Caboto Committee, ca. 1931. Members of this committee to erect a statue of the explorer in Montreal were among the leaders of the *fascio* in Toronto. From left to right: Marco Missori, Tommaso Mari, Antonio Gatto, Rosario Invidiata, and Giuseppe Tomasicchio. (MHSO Collection, Archives of Ontario)

CHAPTER FOUR

Entrepreneurs and the Ethnic Economy

Chapter 6 will examine the formation of a class of notables in Toronto's Italian community between 1885 and 1915. These men were mostly professionals, self-employed businessmen, Italian newspaper publishers, or agents for federal or provincial political parties. This chapter looks at one segment of that class of notables, self-employed men who directed their businesses to the ethnic market or ethnic economy. The ethnic entrepreneurs of the colony included labour agents, retailers of Italian foodstuffs and dry goods, immigrant bankers, steamship agents, and macaroni producers whose activities were often combined under one roof. They can be distinguished from the professionals and political party representatives in that they usually did not play a major leadership role in the voluntary associations of the community.

Ethnic entrepreneurs formed part of the élite of the colony by virtue of the trust they commanded from the grass roots, and of the intermediary role they played between the immigrants and the goods and services they purveyed. Except for one entrepreneur, they remained aloof from the political life of Italian Toronto. Unlike the professionals, they did not become actively involved in the city's Italian fascist movement of the 1930s. This chapter shall analyze the development of the enterprises of these ethnic entrepreneurs, their place in the colony, and the ethnic market to which they catered.

As a banker, steamship agent, or wholesaler of Italian food and dry goods, the ethnic entrepreneur was an immediate descendent of an earlier middleman in North American immigrant communities, the *padrone* or labour agent. The Italian *padrone* was most influential in the United States and Canada during the period stretching from the late 1870s to the early 1900s. It is essential to examine briefly this predecessor in order to understand the evolution of the banker and steamship agent in the post-1900 era.

Among Italian immigrants, the *padrone* system developed on this continent in the 1870s and provided the mechanisms for drawing Italian peasant labour to American and Canadian capital.[1] The agents, who flourished in virtually every city and town on the North American continent, developed networks among themselves, as well as with agents and subagents in Italy and Switzerland, to recruit labour for specific building projects in the new world. Mines, quarries, railroad companies, municipal works departments, and canal and dam contractors depended heavily upon the *padrone* to provide the necessary manpower for their undertakings.

The labour agent played a powerful role among the transient or sojourning population of each Little Italy by acting as middleman between the migrant and other agencies: he provided work, food and clothing for the work season in the northlands, a post office box, and a safety deposit box for savings. He also forwarded remittances to the sojourners' hometowns. When the labourers returned to Toronto for the winter season, the *padrone* attended to accommodations, either at his own boardinghouse or in another home in Little Italy. In other words, the *padrone* provided for all the ancillary needs pertaining to the migrant's main goal: acquiring capital to bring back to the hometown. In 1904, an Italian labourer who had worked for the Grand Trunk Railway was found dead on the job at the foot of Brock Street. His pockets contained $100.32 and a letter "which identified him from Rocco Peretta [*sic*] of Utica, N.Y. written in Italian." The paper with his *padrone*'s name indicated just how the sojourner depended upon his labour agent, not only for a postal address but also for a livelihood.[2]

Canada's most prominent labour agents, Albert Dini and Francesco Cordasco, were located in Montreal. From there they controlled most of the labour market for the doubletracking of the Canadian Pacific Railway (CPR) in the west at the turn of the century. In Port Arthur, the R.F. Welch Company, owned by the Veltri family from the town of Grimaldi, Cosenza in Calabria, imported many of the labourers and contracted a significant portion of the National Trans-continental Railway construction east of Winnipeg.[3] In comparison to Montreal, Toronto was a minor centre of Italian distribution. Nevertheless, the links that the city's *padroni* developed with their counterparts in other American cities guaranteed a steady labour supply for heavy construction projects within and especially without the city. From the late 1870s, labour agents recruited Italians and other foreigners to work on dams, bridges, roadways, and railways outside Toronto. However, they returned to winter in the Ward. By the 1890s, the *padroni* were supplying Italian labourers for the construction and repair of roadways, streetcar lines, and trunk sewer systems in Toronto.

From an early date, occasional reports in Toronto newspapers gave the city's *padroni* a bad name. For example, in late June 1874, 18 Italians who had been promised work on the Welland Canal, Ontario by New York agents were abandoned in a forest not far from one of the work camps near St Catharines, Ontario. In November 1883, the Italian vice-consul in Buffalo, New York, accused labour agents in Toronto of "forwarding large numbers of Italians to points where work is promised them then furnishing them with none, and leaving them in a destitute condition." Apparently 200 men had been shipped to Toronto from Buffalo, but only 60 had found work there. Five years later a gang of navvies paid for a job and passage from New York to Cornwall, Ontario, where their labour agent left them stranded. In Cornwall they were taken under the care of the De Santi brothers, labour agents who promised them work in Toronto and charged them $7.00 each for a $3.50 train fare to the city. When no work was to be had in Toronto, the De Santis refused to refund the fare or even the surcharge. In June 1898, just after the Royal Commission on Crow's Nest labour conditions had been released, 14 Italian workmen arrived in Toronto. A *padrone* "had brought them from Pittsburgh and charged them $9.00 each for obtaining work for them on the Crow's Nest Pass [railway construction] and had left them in the morning to their own resources." The men took the initiative to speak to R.J. Ellbeck, the CPR labour agent for the Crow's Nest Pass, to whom all other labour agents and subagents were responsible. Some local Italian immigrants, however, dissuaded the navvies from signing contracts because of the "horror" inspired by the Royal Commission's report. The labourers then approached the Italian vice-consul and asked to be returned to Buffalo, and in the meantime "camped out under the York Street bridge."[4]

The earliest *padroni* in the city were most likely the Glionna brothers, Giovanni and Francesco. Although they arrived in the mid-1870s, they opened their immigrant saloon, Glionna's Hotel, in

1885. However, they probably had begun recruiting labourers a few years earlier. In the 1880s, agents from Buffalo, Cornwall, Pittsburgh, and Utica supplied Italian navvies to Toronto. In the late 1880s, James Palma settled on Elizabeth Street in the Ward. From there he hired sojourners from Buffalo, Chicago, and other American cities to work on doubletracking the Grand Trunk Railway. On one occasion, in 1888, he was reported to have secured sixty-five Italian labourers from the United States.[5]

Except for the Glionnas with their saloon, the earliest *padroni* were labour agents who lodged sojourners in their boardinghouses. As the colony grew, and as more opportunities opened up for heavy and light construction in Toronto and its surroundings, so did the functions of the *padroni* expand. Francesco Nicoletti and George Glionna, who operated agencies respectively at 78 Edward Street and 126 Elm Street in the Ward, became food wholesalers and importers, and later, bankers and steamship agents for the sojourners as they took advantage of their intermediary role between Toronto capital and Italian immigrant labour. However, they also directed their goods and services to the growing permanent colony of Toronto's Italian immigrants.

Because these entrepreneurs performed various activities under their general function of intermediaries, it became difficult to assign them a specific title. When they were primarily labour agents, as in the late nineteenth century, they were commonly known as *padroni*, the Italian term for boss, whose root of course had much broader connotations. However, as the entrepreneurs catered more and more to a permanent urban population rather than to transient labourers, they became less associated with their labour agencies and more with their banks. Thus a United States Senate Commission on Immigration (Dillingham Commission) of 1907-9 referred to these men as immigrant bankers, and to their agencies as immigrant banks.[6]

The Dillingham Commission surveyed over 100 such immigrant banks in the United States. It distinguished 3 types of institutions. A review of the categories will indicate the kind of entrepreneur who predominated in Toronto:

1) state and incorporated banks, of which there were few;
2) "Privately owned steamship agencies, labour agencies, and real estate offices which masquerade under the name of bank, but which are not legally authorized as such. To this class should be added groceries and

saloons in which the banking functions are clearly defined as apart from the business"; and
3) "Banks which may or may not be known as such but in which [their] functions ... are extended more as an accommodation or as incidental to the main business of the concern."[7]

Toronto had no immigrant banks of the first type. It is almost impossible now to trace banks of the third type except perhaps through oral testimony, even though, in the view of the commissioners, this was the largest and most irresponsible group. James Farano's and Virginio Zincone's banks came under that category. Farano's clients were mostly fellow townsmen from Modugno di Bari (Puglia). The city's significant Italian bankers fell into the second category – steamship agents who had banks set apart from other business concerns.

Eugenio D'Angelo opened the city's first official Italian steamship agency in 1913 on Agnes Street (now Dundas Street), just west of Yonge Street. The following year, Francesco Nicoletti and George Glionna began their own agencies at 78 Edward Street and 126 Elm Street respectively. In 1915, Albert Dini officially listed himself in the city directory as a steamship agent. Three years later, a successful grocer, Carmine Petti, opened his agency at 60 Centre Avenue, and in 1921 Louis Puccini, another successful grocer-banker, established his office at the corner of Chestnut and Elm streets, the site of his Italian Cash Grocery. Meanwhile, on Clinton Street in the second Little Italy at College and Grace streets, Franceso Tomaiuolo had established a steamship agency and bank in August 1913 with only forty-nine dollars. These men were the early ethnic entrepreneurs of the colony. Unlike Peter and Max Dini (Albert's brothers who were responsible for his Toronto operations), they did not remain essentially employment agents for Italian sojourners.[8] Although they offered the same services as the Dinis', they were primarily grocers.

As intermediaries, the ethnic entrepreneurs were an important element among the notables of the colony, even if they were not politically active in the community. If nothing else, the persistent diatribes of the Italian Socialists in the Ward testify to the prestige of these men of commerce. The Socialists viewed them as capitalist exploiters, money-grubbing opportunists who would adhere to any political philosophy or religion as long as the financial rewards were lucrative. In August 1909, one member of the Toronto local of the

Italian Socialist party, Primo Giovanelli, held an open-air assembly at the corner of Elm Street and Centre Avenue, the commercial centre of Little Italy, directly in front of Trentadue Brothers Grocery. He was asked to leave because, according to his own account, "he was blocking commercial traffic to the Trentadue Brothers, wholesalers, bankers (without a vault, of course), Protestants, and in their leisure time captains of the *bersaglieri* [in Italy, the *bersaglieri* were the most prestigious unit of the armed forces], men who do not disdain to accompany priests, prelates, and Catholic madonnas through the streets of the city." The following year another banker, Giuseppe Izzo (also a Methodist, as were the Trentadue brothers), was expelled from the Toronto socialist local for "systematic incoherence of conduct to socialist principles." The notice of expulsion was not detailed but it did remark sourly that Izzo was a shopkeeper.[9]

In March 1910 the Toronto correspondent of *Il Proletario*, a New York-based socialist newspaper, lashed out at the former Methodist minister in the colony, Giuseppe Merlino, who had since become a banker, "as he says during elections, one can vote for the Conservatives and when they do not pay enough, can pick up kit and caboodle for the Liberal camp."[10] He also attacked Merlino's Christian socialism. The correspondent believed that the community's ability to act had been dulled by the ethnic entrepreneurs, and he campaigned to rectify the situation: "Some time ago this Italian Socialist Local initiated a serious and efficacious programme of propaganda to awaken the dormant energies of this mass of immigrants that care for nothing more than working like mules, enduring their bosses' whips, the tyranny of their bankers [*banconai*] and of *prominenti* of any type, and the wastage of money on the part of the raven [Fr Carlo Doglio, pastor of Our Lady of Mount Carmel Parish] who crows every hour for funds in the name of Jesus."[11]

The First World War brought an end to the employment agents in the city. In 1917 the provincial legislature assented to "The Employment Agencies Act" which required licensing, bookkeeping, and governmental inspections of all labour agencies.[12] Under such strict inspection, no Italian immigrant agencies applied for a licence. As a result, the Dinis left the city altogether that year; Francesco Nicoletti sold his business to Giuseppe Gatto in 1920; the Glionnas sold their hotel in 1917, although, as mentioned in chapter two, prohibition and the death of Francesco Glionna prompted that decision. By the end of the war, Toronto's Italian sojourning population had declined dramatically and the vast majority of the population was permanent. The ethnic entrepreneur, no longer primarily an employment agent, was rather a banker, grocer, and/or steamship agent.

Who were the ethnic entrepreneurs? What qualities enabled them to rise to such status in the community? Of the eight steamship agents who operated in Toronto between 1913 and 1933,[13] at least four were either born in Toronto or had immigrated to the city before 1910. One was the son of a *laurenzanese* (Glionna) and a second was married to a *laurenzanese* (Nicoletti): in other words, they came from older and more established families. By 1915, because there was little contact between the *laurenzanesi* in Toronto and the hometown in Italy, these agents did not depend upon their townspeople for a core clientele.

The other four agents, with the exception of Carmine Petti, had few townspeople in the city and did not cater to any specific group of townsmen. Louis Puccini, who operated the Italian Cash Grocery at the corner of Chestnut and Elm streets, was from Ghivizzano (Tuscany). Marco Missori, who after training with a few steamship agents, opened his own agency on Claremont Street in the College and Grace streets neighbourhood in the 1930s, was from Monte Compatri (Lazio). Carmine Petti, who established his office in 1918 at 60 Centre Avenue in the Ward, had numerous townsmen in the city from Oratina (Molise). Giuseppe Gatto, who purchased Nicoletti's shop in 1920, was from Varapoido (Calabria). At least two agents had originally lived in the United States. Petti had travelled to Toronto from Cleveland and Gatto had lived in Drayton, Pennsylvania for one and one-half years – they had seen the success of ethnic entrepreneurial activity in the steamship and banking business in Little Italies south of the border. In the postwar period, the entrepreneurs were Catholic, although, as we have seen, before 1913 three Italian Methodists ran agencies.

Almost all the ethnic entrepreneurs had acquired business expertise and some capital before opening their agencies. Nicoletti's stepfather, Domenico Spada, was a fruit wholesaler, and Nicoletti had operated a confectionery and wholesale grocery store before establishing the agency and bank next door to his store. Glionna of course was from a well-to-do family and had a degree in law. Gatto ran a bakery for fifteen years, first on Elm Street and later on Dundas Street West near Grace Street. When he sold the business in 1919, he went into partnership with Nicoletti, and the following year he purchased his partner's share. Eugenio D'Angelo earned his early capital as a musician, as had his father, Rocco, who had come to Toronto in 1880. Louis Puccini operated a grocery store on Centre Avenue and later a wholesale grocery store at Chestnut and Elm streets (Italian Cash Grocery). In 1921 he entered the steamship agency business in partnership with Marco Missori.

Missori began working in steamship agencies as a young man. He received a high school education in Italy and soon after his immigration to Toronto he worked for Nicoletti, and later, Petti. He then became a partner in Puccini's travel agency and later in Gatto's agency until he opened his own office on Elm Street in 1929. Because he was aware that the focus of Toronto's Italian community was shifting to the St Agnes Church area, he relocated his office to Claremont Street four years later. Francesco Tomaiuolo had operated in the area for sixteen years by that time.

Under his integrated operations, the ethnic entrepreneur met the locus of needs of the immigrants. The Dillingham Commission offered an explanation for the immigrant's tendency to patronize the entrepreneur's "bank." According to the commission, the immigrant's "ignorance and suspicion" attracted him to the immigrant banker as much as the ability of the entrepreneur to offer necessary services no mainstream bank could offer. In addition, he spoke his clients' language. With little difficulty he could telegraph earnings for the client to his savings deposit box in the hometown post office (post offices in Italy offered that service). His bank would remain open in the evening, Saturdays, and sometimes even Sunday mornings. The banker could collect gradually the savings of a customer and remit them to Italy once the depositor had saved a prescribed amount.

At the immigrant bank the patron could purchase steamship tickets, groceries, stationery, books, stamps, or musical instruments. The banker also sold insurance or even real estate – all this under one roof. In addition, the bank itself was pretentiously attractive with its large signs, glass fronts, and wickets – on top of Giuseppe Gatto's agency's entrance door a local artist had painted a fresco of a construction labourer with his pick and shovel. The agency was, however, never too clean. A labourer was less embarrassed to leave a trail of muddy bootmarks on a linoleum floor than on the spotless marble floors of a chartered bank.[14]

It is pointless to try to understand the place of the ethnic entrepreneur in the life and economy of an immigrant group solely in terms of exploitation. Certainly the horror stories of immigrants abandoned by unscrupulous *padroni* after having paid an employment fee, of bankers absconding with the immigrants' hard-earned savings, have given the ethnic entrepreneur a bad name. That in itself, however, does not explain how or why an entrepreneur acquired respect in the colony, or what made him one of the class of notables. As the following case study of two Toronto bankers will show, the entrepreneurs were not necessarily callous swindlers. Like other notables in the hometown, they were primarily capitalists, pre-industrial in outlook and their notability stemmed from pre-industrial notions of deference on the part of the immigrants. The banker's persona, his conspicuous wealth, his versatility with either pure Italian or dialect, his ability to meet the needs of the immigrants, and play an intermediary role inspired trust. Although at least two Italian immigrant bankers defalcated in Toronto during the 1930s, hundreds of immigrants continued to patronize other Italian bankers in the city at the height of the depression. As the Dillingham Commission had described the relationship between the immigrant and the ethnic banker in 1909, "it is solely a matter of trust throughout."

When the disadvantages of an immigrant bank are examined, it seems remarkable that the immigrant rank and file should have patronized them to the extent they did. The banks were privately owned, usually by one investor. Few of them paid any interest and some even charged for services, such as the cost of the passbook. The banks were not incorporated and did not maintain a capital reserve fund. Each client had his or her own account and passbook but all the accounts were deposited collectively in the immigrant banker's own account at a chartered bank. Under verbal and sometimes written agreements, deposits were subject to demand at any time, but no "limitation [is] imposed upon the banks with respect to the care or investment of these funds ... So far as his depositors are concerned, the immigrant banker is at liberty to use their funds to suit himself."[15] In fact, the bankers invested their clients' savings in their own investments, either for purchasing stock for their groceries, acquiring real estate, or making capital improvements to their businesses.

The bankers reached the pinnacle of their financial success and prestige within the Italian community and remained, as stated above, essentially petty capitalists, pre-industrial in outlook. The ethnic economy was based not on production but on a series of middleman roles, and the bankers expanded their enterprises, power, and prestige by envisioning situations where they could act as agents for their clients' needs.[16] Giuseppe Gatto, for example, on Centre Avenue and Elm Street, sold steamship tickets, operated a large grocery store, offered deposit banking services, translated documents, cabled remittances to Italy, sold insurance, purchased a food importing company (from Abramo Puccini) on Front Street, acquired a 10 percent interest in a construction contracting firm, served as macaroni sales agent for a company in St Catharines (owned by Abramo Puccini), operated an immigrant library (which meant he lent books to immigrants for a fee), and supplied coal for home heating. Gatto also invested funds into a short-lived soft drink company but even that attempt at production of goods reflects his pre-industrial perspective: he intended to bottle the drinks in his basement with his children's help. Gatto had eight children and the only two of working age helped in the family business.[17]

Eugenio D'Angelo discovered new economic opportunities by playing in bands, doing secretarial work for the acting vice-consul, Dr Harley Smith, and by translating documents for the Dominion Express Company. Francesco Tomaiuolo operated a private bank and steamship agency on Clinton Street, issued money orders, received payments on gas and electrical bills, and "carried on a retail business which included among many other things Italian books, musical instruments, Italian periodicals, stationery and ... 'dry-goods.' " To draw more attention to his business, Tomaiuolo published an Italian newspaper for the colony, *Il Progresso Italo-Canadese*. (This weekly, edited by his brother, was initiated in 1929 and lasted until Tomaiuolo's firm defaulted in 1931.)[18] These bankers therefore multiplied their goods and services to the community and constantly created new middleman roles for themselves in order to broaden their clientele.

The steamship agents and bankers occupied a unique position in the colony with respect to accumulating capital. Assuredly members of townsgroups in the city did rely upon each other for loans, or at least for insuring loans, but the bankers had at their disposal a large proportion of the savings of the Italian immigrant population. When Francesco Tomaiuolo went bankrupt in 1931, his liabilities against deposit creditors amounted to $21,131.91. In addition, 120 clients entrusted him with $3,405.08 to remit to their hometowns in Italy. Three years later, Giuseppe Gatto became insolvent with $31,780 owing deposit creditors. Gatto and Tomaiuolo may have been excellent middlemen, but they did not know how to invest their funds – or more correctly, their clients' funds – in other undertakings. Gatto invested in a number of enterprises which were never initiated, for example a soft drink company and an Italian newspaper. He lost his investment in a 10 percent share of a sewer construction firm. His greatest error was to purchase the site of his steamship agency and bank at 78–88 Centre Avenue. Gatto's property was mortgaged for over $22,000 in 1933, at the nadir of the depression.[19]

While Gatto accounted $1,250 in food perishables for his stock-in-trade at his declaration of bankruptcy, Tomaiuolo claimed $7,500 worth of books, musical instruments and sheet music, tobacco, and other dry goods. The Clinton Street banker had squandered funds on building a modern, decorous bank and retail outlet and small hotel. Tomaiuolo had taken advantage of his clients' deposit accounts: although his new building was valued at $29,000, his mortgages totalled only $13,386. In addition, he had speculated in two mining lots at Anfuso Mines.[20]

What ultimately made things go awry for both Gatto and Tomaiuolo was the world economic situation. Although Gatto had operated a bakery through the recession of 1907, and both Gatto and Tomaiuolo had run their shops through the immediate postwar recession, neither had learned the importance of maintaining cash reserves in the event that loans should be recalled. When irate depositors demanded their money, the two bankers were unprepared. During a depression it was impossible to transform capital investments or stock-in-trade immediately into cash. The situation was not unique among these immigrant bankers.

In the earlier, more mild depression of 1907, dozens of immigrant bankers on the continent went bankrupt for precisely the same reason. The Dillingham Commission in 1909 examined twenty-five banks which had become insolvent in New York alone during that panic, and the commissioners reported that many others had done so across the United States and Canada. A. Giannetti, a New York banker, who had established an outlet on Front Street in Toronto, became insolvent in the recession of 1907 after speculating on the stock market. He committed suicide in a Queen Street hotel room when 500 Italians in the colony lost their savings. A Macedonian banker in St Louis, Missouri defaulted with a deficit of $4,000 to $5,000 owing his depositors. "He had been in [the U.S.] for only five years, and stated that he had no conception of such a thing as a panic and that the depression of 1907 was to him entirely unexpected, else he would not have tied up his money to such an extent." Gatto and Tomaiuolo found themselves in exactly the same circumstances. When Gatto was asked under cross-examination at the bankruptcy hearings what had happened to all the money entrusted to him by immigrants who wished it sent to their hometowns he answered:

A. Lost.
Q. How did you lose it?
A. You know, the conditions.
Q. What did you lose it on?
A. You know, the depression today.
Q. Never mind the depression, give me some idea what you lost it on?
A. Business bad you know, poor year.[21]

The bank failures were always preceded by a panic among depositors. The clients placed blind trust in the steamship agents, a trust based on his self-assured mannerisms, advertisements, steamship posters, the word *Banca* on the large storefront windows, and the unostentatious yet correct professionalism of his furnishings – a number of wooden chairs, a plain counter, an impressive wicket. Nevertheless, should one major depositor require a large portion of his funds on demand and the banker be unable to comply immediately, word would spread rapidly. Agitated depositors would be at their patron's door instantly, demanding the balance of their accounts. One Italian bank in the United States with $70,000 in deposits kept a cash reserve of $55,000 and invested $15,000 in real estate. Yet even with such a large reserve, a run on this bank during the 1907 panic almost made it go bankrupt. One client trusted the banker enough to accept clearing-house certificates as security until cash should become available; this trust convinced other clients to do the same and the business was saved.[22]

Francesco Tomaiuolo was not as lucky. Although he had maintained low cash reserves, his business was not in particularly bad shape. One client, however, purchased a home and required $2,200 –

his entire account balance – almost immediately. When Tomaiuolo stalled and could provide only a fraction of the amount, other clients began demanding their money. As a result, the eighteen-year veteran of the banking business was placed in trusteeship. The solicitor of the trustees explained that "the bankruptcy created something in the nature of a communal upheaval in the Italian colony in the City and as a result many things had to be done which in ordinary cases are not necessary. For instance from the date of bankruptcy both Mr Martin's [the trustee officer] and my office were visited by a continuous stream of these [deposit] creditors who had come to make enquiry about their savings ... some of these people had their life savings tied up in the estate and could not be dismissed with a gesture."[23]

The proportion of the Italian community which patronized the immigrant banks was remarkably large as were the amount of funds it entrusted with the entrepreneurs. The trustee reported that at the time of his bankruptcy, Tomaiuolo had approximately 300 depositors, about one-third to one-half of whom were trust creditors, "that is, persons who had deposited money with him for transmission to Italy."[24] A tally of Tomaiuolo's and Gatto's list of unsecured creditors indicates 115 savings depositors for the former and 109 for the latter. In addition, Tomaiuolo had 120 trust creditors.[25] The two bankers claimed at least 224 depositors and yet four other Italian steamship agents and bankers in the city each probably had as large a clientele as theirs. In addition, other small grocers may have offered banking services. In all, it would be safe to assume that at least 700 Italians had savings accounts in the immigrant banks; that is, about 20 percent of the 3,850 males over the age of nineteen in the city. Table 14 gives a statistical breakdown of the deposits: The average deposit in Tomaiuolo's bank was $183.76; in Gatto's bank, $291.56; but accounts in the former were more evenly distributed.

In 1909 the Dillingham Commission examined thirty-one American immigrant banks, twelve of which were Italian. The average bank claimed 103 clients with an average deposit of $65.45. The corresponding figures for the twelve Italian banks were 124 clients and $63.73 (American dollars in 1908). Despite the deflated dollar of the early 1930s, the average deposit in Toronto's immigrant banks in that period was four times greater than deposits in United States's immigrant banks in the 1907–8 panic. This attested both to the higher savings of the later immigrants but also to the extensive trust

Table 14
Deposit Creditors of Two Italian Immigrant Banks, Toronto, 1931, 1933

	Tomaiuolo	*Gatto*	*Total*
No. of Creditors	115	109	224
Total Deposits	$21,131.90	31,780.08	52,911.98
Average Deposit	$ 183.76	291.56	237.66
	s[1]=271.18	s=674.63	
	o[2]=270.00	o=671.53	

Source: Gatto and Tomaiuolo Bankruptcy Proceedings, Bankruptcy Office, Supreme Court of Ontario.
[1] standard deviation of sample
[2] standard deviation of population

placed by the community in the private bankers. Twenty-one individuals invested over $500 in Gatto's bank; 9 did likewise in Tomaiuolo's concern (see table 15). One poor soul lost $6,130 in Gatto's failure, while 8 other individuals forfeited their lifesavings of $1,000 to $2,000 (the latter amount would almost cover the cost of a home). One man who had returned to Italy left $1,000 with Gatto for his wife's living expenses, "but at the rate of not more than $50.00 per month during [her] husband's absence from Toronto."[26]

It is unclear, though, through which networks, beyond those discussed already, the Italian entrepreneurs commanded such implicit trust. Gatto was located in the Ward, the commercial centre of Toronto's Italian community, even though by 1933 it had lost many Italian residents. A sample of Gatto's clients reveals that they lived in all parts of the city. Tomaiuolo's clients were more concentrated. His bank was in a residential neighbourhood and virtually all his clients were from the College and Grace streets area. Also they almost all came from the rank and file of the population – unskilled labourers, truck drivers, barbers, needle-trades workers, some skilled construction workers, and a few proprietors of small fruit and vegetable stores.

The system of trust seems to have been based on networks: the faith ultimately placed in a banker was the sum of many "chains" of trust within the community. In other words, one only trusted the banker when one's trusted friend trusted the banker, and so on. If a labourer saw a coworker or friend on the same street patronizing Tomaiuolo's bank, he too would feel less uneasy about doing the same. This was even more true when a prospective client's townsman opened an account at one of the banks. At least ten of Tomai-

Table 15
Number of Creditors with over $500, 1931, 1933

	Gatto	*Tomaiuolo*
$6,130	1	
1,500 - 2,000	2	
1,000 - 1,500	6	4
500 - 1,000	12	5

Sources: Gatto and Tomaiuolo Bankruptcy Proceedings, Bankruptcy Office, Supreme Court of Ontario.

uolo's deposit clients were from the town of Pisticci (Basilicata); five, from Vita (Sicily), and fourteen, from San Sisto (Calabria) or surrounding towns.[27]

Although the immigrant banker often depended upon specific hometown or regional groups for part of his clientele, he usually tried to acquire more business by appealing to the common Italian bond of the community. With the call to patriotism, the banker was able to increase his prestige and the markets for his goods and services. The Dillingham Commission described the typical circulars advertising immigrant banks in the United States in the early twentieth century. Characteristic of all these notices were, "the offer of free advice in all matters, the deep concern expressed for the welfare and safety of the banker's 'very esteemed countrymen,' the benevolent offer of service and guidance, the appeal for confidence, and finally the patriotic valedictory."[28]

Developing an Italian ethnic consciousness was inherent in the very nature of the ethnic brokers' work, in the contracting that went on between wholesalers and retailers, in the networks they established. The centre of Italian wholesale food distribution on the continent was New York, yet producers were established in cities across the continent. In a subtle way, those who entered the network were, through their commerce, moulded into "Italian" ethnics and they, in turn, perpetuated their new identity and tried to pass it on to other immigrants from Italy. Consumers also became aware of this identity as they read the labels on Italian products or simply heeded the advertisements of their brokers.

The statements of affairs of several bankrupt Toronto firms testify to the intricate wholesale networks of the ethnic economy. When Frank Joseph Glionna's General Import Corporation failed in 1928, he owed almost half of his liabilities to the Keystone Macaroni

Company of Lebanon, Pennsylvania. He also imported from a New York wholesaler and a packing company and macaroni firm in Chicago. In 1931 Francesco Tomaiuolo acquired his Italian books from two bookstores in New York. He also sold the New York *Progresso Italo-Americano* in his shop as did Giuseppe Gatto. In addition, as a steamship agent he received most of his tickets from Cosulich Lines and Italian American Shipping Corporation in New York. Giuseppe Gatto imported his Italian books from two Italian distributors in New York. He received his other Italian foodstuffs from Charles Pastene's Montreal branch (the company was based in Boston) or from Toronto's Superior Importing Company. Two Toronto producers, Toronto Macaroni Company and Ontario Macaroni Company, supplied Gatto's retail outlet with pasta.[29]

Gatto and Tomaiuolo's records reflect the state of the Italian ethnic economy's traders in Toronto in the early 1930s. However, Toronto's Italian ethnic brokers entered the Italian-American economic network much earlier. In effect, the immigrant labour exchanges between Toronto *padroni* and their American counterparts during the 1880s introduced the city's Italians to the continental Italian immigrant network. New York immigrant banker A. Giannetti opened his immigrant bank branch in Toronto in 1905. (As noted above, the bank defaulted two years later.) The community's links with the network were given a mark of legitimacy in 1915 when fruit wholesaler Charles Ciceri and Italian foodstuffs importer and pasta producer, Abramo Puccini, joined the Italian Chamber of Commerce in New York. In fact, Ciceri even placed a one-quarter page advertisement in the chamber's monthly news organ, *La Rivista Commerciale*.[30]

The wholesale network, indeed the commerce of the ethnic economy, operated on the premise that all immigrants from the Italian peninsula were Italian. If these immigrants identified with the homeland rather than with their respective hometowns or regions, then the entrepreneur would have a broad market for his goods and services. Although the ethnic economy of Toronto's Italian immigrants was local in nature, it was also part of a larger North American Italian immigrant economy. Some immigrants who had lived in older American Little Italies learned the ways of the ethnic entrepreneur and became bankers in Toronto. Steamship companies and food importers and manufacturers from New York, Chicago, or

Montreal vied for the Italian immigrant market in Toronto. Immigrants who patronized the banks, steamship agencies, or large grocery stores were constantly reminded that as Italians, it was their duty to patronize their countrymen. At home, the housewife constantly read labels of new "Italian" food products, whether it was tomato paste imported by Pastene's in Boston or Montreal or macaroni manufactured by Puccini's in St Catharines. The ethnic economy had helped develop the context for a North American and a local Toronto-Italian ethnic identity.[31]

Advertisement for Francesco Tomaiuolo's Steamship Agency. The agency was located on Clinton Street in the city's second Little Italy from 1913 to 1931.

Advertisement for Angelo's Hotel, 1933. Ernest Hemingway was said to have drunk his liquor from a teacup here during his short stay in prohibition-era Toronto. The building was originally Glionna's Hotel, constructed on the corner of Chestnut and Edward streets in the Ward in 1885.

CHAPTER FIVE

Church, Clergy, and Religious Life

In 1906, an Italian priest by the name of Emiliano Pasteris wrote an article on "Religion and Clergy in North America" following a visit to that continent. Pasteris described his visit to a classroom in Montreal in which he queried the students about the national origin of Christopher Columbus, and he was "moved to tears" when a swarthy, embarrassed, Genoese boy stood up and suggested that the explorer was Italian.[1] Like most religious leaders in North American Little Italies, this priest intertwined religion and patriotism – that is, an innate and deep love for the homeland. Before the Lateran Treaty of 1929, which reconciled church and state, a priest would probably think twice before resorting to the national heroes of the *risorgimento* to draw his flock together. Catholic priests were not the only religious leaders to espouse the national cause in order to foster a degree of ethnic group cohesion among the immigrants. Methodist preachers might extol the virtues of Mazzini or Garibaldi in addition to Giordano Bruno, while Catholic priests could resort to Columbus, Cabot, or Dante in their public addresses.

In the late nineteenth and early twentieth centuries, peasant immigrants were not the only ones who had to adapt to the North American urban setting: church hierarchies and immigrant clergy encountered new problems as well. The Italian clergy responded with a sense of mission to preserve the faith and nationality. In the words of Bishop Giovanni Scalabrini, founder of the Scalabrinian order which was devoted to the care of immigrants around the world, "religion and *Patria* ... were the two supreme aspirations of every noble and generous heart."[2]

Because the church hierarchy and clergy were instrumental in developing and guiding the national parishes, their disposition to, and assumptions about the immigrants are significant. The most important of these was an assumption on the part of bishops, priests, and religious orders that the migrants from many villages in the southern European peninsula were Italians and shared a common national identity. For the bishops of Irish or highland Scottish background, who had previously worked in the United States, such a perspective coincided with their pragmatic approach to problem-solving. This is not to say that bishops did not have the interest of the immigrants at heart. Indeed they dedicated their lives to the pastoral care of these people. Moreover, the bishops were more or less obedient to the spirit of papal apostolic letters and encyclicals which revealed the great concern of the popes, from Leo XIII on, for emigrants and immigrants. Yet because the approach of the bishops was marred by their desire for efficiency, when it came to dealing with the Italian ethnic community they acted more as managers than spiritual authorities. The church in Toronto was Irish in character and peripheral members, like the Italians, could be managed by a delegate. The goal of priests in the archdiocese was to assimilate the immigrants: by removing their old world cultural attributes, they could "civilize" them.[3]

The final part of this chapter is concerned with the participation of the immigrants in the national parish system. The experience of forming or joining an ethnic parish made immigrants more aware of their Italian national background and of their homeland. At the same time, the immigrants continued to practise traditional forms of spiritual worship imported from their hometowns. From the turn of the century until the Second World War, the dialogue between immigrants and clergy, or lack thereof, had a marked influence on the texture of the city's Italian community.

From its earliest "mission work" among Toronto's Italians, the archdiocese faced the difficult problem of how to deal effectively with this immigrant group centred in the Ward but also dispersed throughout the city. By 1902, when Rev. Cyril Dodsworth of St Patrick's Church, an Irish parish, began to celebrate Mass for about seventy Italian families in his parish, the Italian population had been established in the College and Grace streets area, along Queen Street, and around Dufferin Street and Davenport Avenue for a long time. In December 1906, Dodsworth hurt himself in a fall and was unable to continue his work among the Italians. That same month someone sent anonymously an article from *The Toronto Star* describing the efforts of the Italian Methodist Mission in the Ward to the archdiocesan offices. A message accompanied the clipping: "this with other documents illustrating the disgraceful condition of affairs prevailing here will be forwarded to the Propaganda [Fide] and to the Holy Father himself. Desparate [*sic*] needs require desparate [*sic*] remedies." However, it was not until the apostolic delegate, Monsignor Sbarretti, pressured Archbishop Lynch's successor, Fergus McEvay, that the archdiocese found a replacement for Father Dodsworth.[4]

In searching for a replacement, the archdiocese examined the possibility of setting up a national parish for the Italians. A national parish differs from the more common territorial parish in that membership is based on ethnicity rather than place of residence. National parishes were introduced in North America to meet the needs of immigrants who spoke a language foreign to the host diocese. Under normal circumstances a Roman Catholic is obliged to belong to the parish in which he resides. However, if he belongs to a particular ethnic group which has a national parish in the diocese, then he can belong to the national parish. A Catholic must make a commitment to one or the other and cannot belong to both the territorial and national parishes. If there is more than one national parish for a particular ethnic group in the diocese, then each is given a geographic territory, and the Catholic must belong to the appropriate parish.

To verify the viability of a national parish, Archbishop McEvay asked his secretary, Mgr Kidd, to take a census of all Italians in the city because "they may be so far apart that a Central Church would not be of much use." When the census, which unfortunately has not survived, was completed, McEvay determined that a national parish was indeed viable. The clergy would have to be "men of zeal who will visit the homes of these people not merely in your parish but also in the adjoining parishes for ... the boundaries for the Italians can be extended to any reasonable distance from St Patrick's parish." In November 1908 the Irish relinquished St Patrick's to the Italians and the church was reconsecrated Our Lady of Mount Carmel.[5]

The diffuse nature of Italian settlement in the city became a persistent source of anxiety for the clergy and the hierarchy. The absence of tenements in Toronto resulted in a low density of immigrants from any particular ethnic group in a given block. In 1913 the archbishop transferred St Agnes Church on Dundas and Grace streets, in the second Little Italy, from the Irish to the Italians, and he arbitrarily chose Spadina Avenue as the boundary for the two Italian parishes. The Irish moved to the imposing stone structure of St Francis Church farther north on Grace Street. St Clement's Church was partially constructed as an Italian mission in 1915 at Dufferin Street and Davenport Avenue. Masses were celebrated in the basement until the structure was completed in 1934. It was renamed St Mary of the Angels. Italians north of Bloor Street and west of Spadina Avenue were under the jurisdiction of that parish.

Despite the neat division of national parishes, there was much uncertainty about their scope and jurisdiction. As late as 1922, the pastor of St Agnes, still confused about his jurisdiction, inquired about those Italians whose homes were "extra limites parociae of St Agnes, but extra limites of any other Italian parish." When the Franciscans sent Patrick Crowley to St Agnes Church in 1934 (they had just taken over the parish from the Salesians), they found their confrère apprehensive about his new ministry. He noted that Mount Carmel Church had "dwindled to a handful" whereas St Clement's numbered 300 families, and St Agnes, 500 families. Large settlements had also opened up in the extreme east and west ends of the city. "The rest [of the Italians] are scattered all over Toronto. When you consider the area of Toronto is as large as Manhattan and the Bronx together you can get some idea of what it would mean to take over the care of all the Italians in the City." Crowley went on to question the usefulness of erecting an Italian National Parish. He suggested that Italians go to the nearest church since he felt that eventually they would be assimilated.[6]

The national parish structure in Toronto had been established in 1908 with the help of an immigration specialist from Vercelli (Piedmont), Father Pietro Pisani, on the recommendation of the apostolic delegate. The local church hierarchy, religious orders, and clerics shared the attitude that the shortcomings of a national parish among a dispersed ethnic group could be countered by missionary zeal. The zeal, however, was dampened by the condescending attitudes of the hierarchy and clergy. In the search for a priest for Toronto's Italian immigrants, Archbishop McEvay requested of the Redemptorists that two clerics who knew "both English and Italian [be] set apart to save their people." In his response to the archbishop, the provincial of the Redemptorists in Baltimore, W.G. Licking, relayed what he took for common knowledge: "While we know that the spiritual betterment of these Southern Italians is an almost impossible task, partly on account of the inborn indifference of this people: still we would gladly do all in our power to second your efforts if satisfactory arrangements could be made."[7]

The term "mission" was a favourite among the early clergy in the Italian national parishes. Technically they were correct in applying the term to St Clement's because in fact it was a mission and not yet a parish: the Italian Catholic population in the area was small and its stability uncertain. It became a parish in 1934 when St Mary of the Angel's Church was completed. The early directors of St Clement's, Father Aloysius Scafuro and Father Joseph Longo, read much more into the term "mission." For them a mission connoted a sense of foreigness, of new lands to open up, of strange peoples who must be approached warily. Rather than approach the faithful – these were baptized Catholics after all – with a sense of authority and charity, they advocated sly tactics, calculation, and efficiency. It might be that they acquired this disposition in Toronto, for in 1924, Fr Scafuro criticized the anglophone clergy in the city for precisely the same attributes. In 1920, Fr Scafuro wrote Archbishop McNeil that "the little experience that I got from missions in different parts of America has taught me that the Italians, in the beginning, submit the poor priest to a cruel and shameful examination. No priest can work without a little prestige. The sinners and the open and concealed enemies of the church not been [*sic*] able to find faults in my life ... are continually setting traps for me ... If they succeed to trample the priest under their feet, the mission would be ruined."[8]

Despite his warning to the archbishop that these cunning parishioners must be scrutinized, Scafuro added that "some questions brought up are above the average intelligence of the working people of my parish." Ten days earlier he had advised Mgr Treacy, pastor of nearby St Cecilia's in the Junction, that "our talking must be soft and light to accomodate ourselves to the intelligence of the women and children." It seems that sixteen years later, either the pastor's outlook had changed or the parishioners had remained intransigent. Scafuro's successor, Joseph Longo, wrote Archbishop McGuigan that "this parish [St Clement's] may be rightly compared with an african [*sic*] Mission; greediness, the war, the depression and communism made many Italians [not] only to forget their religious duties but to hate the priests ..." In his first report to his superior in

1913, Father Coughlan of Our Lady of Mount Carmel Parish wrote that the Italian immigrants "are an altogether different people from others and must be treated altogether differently too ... I hope we have struck upon the right plan of managing them."[9] The premise of the rector at St Cecilia and of the Redemptorist provincial was that the priest among the Italian immigrants was a zealous missionary "saving" an irreligious people. This frame of mind was almost identical to that of the Methodist home missionaries who somehow seemed always to be one step ahead of the Catholics in setting up missions among the immigrants.

The Church of England Mission to the Italians, which opened in November 1899 at 88 Edward Street in the heart of the Italian neighbourhood, was run by an ex-Roman Catholic priest from Calabria. In October 1905, the Methodists opened an Italian mission in the neighbourhood and within a few months took over the Edward Street site abandoned a few years previously by the Church of England. Rev. Giuseppe Merlino was placed in charge of the forty-five regular members of the mission until 1908 when he was succeeded by Alfredo Taglialatela. In June 1907, a branch mission was inaugurated at the corner of Clinton Street and Mansfield Avenue in the heart of the second Little Italy. Three years later it was replaced by the Claremont Street mission. In 1912 a store was purchased at the corner of Chandos Avenue and Dufferin Street for a mission for the third Little Italy. Preachers had been holding outdoor assemblies in that neighbourhood since 1910.[10]

Some of the missionary fervour clearly was fuelled by the competitive spirit between the clergy of both religions. When the Church of England Mission to the Italians celebrated its first anniversary in 1900, Rev. John Langtry stated that, "each year will see an increased immigration to our shores and City of Italians, who in Italy have already broken away from the Roman communion, and who if spiritually and morally neglected are in danger of falling into open unbelief."[11] Neither side ever had a clear idea of the activities or program of the "other side." One undated notice from the 1920s in Archbishop McNeil's files gave the location of the three "protestant" missions and a short list of some of their activities: kindergarten classes, sewing, evening language instruction in Italian and English. The pastor of St Clement's, Father Scafuro, as well as the Carmelite sisters, who helped Italian immigrants in the city, saw the Methodists as the devil's instrument and felt their attempts to influence the

Italians must be thwarted. The establishment of a crêche at St Clement's in 1917 was a response to the Methodist kindergarten next door. In any case, Scafuro felt that his counterattack had produced favourable results. He informed his archbishop in 1920 that "the Methodists [*sic*] Mission next to my door is killed already. The school is practically closed. No Italians go there any more. These Prtestans [*sic*] may make some more futile efforts but the question is settled."[12]

The Carmelite nuns were also active in staving off the Methodist onslaught. Their annual reports of activities from 1911 to 1916 were replete with examples of Italian families they had "saved" from the Methodists. One case from the May–June 1913 report to Archbishop McNeil captures the general thrust of their program: "One Italian lady whose brother is a Methodist Clergyman and therefore does try to get her with her family to the Methodist Church, we helped with food and clothes and also through the Holy Name Society of the Italian Parish with money to pay the rent. She and her husband were willing to let their baby be baptized in the Methodist Church. Both received the Holy Sacraments, are going to Church now and the baby was baptized a Catholic."[13] Even more than the Catholic clergy, the Carmelite nuns were ready to use a "fight fire with fire" approach against the Methodists: they came to the aid of poor Italians with food, clothing, and fuel in hard times.

The backgrounds and personalities of individual priests at the Italian parishes accounted more for the prevalence of a condescending attitude towards the immigrants than a uniform deprecating church perspective. Most of the clergy assigned to Italian parishes were either Irish or northern Italian. The first cleric to say Mass regularly for the Italians, Rev. Cyril Dodsworth, a Redemptorist, had worked in North East, Pennsylvania, and in French missions in St Louis, New Orleans, and Saratoga before coming to Toronto in 1894. Pietro Pisani, who was chosen by the apostolic delegate in Ottawa to form the first Italian parish in Toronto in 1908, was from the archdiocese of Vercelli. Joseph Longo, pastor at Mount Carmel, St Agnes, and St Clement's in different periods between 1910 and 1936, studied theology in Turin and had served as vicar in a church in that archdiocese. He had wanted to go to an African mission soon after taking holy orders but became entangled in an infamous national scandal involving orphanage finances in Turin between 1906 and 1908. Even though he was found innocent of all charges, his plans for a missionary career were thwarted. Dominic Viglianti, who served at Mount Carmel between 1913 and 1927, was from the province of Veroli. His Redemptorist partner, Umberto Bonomo, from Asiago, Vicenza (Venetia), arrived in 1915. St Agnes's first Italian pastor, Joseph Bagnasco, came to Toronto from the northern city of Tortona (Piedmont). Until the arrival of the Franciscan fathers in 1934, Aloysius Scafuro was the only other priest besides Viglianti who came from southern Italy. Born in Lauro in the southern province of Avellino (Campania), the Resurrectionist priest first served in his order's convent in Kitchener, before coming to Toronto in 1915.[14]

Except for these two, all of the pre-1934 Italian priests were northern Italians who had studied in Italian seminaries between 1885 and 1915. Perhaps they even shared in the northern Italian's condescending attitude towards the southerner. Social and geographical background, however, cannot explain totally the near disdain in which some of the Italian clergy in Toronto held their parishioners. At least two of the priests seemed to have had serious difficulties in their dealings with people. Their personal shortcomings rather than ideological or regional differences alienated parishioners and accentuated the tension between clergy and laity within the community.

Scafuro and Longo shared a fear or suspicion of parishioners and other clergy, and the ecclesiastical hierarchy – a fear bordering on paranoia. Almost all their correspondence from their earliest days in the archdiocese (1910) to Longo's death in 1936 either alludes to their having been wronged by others or describes a method of keeping "the enemy" at bay. Scafuro was in trouble almost as soon as he arrived at St Clement's. A petition opposing his appointment as pastor was circulated throughout the parish; some parishioners even destroyed a boys' club he had recently established. Scafuro labelled the episode a "diabolic" revolution.[15]

As pastor, Scafuro felt a responsibility to be in control of his parish. His correspondence suggests that he intended to achieve this surreptitiously through various schemes. In 1919, for example, Scafuro introduced envelopes for money collections at each Mass. This method of keeping track of offerings was always practised in other parishes. Scafuro, however, went one step farther in his effort at "trapping the enemy" – he instituted at St Clement's in 1919 an almanac which included a complete listing of all donors and the amount of their respective donations. "Thus they [i.e., those who were not contributing] saw with their own eyes that they were detected."[16]

Scafuro obviously had a grim outlook on life and not surprisingly his view of St Clement's Italian National Parish was also bleak. In 1920 he described St Clement's (to Mgr Treacy, the doughty Irish pastor of St Cecilia's Parish, adjacent to St Clement's) as being "in a very pitiful state." He suggested in the same letter that St Clement's "may be worked out in [*sic*] good parish which, some day will be a happy [*sic*] next for some young Levite while the poor old Fr. Scafuro will be either underground or in some corner of the world praying the Rosary or saying Mass for the Sisters."[17] Evidently, his disposition did not change after he retired to Italy. He wrote to the episcopal secretary in 1925 that his successor, Fr Stephen Auad, would be in trouble as long as there were social workers in the parish for "they will make him climb the ladder in order to dump him quicker in due time." In another letter to the secretary, Scafuro remarked that some of his former parishioners from Terracina (Lazio) whom he chanced to meet in their hometown, kissed his hand, "although I was still dressed in American clothes." He ascribed this respectful gesture to "the effect the surrounding has on these people! These very people in Toronto hardly even looked at a priest."[18]

Scafuro's successor, Joseph Longo, who arrived in Toronto from Turin in 1910 at the age of forty-one, was an even more tragic figure. As noted above, he had been involved in a scandal regarding orphanage funds, and although he was acquitted of any wrong-doing, the case was to haunt him for many years. In fact, when the Toronto archbishop discovered this information, he transferred Longo to Midland for one year. After that, Longo returned to Mount Carmel and St Agnes parishes for three years. He then served in the rural areas of Albion, Grimsby, and Stayner, Ontario from 1914 until 1927, after which he began his nine-year pastorate at St Clement's. Longo's lack of tact was a major drawback in his dealings with the public. With the important exception of James McGuigan, who became archbishop of Toronto two years prior to Longo's death in 1936, no clergy or diocesan authority seemed able to get along with him. When Longo was appointed pastor at Mount Carmel in 1910, he expressed his belief that "my inability to handle administrative matters and special painful conditions of my life for which I have suffered so much, scare me, as I think that I am destined for the Italians." Longo, however, was also destined to walk a tight rope with the local church hierarchy constantly; that, in turn, resulted in numerous transfers from one parish to another.[19]

The Redemptorist fathers were invited to assume control of the pastorate at Our Lady of Mount Carmel in 1913 by Archbishop McNeil because "serious difficulties" had arisen between Longo and his parishioners. When Father Coughlan and Viglianti, the two Redemptorists, arrived in Toronto they found that their greatest obstacle was Longo. By that time, the archbishop too had tired of that cleric. Arthur Coughlan, who replaced Longo as pastor, wrote his superior that his excellency "thanked me especially for maintaining such a friendly attitude towards Fr. Longo."[20]

Archbishop Neil McNeil had a much more strained relationship with the Piedmontese cleric. In 1922, a petition against Longo was passed among the Catholics of Stayner – this was not an Italian parish – where he was serving at the time, and McNeil sided with the petitioners (the exact details of the case are not clear). Longo sent a harsh message to the archbishop: "You cannot be my judge in this case, because you are my bitterest enemy, for which I never knew the reasons ... by your letters to my people you were exciting them against me." He went on to inform McNeil that he would write to Rome to have a judge appointed to examine his case. But not even the apostolic delegate in Ottawa could penetrate this man. When McNeil received a hostile letter from Longo in 1930, Mgr A. Cassullo, the apostolic delegate, informed the archbishop that "the tenor of the letter does not surprise me, knowing Longo's character and his state of mind."[21]

This attitude coloured the relationship between Longo and McNeil. At the base of the feud between the two, and later between Longo and the apostolic delegate, was Longo's conviction that his superiors had treated him shabbily by transferring him from parish to parish, including to many rural churches. In 1930 he complained to the delegate, Archbishop Cassullo, that "I can't remember the enormous cruelty that I received from him [McNeil]; he wished to punish me, dishonour me in front of the whole diocese; he suspended me from my jurisdiction and *a divinis*; He forced a Syrian priest [Stephen Auad] from the parish of St Clement's where he could have done a lot of good, to send me here at the cost of falsehoods."[22]

Six years later Longo still could not forget the "injustice." He related to Archbishop McGuigan, perhaps the only man he trusted, that the apostolic delegate "promised that he would always take his [McNeil's] part, and a few days after, though sick and absolutely incapable of taking charge at St Clement's Parish, I was sent there, and compelled to go there, and remained there for nearly nine years, successful only in keeping lit the light of faith and diminishing a little the hatred against the priest which was kindled a few years before." One can surmise that Longo's frustration with his superiors, and perhaps more to the point, with his unfortunate circumstances, was largely responsible for his condescending attitude towards his parishioners – and thus for his conviction that he was saving a lost and spiritually dead people. The persistence with which both he and Scafuro sought fault in their flock created tensions between clergy and laity at St Clement's Church on numerous occasions. It must be noted, however, that these men worked under severe pressure and their job was thankless. They had little moral support from the bishop and were totally ostracized by the anglophone clergy who had a different understanding of Catholicism.[23]

The correspondence between Longo and the archbishop and Longo and the apostolic delegate also gives some insight into the special relationship between an Italian immigrant priest and the church hierarchy. A priest usually referred his problems regarding his religious duties to a bishop. Except in dire circumstances priests did not correspond with the apostolic delegate. Italian immigrant priests, however, had easy access to the delegate in Ottawa. Because the apostolic delegate to Canada was always Italian, he took a keen interest in his country's immigrants in Canada. It was Mgr Sbarretti who in 1908 urged McEvay to be more concerned about Italian immigrants and to initiate an Italian National Parish in Toronto.

Archbishop McEvay and his successors found the administration of the Italian national parishes a tedious, time-consuming task. The most efficient method of dealing with the immigrants was to have a religious order with some experience in American ethnic parishes look after the Italian Catholics of the city. Certainly the serious problem of drawing Italian-speaking priests to the city might be solved that way. Until 1909, McEvay could depend on Father Pietro Pisani to provide priests. As an immigration specialist, Pisani had a penchant for locating and supplying clergymen for Italian parishes in North America. However, the turnover rate at Our Lady of Mount Carmel in its early years was high – three priests in just over four years. McEvay must also have understood that some of the clerics

Pisani was supplying were outcasts from the old country. Joseph Longo had, after all, come to Toronto to create a fresh start after the orphanage scandal in Turin, and rumours spread that Carlo Doglio, the first pastor at Mount Carmel in 1908, had a questionable relationship with one of the women who ostensibly served as his housekeeper. McEvay, after ordering Doglio to leave the archdiocese, recommended him very strongly to the bishop of Rochester, New York.

When Longo's past was discovered by the Toronto hierarchy, the first reaction was to pass him off to some unsuspecting bishop elsewhere: "Pisani ... also says he can get places for Italian Priests in the States but for some reason this priest does not want to go."[24] McEvay himself had entered the less than reliable network, and just as he was conveying questionable clergy to other dioceses, so could he expect that more of the same was being deflected in his direction. If a religious order committed itself to a parish, at least the replacements of pastors and assistants would no longer be his responsibility. The dearth of dependable clergy to look after the immigrants seems to have injected a spirit of competition among the North American bishops in their search for adequate priests. However, when the episcopal leaders turned for help to the religious orders, they discovered an even more intense spirit of rivalry.

The male religious orders serving Toronto's Italian immigrants before 1940, as well as orders that tried to obtain parish work there – the Redemptorists, Salesians, Dominicans, and Franciscans – vied for control of Toronto's Italian national parishes. In 1907 Archbishop McEvay contacted the Redemptorist's superior in Baltimore, Rev. W.G. Licking, regarding the possibility of providing Italian priests for the Toronto archdiocese. He was dealing with a man who seven or eight years previously had embarked on a program to expand missionary work in his order among North American immigrants. A shortage of personnel scotched the movement, and in 1907, in an attempt to alleviate part of the problem and in response to McEvay's request, Licking asked superiors in Rome for a few students who had taken vows to remain in the order. Because the Baltimore superior was unable to produce immediate results, the following year, with the help of Pisani, McEvay obtained a secular priest, Carlo Doglio, as Mount Carmel's first pastor.[25]

Nevertheless, the Redemptorists did not abandon their effort to expand and less than five years later they acquired control of Our Lady of Mount Carmel. Clearly, Father Arthur Coughlan, the first

Redemptorist pastor of the parish, was well trained in ingratiating himself with the hierarchy and insuring that his order's latest foothold in the archdiocese should remain firm. Upon his arrival with his assistant, Dominic Viglianti, at Mount Carmel, Coughlan made every attempt to make sure the archbishop would notice the improvements the new team intended to make over the parish's previous pastor, Joseph Longo. Coughlan and Viglianti arrived on Palm Sunday, 1913, but they did not attempt to deal with the general disorder of the church before the archbishop's first visit one week later. "We did nothing in the church until yesterday, first of all because Father Longo did not ask us and secondly to let the Archbishop see for himself the filthy condition of the sacristy, etc."[26]

Toronto's second national parish also passed from the control of secular to regular clergy in 1924, when the Salesian fathers began a ten-year term at St Agnes Church. Until 1932 this order constantly queried the archbishop about the possibility of taking on other Italian parishes in the city. By the end of that year, however, the provincial in New Rochelle, New York, Richard Sittini, asked McNeil to begin looking for another order to run St Agnes. He argued that according to Salesian rules, two priests at their Toronto parish could not be considered a religious community. McNeil had not responded to Sittini's earlier plea to administer another parish in addition to St Agnes. Thus the Salesians gave up Toronto's Italian parishes in 1934 for that very reason.[27]

In August 1931, Archbishop McNeil invited the Dominicans to administer St Clement's Parish. The negotiations were unsuccessful for the Dominicans because the Canadian provincial hesitated in giving permission for the Bologna province's entry. The religious order that eventually replaced the Salesian fathers, the Franciscans of the Province of the Immaculate Conception, New York, were confident that they were bestowing a favour on Toronto's Italians when they sent their first confrères to Toronto in 1934. The provincial, Alfonso Parziale, mailed a statement of intent to expand parish work among the Italians to Archbishop James McGuigan on 1 January 1935: "It would be a real blessing for the Italian people, a great advantage to us, and a benefit to the diocese ... I assure you that the Franciscans of the Immaculate Conception Province are ready and most willing to work for ... the welfare of the [I]talian people, who are negligent, but still keep their faith: we wish to help them save their immortal souls."[28]

Parziale hoped to impress the new archbishop, James McGuigan, when he observed that "with all the Italians under one direction, a system of mutual cooperation could be worked out with great advantage." The overture was successful and by the end of the year St Clement's was under the control of the Franciscans. Father Longo proved to be the main stumbling block as he had been for the Redemptorists at Mount Carmel in 1913. He refused to give up his pastorate until he reached favourable terms. Longo finally settled for an annual pension to be paid by the Franciscans, although for many months the latter complained about those payments.[29]

No sooner had matters been settled at St Clement's than the Franciscans pursued their attempt to control the Italian parish network of Toronto. The Redemptorists, on the other hand, who had not placed a confrère in Mount Carmel since 1927, even though they had a right to the church, intended to reinstall their own clergy there in 1937. This was a cue for Parziale to send a memorandum to Archbishop McGuigan in June of that year. The letter combined the same old tactics that Franciscans and other religious orders had used previously to ingratiate themselves with the city's Catholic hierarchy: criticism of predecessors ("if the Redemptorists are allowed to take over this parish the poor Italians will be worse off than they are under the present pastor"); missionary zeal ("we have taken over the care of the Italians of Toronto with all enthusiasm that we may get them back to the practice of their religion. Ours is a missionary work devoid of any material interest."); the cult of efficiency ("the Franciscan Fathers already having the care of two of the Italian parishes could work more satisfactorily and profitably if they had jurisdiction over all the Italians of Toronto"); and the astuteness to use cash as a last resort ("the proposition of Your Excellency to offer the Redemptorist Fathers some recompense is agreeable to me. I think that the limit shall be $15,000, however, I think that the sum of $10,000, subject to modifications, should be enough.").[30]

The attitudes of hierarchy and clergy towards the Italian immigrants, and the eagerness with which religious orders sought new territories in Toronto's Italian parishes may give the impression that these immigrants were mere pawns. Laymen, however, showed concern for their parishes and their relationship with the clergy. From the earliest days of Mount Carmel Church, the Italians took an active role in parish organization and in voicing their opinions to the priest or archbishop. It is against this backdrop of lay initiative and interest that we can understand the immigrants' reluctance to yield to the capriciousness of Fathers Scafuro and Longo.

In fact, the involvement of the Italian-Catholic laity in Toronto predated the establishment of Our Lady of Mount Carmel Parish in 1908. When, in June 1908, Mgr Sbaretti, the apostolic delegate, came to Toronto to attend the investiture of Fergus McEvay as archbishop of the city (his predecessor, Joseph Lynch had just passed away), some Italians seized the opportunity to address the apostolic delegate at St Paul's Church where "they expressed their desire that some Italian priest might be particularly appointed to look after their spiritual interests."[31]

McEvay's solution was to have the Redemptorists allow the Italians use of the old St Patrick's Church as its Irish parishioners were moving to larger premises nearby. However, he did not finalize his decision before being warned by W.G. Licking, Redemptorist pastor of St Patrick's Church, that he was treading dangerous waters: "I understand that the Italians have already expressed their opinion of this view to the effect that if the old church is not good enough for the Irish, it will not be good enough for the Italians. They would probably refuse to go to the old church and such as come would mingle with the Irish in the new church."[32] Eventually the Italians did find the building acceptable, but as their parish sprouted they directed their criticisms to other issues.

The initial major problem in the parish involved the first pastor of Our Lady of Mount Carmel. Rev. Carlo Doglio claimed that the three women who lived with him at various times between 1908 and 1910 were his housekeeper, cousin, and sister. This may well have been true but the parishioners, aware of his reputation, were suspicious. The archbishop's secretary, Mgr Kidd, informed Doglio "that the trouble in the Italian colony regarding your household has arisen from the persons whom you brought there yourself. On account of their scandalous talk it is no wonder that some of the people are shocked." Archbishop McEvay enlightened the apostolic delegate about the refusal of the colony to put up with the scandal: "I suggested to him [Doglio] to put away the present cousin ... I sent another Italian Priest to live with him but the reports continued and his usefulness here is gone and many Italians will not attend the church on account of these reports and other quarrels with some of the people."[33]

Certainly the archbishop took the immigrants' criticisms very seriously. When he discovered in 1909 that his newly arrived prelate, Joseph Longo, had been involved in the above-mentioned orphanage scandal, he tried to place him elsewhere in the diocese: "I have enough troubles here among the Italians and the matter would be sure of falling into the papers."[34] Perhaps the archbishop was expressing his fears of the small enclave of Italian Socialists in the city who had nicknamed Father Doglio "the Raven." In a footnote to an article in the Buffalo, New York Italian socialist weekly, *La Fiaccola*, the author attacked Doglio's Christmas 1909 message which had been sent to all Toronto Italians: "Poor Christ! ... Although you anathemized the idle rich, they, in your name, plunder he who works for a living, so they may live in idleness and gluttony."[35] Even if the members of the Italian Socialist Committee wrote from the viewpoint of agnostics or atheists rather than disgruntled parishioners, the hierarchy justifiably still feared the infiltration of their ideas among the laity.

Within the Italian national parishes the laity kept a close watch on the clergy after the First World War. Unfortunately, because most of the evidence is in the form of official correspondence, it is difficult to ascertain the true causes of intraparochial conflicts. For example, in 1923, a great deal of bickering occurred in the St Agnes Parish Committee regarding the pastor's alleged misappropriation of funds. Some members resigned to give the pastor control of the parish until the archbishop returned from a trip.[36] In the late 1920s the parish committee of Our Lady of Mount Carmel Parish – all notables of the colony – filed a complaint in Italian with the archbishop regarding their pastor, Fr Stephen Auad. Auad was a Syrian Maronite priest who had become a biritualist (i.e., had the power under canon law to celebrate Mass in the Maronite and Roman rites of the Catholic church) after studying in Rome. The committee was highly critical of Auad, but at the same time assured the archbishop that it was not unfair in its comments: "He is not a bad priest, in fact excellent from any point of view, but for a number of reasons we do not think him fit for the post to which you have assigned him, Your Excellency." The committee members followed the apology with a litany of valid objections to Auad's pastorate: he was too busy to hear confessions; it was difficult to find him in the rectory or in the church; he rarely visited school children; his masses were too short, etc. The first objection was the main one – that Auad took little care of the Italians and rather depended on the "English" of the parish. The immigrants wanted a pastor of their own national background, a cleric more responsive to their needs.[37]

Lay initiative of course was not defined by criticism of the clergy. The national parish was the focus of many activities which can be divided into two main spheres – the religious and devotional on the one side and the social and patriotic on the other. The distinction is important for an understanding of social organization within the community. The clergy had prestige among Toronto's Italian immigrants because they provided for spiritual needs. However, it was never the only power within the ethnic group – there was also the élite of bankers, wholesale grocers, steamship agents, and later, the fascist club directors. When a patriotic gathering was held in the parish, it was almost always organized by the nonclerical élite. These social events will be described in more detail in the following chapters.

Unfortunately, few documents have survived which allow one to catalogue the extent of religious and devotional life within the early Italian parishes of Toronto. The impression received from reading the correspondence of prelates, pastoral visitations, and newspaper accounts is that a relatively small part of the Italian Catholic population attended Mass regularly and those who did practise their faith were active at the various church functions. There is little statistical evidence to prove this and the impressionistic statements of the various priests on the subject may very well have been biased. For example, Carlo Doglio, Mount Carmel's first pastor, contended that in 1910 the parish was as effervescent as at its inception two years earlier: "Today I examined the offertory's collections of the last six months (1910) and I found it exactly the same as on the first six months of the opening when the Italians were enthusiastic of their Church and priest – This demonstrates that my enemys [*sic*], or better, religion's enemys have done not very much." Doglio was very optimistic about Italian church attendance in Toronto but he was also under scrutiny from the bishop at the time, and was about to lose his post. His observations were most likely a last attempt to retain his pastorate at Mount Carmel.[38]

John F. Byrne, author of the *Redemptorist Centenaries* (a chronological and documentary account of the religious order), estimated that in 1913 "there were about 2,000 Italians in the Parish [of Mount Carmel], and some two hundred of the children attended St Patrick's school ... But in the course of years the parish dwindled numerically, and everything considered, the results obtained were hardly commensurate with the effort put forth." This statement seems to suggest a low rate of church attendance but the author's statements were very vague. Was the effort no longer worthwhile because the parish was smaller in the 1930s then twenty years previously, because fewer immigrants attended Mass, or because collections had dwindled? Byrne might have been looking for some justification for his order's abandonment of the Italian pastorate in the city in 1927.[39]

Father Arthur Coughlan's first report from Mount Carmel to his superiors in 1913 was very optimistic about spiritual activity in the parish: "With regard to the Italians, they are very enthusiastic over the changes; they are flocking to us to assure us of their joy and of their good will. What is better they are coming to church in greater numbers than ever." However, Coughlan's correspondence, like that of the Salesian and Franciscan fathers in the city, tended to compare favourably his religious order's work to that of the previous clergy in order to demonstrate to his superior and the archbishop that the right man had been chosen for the job. Coughlan was to the point when discussing confessions during Holy Saturday and Easter Sunday, 1913: "I did not have time to take a shave before singing the High Mass! We must have had about 200 Italian confessions yesterday and today, and F. Longo told us he did not have more than 200 during the whole Easter Season." Coughlan added that "there were more people in Church this morning (Easter Sunday) than were ever before in this church. They are contributing quite generously to the collections, surprising ourselves as well as Father Connolly [pastor of St Patrick's]."[40] A few years later, Fr Scafuro claimed that "about five hundred children" attended St Clement's Church. In one of his more positive letters he asserted that the "majority of the people are good and will be brought back to the Church." However, in the following decade, his successor, Joseph Longo, claimed that there were "hundreds of Italians" who refused to go to church: "As you know, a very small percentage of the Italians go to Church; but for Baptisms, Weddings, and Funerals, they like to make a big splash. Consequently the almost common saying: 'These people go to church three times in a life.' "[41]

The pastor of St Clare Church (the next parish north of St Clement's, in Fairbank) probably based his church attendance figures on assumptions as well, when, in 1939 he claimed that a large percentage of the Italians in his parish did not attend Mass. Of 904 parishioners, "149 are Italian of which 20 definitely attend the church. The remaining 129 claim that they attend [St] Mary of the Angels but I doubt if any more than one-half of them attend any Church." The pastor's comments spoke also of the sloppiness of parish boundaries when a territorial parish was located near a national parish. It would seem that an optimistic statement by any of the above clerics meant that church attendance by Italian immigrants was better than expected but still not particularly impressive.[42]

Although the city's Italian immigrants had a low rate of church attendance, they participated in parish activities and especially in events involving their hometown churches in Italy. One of the best indicators of parish activity is the pastoral visitation, the report of the bishop's visit to, and examination of the parish. The earliest surviving visitations for the three Italian national parishes are for 1948; there is no evidence of earlier visitations. However, since virtually no new Italian immigrants had arrived in Toronto during and immediately after the Second World War, the 1948 visitations give at least some indication of the religious practices and associational life of prewar Italians in Toronto. Allowing for the effects of acculturation, the extent of lay participation in the Italian parish can still be determined.

Table 16 lists the organizations in the three parishes and membership totals, while table 17 indicates the population of the parishes, 1902–37. Lay participation in the parish clubs was not impressive but neither was it extremely low. For example, memberships in associations at St Clement's amounted to 441, not accounting for the possibility of parishioners having dual or triple memberships in other clubs, of a total of about 400 or 500 families or 2,000 to 2,500 people. The proportion of active members is rather high considering that the Dufferin-Davenport Little Italy had many young families with children who could not hold memberships; that many parishioners were active in the Fratellanza (Brotherhood) and *Famee Furlane* (Friulan Family) mutual benefit societies; and that most of the men worked long hours in construction, and their older daughters, and some wives worked in the needle trades downtown and arrived home fatigued in the early evening.

The associations listed in the pastoral visitation were established North American parochial organizations, many of which did not exist in the small Italian agrotowns from which most of Toronto's

Table 16
Membership in Parish Associations, 1948

Association	*Parish*		
	Mt Carmel	*St Agnes*	*St Mary of the Angels*
Holy Name Society	90	60	94
Catholic Women's League	?	n/a	n/a
Sodality of BVM	35	80	87
Christian Mothers	n/a	n/a	45
CYO	270	60	50
St Vincent de Paul	n/a	n/a	6
St Francis Third Order	n/a	50	45
League of Sacred Heart	n/a	70	n/a
Altar Society	n/a	n/a	74
St Anthony Society	n/a	n/a	40
Totals	395	320	421

Sources: Pastoral Visitations, 1948, Our Lady of Mount Carmel, St Agnes, and St Mary of the Angels parishes, Files, ARCAT.

immigrants came. It is understandable that membership would not have been very high because these clubs required acculturation on the part of the immigrant: they were not authentic forms of old world religious practice. The few recorded accounts that have survived describing participation of Toronto's immigrants in their old world hometown parish events – usually fundraising drives – suggest that these "urban villagers" were indeed very active in their "other" or former parishes, even though they lived in Toronto. A number of reasons probably dictated the choice to donate to the hometown's fundraising drives: genuine generosity; village traditions which prescribed that money be sent back to the village by those whom its pastor might still consider his parishioners; or one's ascriptive status among one's village group in Toronto. In other words, one was expected to give, if possible. Not to do so was to stand aloof from the hometown group in Toronto.

A hometown group in the city delegated one person to collect money from fellow townsmen and to send it back to their hometown for the celebration of the town patron saint's feast day. In the 1930s, Mrs Rosa Panzini was responsible for collecting among the immigrants from Villa Santa Lucia (Lazio) in Toronto, for the feast day of *Madonna delle Grazie* (Our Lady of Grace). Pietrangelo Di Franco

Table 17
Population of Parishes, 1902–37

Year	*Mt Carmel*	*St Agnes*	*St Mary of the Angels*
1902[a]	70 families		
1913[b]	2,000 people		
1919[c]			500 families; 2,000 people
1934[d]	"a handful"	500 families; 2,500 people	300 families; 1,500 people
1937[e]		1,009 families; 5,031 people	

Sources: [a]Byrne, *Redemptorist Centenaries*, 374.
[b]*Ibid.*, 376.
[c]Scafuro to McNeil, 17 May 1919, "National Parishes," McNeil Papers, ARCAT.
[d]Crowley to Parziale, 6 Oct. 1934, Parziale Papers, AFPIC.
[e]Crowley to J.C. Harris, 31 May 1937, St Agnes Parish Papers, AFPIC.

did the same for the townsmen from Montorio nei Frentani (Molise) for their *San Rocco* (St Roch) celebrations. In 1931, Michele Pucacco, who normally canvassed Toronto's families from Casacalenda (Molise) for the *Maria S.S. della Difesa* celebrations, "knowing the actual conditions of his townspeople [in Toronto because of the Great Depression] abstained from doing so, and was content with sending fifty lire back to Italy." The previous year, Pucacco had collected $28.50 from 38 of his townspeople. Only 4 donors were listed from Villa Santa Lucia, and 10 from Montorio nei Frentani in 1931, but the *Progresso Italo-Canadese* assured readers that only a few of the donors had actually been listed in the newspaper. In June 1931, Salvatore Domenico Graziadei began a fundraising drive for construction of the new *San Rocco* church in his hometown, Pisticci (Basilicata). He exhorted his townsmen in Toronto to be "generous with their offering. That which we give is for a good cause; we are giving to Pisticci, to our protector [patron saint], towards beautifying our hometown, because the planned church will be a work of art." Vito Cammisa and Antonio Iannuzziello were in charge of collecting funds, and by November had collected over $120 from 135 *pisticcesi*.[43]

Some of the townsgroups were able to insert their hometown celebrations into the activities of the Italian national parishes. Indeed, Mount Carmel internalized two such feasts to the point of making them important annual events for the entire Italian population. For years, the immigrants from Termini Imerese (Sicily) reproduced the Good Friday Passion Play in vivid detail. One Salesian priest advertising the "Sicilian colony's" event in 1930 quipped that "the tragedies of Aeschylus and Shakespeare are 'kid's play' compared to the one being staged at the Church on Good Friday."[44]

Another hometown tradition continued by the *termitani* was the weekly Tuesday afternoon devotions to St Anthony. Other Italians also attended but the largest group was composed of women from Termini Imerese. For these women dispersed throughout the city in fruit stores, the devotions provided an opportunity to keep in contact with one another. As late as 1938, the Mount Carmel pastor informed the chancellor of the archbishop that "we are continuing the devotions to St Anthony in the Church of Our Lady of Mount Carmel and would like to have your permission to have two benidictions each Tuesday afternoon." The annual feast day of Our Lady of Mount Carmel would most certainly have been celebrated by various townsgroups in Toronto because she was the patron saint of numerous Italian towns. St Agnes Church, too, began observing the feast day in 1930.[45]

Next to the Good Friday Passion Play, the most important feast day in the community was that of *San Rocco*, patron saint of two of the most prominent towns represented in Toronto, Monteleone di Puglia and Modugno di Bari (Puglia). Ten of the twelve members of the 1929 organizing committee for the *San Rocco* feast were from either of the two towns. In the 1950s the archbishop was approached because of a controversy over which group of townspeople – the *monteleonesi* or the *modugnesi* – owned the *San Rocco* statue that was carried in the procession. It took five years for the archbishop to find a happy solution to the small crisis which for years had kept the two hometown groups segregated across the aisle from each other at Mount Carmel's Sunday services.[46]

Even within their religious life, then, Italian immigrants were able to live on two levels of identity. On the whole they rejected Italian Protestantism but they were not prepared to accept Irish Catholicism. They were open to the Italian national parish structure organized by the Italian clergy through the Canadian hierarchy, but they often defined the limits of acceptable behaviour for priests. The immigrants demanded lay participation in the parish and resisted overbearing or uncaring prelates, or priests who caused scandals. They also adapted to the national parish structures by merging their hometown celebrations with those of their Toronto parish, and by providing financially for the feasts and churches of their hometowns, as well as for religious celebrations of parishes in Italian Toronto.

In that sense, Toronto's Italian immigrants had come a long way since 1908. At the opening of Mount Carmel Parish in that year, Father Casassa of St Anthony's Italian Parish in Buffalo had preached the sermon at the inauguration ceremonies. Aware of the fragile bonds of a consolidating community, Casassa stressed the ideal of "Christian citizenship": "Now that they had their own church," said the priest, "they wauld [*sic*] join in attendance and activities, they would unite with their compatriots and bury all Old Country prejudices of locality or politics, in working side by side as good Catholics in the new land of their adoption."[47] By 1935, the Italian immigrants in the city lived in both worlds for they could identify with one of the Italian national parishes in the city and also with one of the hometown groups which comprised it.

CHAPTER SIX

The Way of the Notables

The Italian immigrants who settled in Toronto arrived with some sense of Italian nationality. If nothing else, taxes, or myths of the *risorgimento* made them aware that they came not just from a hometown but also from an Italian nation. In Toronto the immigrants became even more conscious of their nationality. People from different hometowns lived on the same street or worked or worshipped side by side, boarded in the same house, or patronized the same labour agent, and were recognized as Italians by Canadians. In addition, similar needs and circumstances reinforced the common ethnic bond with immigrants from other parts of the peninsula. These factors, however, do not account completely for the development of group identity in the new world urban setting.

Historians and sociologists have proposed a number of theories to explain the formation of group consciousness. Most prevalent until the 1960s was the view of Robert E. Park and Herbert A. Miller that group solidarity was a defensive device against discrimination from the host society. Some popular writers of the immigrant experience have perpetuated this point of view but it has been generally dismissed as inadequate. W. Lloyd Warner and Leo Srole, in their Yankee City series of the 1940s, underlined the correlation between religion and nationality. Victor Greene and Timothy Smith have extended this argument by demonstrating that the struggle for lay control of the church developed the national consciousness of various eastern European groups in America.[1]

Without downplaying the significance of Smith's or Greene's studies, one could suggest that the tie between religion and ethnicity is much more crucial among eastern European immigrants than among their Italian counterparts. The Italian peasant's national identity was intertwined with his Roman Catholicism: he grew up in a religiously homogeneous town and his Catholic identity did not form the same conscience border of identity as did, for example, Uniate Catholicism or Orthodoxy for Ukrainianness. Some historians, therefore, have given less emphasis to religion and have examined more closely the relationship between group leadership and ethnic identity. Nathan Glazer and John Higham, for example, have indicated that ethnic groups, that is, immigrants forming a national group in the new world, are amorphous and very much what their leaders make them. Victor Greene has argued that ethnic group leaders help immigrants to preserve some of the old ways and also to adapt to the new urban milieu. Leaders, of course, do not create ethnic groups but they can help to strengthen group solidarity, and consequently heighten ethnic consciousness among group members. This chapter studies this process.[2]

A strong correlation existed between leadership and group consciousness within the Italian community of Toronto. An ethnic leader or notable could achieve his status in a number of ways but all of these depended either upon his stressing the homogeneity of the ethnic group or paying patriotic lip service to Italy. The emerging leaders' confident assertions that those from the Italian peninsula in Toronto formed a single community – for which, of course, such leaders could speak – and their sentimental, patriotic references to the homeland, eventually heightened the immigrants' sense of belonging to a Toronto-Italian ethnic community. In other words, the notables or the élite helped to shape the ethnic group boundaries of Italian Toronto.

An élite did not appear spontaneously. The very process by which notables emerged in the colony helped to shape the boundaries of the ethnic group. Briefly, the routes to élite status included: (1) taking advantage of a situation which threatened the Italian immigrants as a collectivity in the city, and standing up as a defender of the Italian population; (2) creating institutions to focus the attention of the Italian population across local or regional boundaries – mutual aid societies, recreational clubs, newspapers, churches, immigrant banks; (3) forming contacts with mainstream Toronto and acting as a representative of the Italian community to these contacts; (4) holding an official position in the community, such as priest, minister, court interpreter, or Italian consular representative;

(5) long-term residence in the city, i.e., being a pioneer of the Italian neighbourhood; (6) an education beyond the elementary grades and the ability to speak perfect Italian rather than only a dialect; (7) business success or high occupational status.

The élite included the steamship agents discussed in chapter 3 and the Catholic and Methodist clergy examined in chapter 5. However, this chapter will concentrate on other notables more active in the political life of the community who undertook positions of leadership in the emerging community. The two processes – the formation of an élite and an increasingly widespread and articulated ethnic group consciousness among Italian immigrants in Toronto – fed on one another. A group of community leaders could not exist without a quorum, without an ethnic community; and yet the notables to a great extent expanded the ethnic consciousness of the immigrants and inscribed the ethnic perimeters of the community.

The immigrants who arrived in Toronto in the mid to late nineteenth century from Pisticci, Laurenzana in the Basilicata, or the hinterlands of Chiavari (Liguria), or the province of Cosenza (Calabria) came primarily as people of their respective villages, as part of the socio-economy of the villages' migration streams to particular destinations in the new world. However, the events and atmosphere of Italy's *risorgimento*, and the postunification government's program of bringing the regions of the south within the national orbit had instilled at least a modicum of Italian national consciousness into these peasants and rural day-labourers who became emigrants a decade later. When the various groups of townspeople had settled in Toronto, they realized that certain needs must be attended to in this North American urban centre – mutual aid in the form of voluntary associations as had been practised in the home village, English classes for their children, a national parish. Some of these needs could be met by the pioneers of the respective hometown groups, who, in effect, were the first notables. Because they had welcomed new arrivals from their villages into their homes, and had sponsored many of the greenhorns, pioneers such as Nicola Majorana from Modugno di Bari (Puglia), Giovanni and Francesco Glionna from Laurenzana (Basilicata), or Pietro Lamantia and Antonio Gatto from Termini Imerese (Sicily), earned respect from their townspeople.[3] However, any form of self-help was difficult for a group of townspeople to undertake if their numbers were small and they had little or no experience with associational life and dealing with government. In 1897, Toronto's Italian population stood at only 750, and no particular townsgroup was large enough to support a mutual aid society based exclusively on membership from one hometown.[4]

Voluntary organizations required leaders who could rally immigrants from different towns to meet common objectives. In Toronto, Italian community consolidation began in the late 1880s, mainly under the impetus of the immigrants from Laurenzana, the largest and wealthiest hometown group in the city at that time. Most prominent among the *laurenzanesi* was the Glionna family, the largest clan in the Italian community, and its inlaws, the Laraias, Laurias, and Lobraicos. The Glionnas, as noted, owned the northwest corner of Chestnut and Edward streets in the early 1880s, including Glionna's Hotel, which also served as a labour agency and immigrant bank. The *laurenzanesi* and especially the Glionnas were the main organizers of the city's first Italian mutual aid society, the Umberto Primo Benevolent Society, established in 1888. Donato A.G. Glionna, son of Francesco, was president of that society almost every year until 1911. From that position he emerged as the federal Liberal party's chief political link with the Italian community. Until 1906, the *laurenzanesi* had virtual control over the board of directors of the society and continued to maintain a high profile on the board until 1912. For example, in 1893, at least five of the seven members of the board were from Laurenzana (four were Glionnas or their inlaws); in 1896, six of eight; in 1897, seven of nine; and in 1904 all four members were from the Basilicatan town.[5]

Previous to coming to Toronto, some of the Glionnas had lived in New York and from their experience in that Little Italy had undergone some of the ethnicizing process; they sought or accepted leadership roles not just as *laurenzanesi* but as Italian Canadians, and the articulation of their goals contained Italian patriotic themes. In drafting the constitution of the Umberto Primo society, they stressed the common Italian origin of the society's members. The "supreme goal" of the society was "to remind its members to make progress in civilizing and educating themselves, to encourage relations among Italians, to promote reciprocal love among them as well as moral and financial assistance, and finally to honour the distant fatherland with hard work and industry."[6]

Until 1888 any semblance of an Italian community in Toronto had been created through informal contacts, but the Glionnas and their townspeople began to inscribe more distinct ethnic boundaries around the 400 or so nationals from the Italian peninsula by creating a formal, functional institution for the entire community, the Umberto Primo society, named after the Italian king. That is not to say that the Glionnas' patriotism was feigned – however, as good entrepreneurs, they realized that the appeal to patriotism brought financial gain and prestige.

Contacts with the "outside," mainstream society of Toronto also helped define the boundaries of the city's Italian population. Torontonians, like most Canadians and Americans, perceived of the foreigners in their midst as belonging to recognizable nationalities or races. Aliens from the Mediterranean peninsula were simply Italians, or, at best, a hierarchy of northerners, southerners, and Sicilians.[7] Thus immigrants from the different towns and regions referred to themselves as Italians in their official dealings with the rest of the city's population. In early January 1889, a board meeting of the Roman Catholic Separate School Board (RCSSB) recorded that "a *petition* was presented from the *Italians* of the City praying that a night school be established for the purpose of teaching young children the English language [secretary's italics]."[8]

A few weeks later when an unpopular *laurenzanese* applied for that teaching position a second petition was drawn up which referred to an homogeneous Italian community. The petition complained that "such an appointment would cause great dissatisfaction among and entail great disgrace upon the Italian body." Although the board secretary's entry noted that the document was signed "by 40 Italians," most of them were from Laurenzana: "*The majority of* your Petitioners are natives of the same town as Mr Napolitano [i.e., Laurenzana] and can establish the fact that he served several years confinement for a criminal offence committed in that town."[9]

The petition testifies to the conflict among such a small population (ca. 400) at an early date. Yet even conflict was a unifying force and helped define the boundaries of the Italian community. The English night school issue was part of a larger struggle in the community; otherwise Saverio Napolitano's opponents would not have gone to such a great extent to have the teaching application dismissed.

The tendency of anglophone society to identify all the immigrants from the peninsula simply as Italians or by some less polite name (Sicilians were often singled out for connections to the Mafia or the stiletto), the desire for mutual aid societies and language classes among the immigrants, and even the need for a common ground for internal conflicts among the city's Italians all contributed to the early formation of an Italian community in Toronto in the late 1880s. In addition, the Italian government made its presence felt in this period when A.M.F. Gianelli, honourary Italian consul, moved his fruit wholesale business from Montreal to Toronto where he exercised his consular duties. The arrival of an official responsible to Italy contributed significantly to the emerging sense of an Italian ethnic group.

If the development of an Italian community in Toronto went hand in hand with the formation of a recognized leadership for that community from among the respected or financially successful immigrants – mostly *laurenzanesi* or *genovesi* – a significant number of Italians who lived in the Ward as early as the 1880s nonetheless remained relatively unaffected by the élite, its activities, and by the sense of community developing within the colony. The transient population of construction labourers who returned to winter in Little Italy after a season on the northern railroads, canals, dams, and bridges had their own hierarchy.

For these sojourners, Toronto was not a permanent settlement but a labour distribution centre, and they had no obligations towards Little Italy's emerging élite, but rather only towards their *padroni*. Ethnic entrepreneurs realized the value of the market provided by the transient labour force, but they also understood the importance of catering to the permanent Italian population by providing Italian foods, a safe mailing address for transient boarders (a series of pigeon-holes served as post office "boxes" for clients), steamship tickets to return to Italy or to send for relatives, savings deposit accounts, money orders for remittances, jobs, or lodging. By supplying the immigrants needs, by acting as middleman between the sojourner and contractor, housewife and Italian food wholesaler, wage-earner and the Banco di Napoli (which sent remittances to the hometown post office savings account), and between the immigrant and the often inept Italian consular officials, the bankers or ethnic entrepreneurs built up a broad-based "Italian" clientele, rather than a clientele from a single village.

These individuals responded to a locus of needs for each hometown group, and by reinforcing in these immigrants their common circumstances they also reinforced their shared ethnic identity. Some entrepreneurs stressed their pan-Italian identity in their advertisements. After the First World War Louis Puccini renamed his large wholesale store "Italian Cash Grocery," while Queen City Bakery boasted itself "the first Italian Bakery in the city." The Italian ethnic identity which emerged in the colony was therefore not simply the progeny of shared cultural emblems but also of shared sociocultural communication.

Structurally, there were many different routes to élite status within the Toronto Italian community. Wealth, education, or a high-status occupation could almost guarantee one's entry into the select group but so also could a connection to a Canadian political party or a prominent person of Toronto's mainstream, anglophone society. Others commanded respect because they had begun one of the larger townsgroups' migration chains to Toronto, or because they had lived in the city for so many years that they were regarded as precursors of the colony. All of these avenues to notability depended upon one condition: those who recognized such an élite, the immigrants from the various areas of the Italian peninsula, had to be aware of living within an *Italian* community in the city. As long as this was so, the élite could maintain or enhance its prestige and in some cases expand its market for goods and services.

A three- or four-tiered class structure did not truly exist in Little Italy before 1915. The common experience of settling in a new land, the small population of Italians in Toronto, and the ease with which all Italians could meet informally along Centre Avenue or Elm Street or on other roads in the Ward had a levelling effect within this immigrant community. Toronto's Little Italy could be compared to the internal colony described by students of black neighbourhoods in the United States. The great majority of the population consisted of rank and file workers. The small number of élite members – perhaps 50 in a population of about 10,000 in the 1910–15 period – maintained contacts with mainstream Toronto and represented the Italian community of the city to the society outside the colony, and drew much of their social and economic strength from their role as intermediaries.[10]

In 1908 one businessman, Serafino Castrucci, summed up a number of routes to notability in a review in *The Catholic Register* (Ontario's official Roman Catholic weekly) of an Italian play assembled by a few actors from the community. Castrucci commented that the "entire drama was haled [*sic*] by the fine Italian audience present, amongst whom were some of our distinguished old Italian residents of the city. Messrs Glionna, Castrucci, Giassi [Grossi], Toghietti [Taglietti], Nicoletti, Merlino, etc." Glionna, Castrucci, Grossi, and Taglietti were among the earliest immigrants to Toronto still living and were all wealthy by community standards. Nicoletti arrived much later and was at the time the most successful banker in Little Italy. Merlino, a Methodist minister, was well educated and very active in community work. Castrucci's list of distinguished persons underlined some of the qualities of the notables in the Ward.[11]

It is difficult to isolate the most common attributes shared by the *prominenti*. Certainly one can single out wealth, occupation, long-term residence, or the provision of key goods and services, but many notables did not fit into simple categories. For example, John Abate had risen from fruit pedlar to fruit stall operator in the West Market, and in 1902 opened a concession in the St Lawrence Market. For that reason he had a prestigious place in the Italian community, but he also derived prestige from being an early immigrant and a *laurenzanese*, the wealthiest group of townspeople in the Ward. The same was true of Harry Castrucci who had arrived from Lucca (Tuscany) in 1861 as a plaster figurine vendor, and established a company to manufacture artists' casts. His business success, early arrival in the city, the fact that his enterprise served all of Toronto rather than only the "colony," his northern Italian background, and the financial success of other *lucchesi* in the city assured Castrucci an eminent place in the community. Some of the prominent fruit dealers, such as the Deferrari brothers, Angelo and Salvatore, or the Garbarino family, attained a prominent place in the prewar community not only because of their financial successes, but also because they were among the early families from the province of Genoa in Toronto. It is difficult, therefore, to isolate a single factor responsible for an individual's rise to power and influence.[12]

Occupation and income were important determinants of where one stood on the more detailed status ladder. In 1900, a pedlar with horse and buggy, for example, occupied a higher category than a pushcart hawker. Musicians – the wealthiest occupational group in early Italian Toronto – had a greater standing than a barber, and a barber, greater standing than a bootblack. In addition, each village group had its own status ladder based on the individual's former social position in the hometown, the date of arrival in Toronto, occupation, or ability to find employment for townsmen. The detailed multistoreyed notions of status which the peasant had developed in the hometown were transferred to the new world.[13] However, as an Italian community developed in Toronto, it became apparent that the immigrant society was divided into two general categories – the rank and file and the élite or notables.

Brief profiles of the careers of three of the city's notables will crystallize some of the important themes on qualifications for and routes to élite status. The profiles are of three typical, prominent men of the colony: one had connections to a Canadian political party, another had important links to an institution in Italy, while a third individual was politically active but remained in the community for only a few years.

Donato A.G. Glionna's public career clearly shows how the homogeneous ethnic group was used as a base to launch one *prominente* as *the* representative of Toronto's Italian community to mainstream society. Glionna was born in Laurenzana in 1869 and arrived in Toronto in the early 1870s. His father, Francesco, was the proprietor of Glionna's Hotel and owned numerous building lots in the Ward, as well as farmland in Scarborough. The Glionnas were certainly the most distinguished clan in Italian Toronto. The family included many musicians, the colony's first doctor, a real estate agent, and importers. Two family members served as Italian consular agents in the city from 1917 until the early 1920s. During his 1908 visit to Toronto, Father Pietro Pisani praised the Glionna family, whom he described as "noted and admired for their musical talents," and observed that the family included "eighty members from the grandparents down."[14] They dominated the colony if for no other reason than by sheer family size.

As indicated earlier, Glionna emerged as a community leader in the 1890s when he assumed the presidency of the Umberto Primo society. It was probably that office that made him attractive to the Liberal party as its agent in Little Italy; and it was probably the Liberals who found him a position as a fireman with the Drill Hall in 1896. By 1910 he had moved through the ranks to become a vice-president of the Centre Toronto Liberal Association.[15]

In May 1910 the colony's élite and local Liberals began a year-long effort to place Mr Glionna in the federal bureaucracy, specifically in the immigration department. The secretary of the Centre Toronto Liberal Association wrote an official letter to the minister of the Interior, Frank Oliver, recommending that staff officials of various nationalities be placed at ports of landing to search baggage for weapons and to advise immigrants on the laws of the country. The letter recommended Glionna as "a member of one of the best-known Italian families [in] Canada – a man of character, probity and ability – who would if appointed as Italian officer, 'make good.' "[16]

The excuse used by both the local Liberals and the Italian community to promote Glionna's career was the series of knife-woundings and brawls involving foreigners, and especially Italians, during the two previous years. The problem had come to public attention during the recession of 1907–8 when 1,200 to 1,500 Italian immigrants in Toronto were unemployed. At a meeting of jobless Italians at the Italian Methodist Mission Church in May 1908, Michael Basso, the former court interpreter, blamed much of the unemployment on poor press coverage which stressed the use of the stiletto by Italians: the "employers and contractors ... instructed the employment agencies to engage other foreign labourers in preference to Italians." A series of murders – usually the result of love triangles – occurred in the ensuing months, especially in March and April 1911. During a one-month period, four separate murders or attempted murders in Toronto involved Italian immigrants, and three of the incidents happened in the Ward, on Agnes (later Dundas) Street.[17]

Another request to install Glionna in the immigration office was delivered to the Ministry of the Interior in March 1911. The superintendent of Immigration, W.D. Scott, wrote a memorandum to Frank Oliver citing the request that a position be created for Glionna to educate his countrymen regarding concealed weapons. The superintendent discouraged the hiring because "it is not part of the policy of the department to encourage the immigration of Italians."[18]

The Umberto Primo society took the next step by passing a resolution at a special meeting on 30 April 1911. Exploiting the recent string of Black Hand murders in Toronto and other cities, they expressed their "indignation at the disgrace that has been brought upon the Italian residents of Canada by the repeated crimes that are from time to time committed by men who, we regret to have to admit, are of Italian birth ..." The resolution indicated that these men had been residents of Canada for a short time only and were ignorant of the English language and Canadian law. The society requested that the government "appoint an officer conversant with the Italian language, whose duty it would be to instruct them in the laws of the country upon such matters." Copies of the resolution were to be mailed to Prime Minister Laurier and all cabinet ministers by the president of the society.[19]

More interesting than the resolution itself were the covering letters to the politicians that accompanied it. The secretary of the Umberto Primo society, Francesco Ungaro, a *laurenzanese*, signed the letters because the president was none other than D.A.G. Glionna, candidate for office. Ungaro emphasized that the resolution reflected the wishes of all Italians in Toronto. In the draft mailed to Sir Richard Cartwright, he asked the Trade and Commerce minister to "support the views of the Italians of this City and urge the same before cabinet." Four months later, Laurier received a second copy of the resolution and a newspaper account of a recent Black Hand murder in Toronto. The accompanying letter again accentuated the representative nature of the society: "In having Mr Glionna appointed at once, the Italian citizens of Canada would recognize that the Dominion Government are willing to help the majority of their people who do not wish to be classed as Murderers even though they were born on the sunny shores of Italy. By giving this matter your personal attention you will merit the confidence of every true Italian citizen of Canada."[20]

At the same time, Frank Oliver received a letter from Father Marco Berardo. The pastor of Mount Carmel Parish had arrived in Toronto from Italy one year earlier and could not have composed the gracefully written English of the letter that bore his signature. The letter noted that the attention of the government had been drawn to "the horrible condition of affairs" and that no action had been taken. It also referred to the resolution asking for Glionna's appointment "as an officer to look into the situation and educate the ignorant of the laws of Canada." Berardo's message ended with one request: "I must say that the wishes of the society is the unanimous wish of all the Italians, and I trust the appointment will be made at once." Thus the pastor of the Italian National Parish assured the honourable minister that the Umberto Primo society truly represented the Toronto-Italian colony.[21]

However, Oliver refused to be backed into a corner. W.D. Scott, superintendent of Immigration, skirted the issue of how representative of the Italian community the request for an immigration official actually was. Scott replied astutely that an Italian subject could receive a passport only if his or her record was good, and "if Italians are desirable when they come into Canada, I do not see that there is anything in our national life here which would corrupt them." As to Glionna's plans to educate fellow Italians, the superintendent remarked dryly that "the education of residents of any province comes under the control of the Provincial Government." Thus he washed his hands of the problem. However, not for long. Somehow, probably because of partisan politics, upper levels in the Ministry of the Interior were convinced otherwise. On 10 August the deputy minister advised Scott that Glionna would be hired for six months to work with the exclusion service of the Immigration branch in Union Station, Toronto.[22]

The new office did not prevent Glionna from continuing his ward politics. He was relieved of his duties in February 1912, when his six-month contract expired. The decision not to rehire him probably resulted from the Liberal defeat in the 1911 federal elections. In fact, Glionna was out of the limelight until 1920, after the federal Liberals came back to power when he initiated, for example, the Italian Aid and Protective Society and was the liberal "Ward-Leader" among Italians. During the period of private life, Glionna, with a Jewish partner, opened a real estate office on Elm Street in the Ward. By the end of the war he had returned to his original occupation, musician.[23]

The second notable, Giuseppe Merlino, was one of a number of "travelling *prominenti*" who journeyed from one North American Little Italy to another, establishing themselves in the élite of each colony, usually because of their educational background. This type of leader was active but never truly became a part of the community and usually remained only a few years before moving on elsewhere. Giuseppe Merlino was from Messina (Sicily) and first appeared in Toronto in 1905 when he became minister of the Italian Methodist Mission on Elm Street. He made his mark on the community as a Methodist missionary and a petty entrepreneur. In 1908 when Michael Basso addressed an assembly of unemployed men in the colony, Merlino allowed them to use the Italian Mission as a hall. Merlino strove to make himself known in the Italian community and in Toronto's mainstream society. In 1906 an article appeared in *The Toronto Star* describing his missionary work among "irreligious Italians" in the city. During the 1908 Messina earthquake aftermath, *The Toronto Telegram* reporters gave him more press coverage than any other member of the colony. He and other immigrants contacted

Italian newspapers in New York to obtain a list of the victims. Merlino involved himself in the community on many fronts. In June 1906 the director of the local *Società Nazionale Dante Alighieri* complained that every committee had a note of discord. In the Dante society committee, an Anarchist "and a certain Merlino, a religious renegade seek to cause trouble. However I am keeping an eye on them and they must stay in their places."[24]

By 1908 Merlino had been tempted from the clerical garb by more remunerative possibilities – as a teacher of Italian and official interpreter. The 1909 *Might's Toronto City Directory* edition, under "Colleges, schools, etc.," referred to "*Signor* Merlino Teacher of Italian Grammar, conversation and literature." In 1910 the former minister had become an "insurance agent" on Centre Avenue. The community's Socialists were more precise about the job description: "ex-reverend, ex-banker, wanderer emeritus." Merlino had quit the ministry, opened an immigrant bank, and called it a Business Intelligence Office. Apparently, he and a lawyer had received $890 compensation for two injured labourers and pocketed $540 for themselves. In early 1910 he left for Boston and once again returned to the ministry.[25]

Edward Joseph Sacco was typical of a group of early professionals in the city – teachers, musicians, artists – who participated occasionally in the immigrant community's events but usually kept a distance from its activities. Yet they were respected in the colony for their learning, culture, and knowledge of the Italian language. Sacco was atypical in one respect: he used his associations with upper class Torontonians and with an Italian institution to enter the cultural and commercial arena of the Ward's Little Italy.

Sacco arrived in Toronto in 1892 and by 1895 was a special instructor in Italian language at the university. On the one hand, he was part of a long line of Italian artisans and professionals who had imported aspects of urban culture to the growing city – gastronomic delights, plaster statues, or in this case, romance languages. By 1905 he had formed a Canadian-Italian Club "with the most select persons of this [Toronto's] aristocracy as regards talent or influence." On the other hand, Sacco was simply an immigrant in search of work and opportunity. In 1899, as well as his duties at the university, Sacco took on a night school Italian class with the RCSSB. In 1902 he taught evening school for the RCSSB at St Patrick's in the Ward, and by 1904 was teaching five nights a week at another school, also in the Ward, for the same board. When his appointment at the university terminated in 1905, he fell back on his class of rich and influential Torontonians, one of whom probably found him a place as an official interpreter at the Ontario Immigration Office in Union Station in 1907. He continued in this post until 1915, when he left the city.[26] The office of official court interpreter was prestigious. Michael Basso had been seen as the representative of the Italian community when he was court interpreter in the 1890s and 1900s. (Frank Motta, who held the same post in 1911, received photographic coverage in *The Evening Telegram* while he was working as an interpreter on a murder case involving Italians in March of that year.) Yet Sacco attempted to keep open all avenues. In 1905, probably when he was about to be dismissed from the University of Toronto post, Sacco applied for a charter for the Toronto local chapter of the Dante society. He stressed the "aristocratic" element of his club and the patriotic motives behind his request.[27]

Sacco maintained his public profile by involving himself in three projects in the following five years. In July 1908, as part of his duties with the Department of Agriculture, Bureau of Colonization, he undertook an investigation of camp conditions among Italian railway labourers in northern Ontario. In January 1909 he delivered a series of addresses to raise money for the victims of the Messina earthquake. In the same year he began his most ambitious though unsuccessful project – the construction of an Italian pavilion at the Canadian National Exhibition (CNE). Again he used his important connections from his Italian language class to get the project underway and he also struck the patriotic motif: "I have influence and capital so that our Italy will be represented with a building." Magistrate Kingsford, president of the Toronto Dante society, did, in fact, present the proposal to the CNE manager, Don Orr. The building would be for the "exclusive use of the Italian colony" and would be available for community reunions. The CNE project was unsuccessful. Sacco remained in Toronto until 1915, continuing as an interpreter, but he played no further leadership role.[28]

The three *prominenti* just examined were from diverse backgrounds. Glionna belonged to an established, distinguished, and relatively wealthy family in the Ward and to a large hometown group. He gradually built up his leadership in the community. Giuseppe Merlino was one of the many ethnic brokers – legitimate, but always suspect – who travelled from one Little Italy to another, immediately making his way into the élite. Merlino was a highly educated Italian and Methodist minister. E.J. Sacco was typical of a group of professionals who were respected in the immigrant community. They had significant social standing in Toronto's mainstream society, which gave them independence from the colony.

More important than the differing backgrounds of these three notables were their similar approaches to attaining and maintaining power. First, they convinced Italian immigrants that they cared for and protected them, and although these notables understood the benefits of publicizing this attitude, they were not totally insincere in their belief that they were helping the immigrants. Advertising their mediating role required establishing a high profile during significant events for or in the colony and exploiting these situations to increase their reputation for effective leadership. Glionna's bid for placement in the Immigration office was effected against a backdrop of Black Hand murders in Canada and especially Toronto. Merlino was on hand to contact New York newspapers for casualty lists during the Messina earthquake. In 1907 the Toronto branch of New York's Giannetti Bank suddenly closed its doors on Front Street, leaving scores of Italians in despair. *The Toronto Daily News* reported that four men "are interesting themselves on behalf of the Italians." They were E.J. Sacco, government Immigration agent, Rev. Giuseppe Merlino, Italian missionary, Donato A.G. Glionna, and Michael Basso, the court interpreter.[29]

Second, by persuading Italian immigrants that they were working in their best interests, Sacco, Glionna, and Merlino appeared as representatives of Little Italy to Toronto's mainstream society or Italian officials. They could maintain their status by virtue of their role as mediators between the colony and the larger society. Thus, Sacco assured the director of the Dante society in Rome that the prospective Italian pavilion at the CNE would be for the exclusive use of the colony. Glionna had Father Berardo convince the superintendent of Immigration that it was the Italian community's wish that Glionna be placed in the Immigration office.

Third, the three notables were truly mediators between colony and outside world because each was associated with an external agency. Glionna had connections with the Liberal party machine and Merlino was a Methodist missionary. Sacco was linked to the Dante society in Italy and to artists and influential persons in Toronto high society. These associations helped the three individuals develop their mediating role as they convinced both Italian immigrants and mainstream society of their ability to function as intermediaries, spokesmen, and leaders.

There were other notables: Vanni Oranova (his real name was Giovanni Danovaro) found his immediate path as a publisher and publicist, launching a short-lived journal and newspaper, organizing a grand lodge of Sicilian mutual aid societies, and even attempting to found a band.[30] He then travelled to Welland, Ontario where he became Italian consular agent. In the postwar years, Professor Giuseppe Angelo Carboni, a musical maestro at Toronto's Royal Conservatory of Music, and a future secretary of the Toronto *fascio* (fascist club), would follow a career much resembling Sacco's. He, too, would become a notable and at the same time maintain a certain distance from the community.

Connections to outside agencies gave some members of the élite a legitimate claim to leadership. However, a leader also had to depend upon some agencies within the city's Italian community to maintain his power and status. If he was to act as a middleman between the colony and Canadian or Italian political or cultural institutions, he must legitimize his role as a representative of an *Italian* community. One of the most effective means of achieving this was to involve himself in the offices of the self-help societies and recreational clubs of Italian Toronto. If such a society did not exist or if there were barriers to entry to the offices of some societies, the notable could with time organize a new association. The Glionnas did so in 1888 as the key promoters of the Umberto Primo society. In 1902, Giuseppe Bagnato, who would emerge as one of the respected notables of the colony, was instrumental in organizing the Vittorio Emanuele III Society; again in 1919 he was the moving force behind the amalgamation of the city's three main mutual benefit societies into the *Società Italo-Canadese*. In 1913, Vanni Oranova, who had arrived in 1908 after years in American Little Italies, formed the *Ordine Unione Siciliana* with three Sicilian-Torontonian mutual benefit lodges within it. As founder, he became Grand Supreme Orator. Later, he was unsuccessful in re-establishing the Toronto local of the Dante society.[31]

In 1909 five wealthy men who had been among the early settlers in the Italian neighbourhood enhanced their prestige by forming the Italian National Club. Francesco Nicoletti, whom we have already encountered, was an immigrant banker who married a *laurenzanese*; Donato D'Alessandro and Nunzio Lobraico were musicians from Laurenzana; Antonio Mandarino was a tailor from Cerisano (Calabria); and Harry A. Castrucci a sculptor from Lucca. The organization was to provide a sociorecreational club for the élite – a *circolo dei signori* as in the Italian hometown – and thus was very conspicuous in the Italian neighbourhood. A house was purchased on D'Arcy Street, immediately outside the Ward, and a bar, billiard tables, and a bowling alley were installed. This organization gave its membership exposure to provincial and federal politicians and also made these politicians visible in the community. E.W.J. Owens, Conservative party member for Toronto South (Seat A) from 1911 to 1917, and Arthur Roebuck, unsuccessful Liberal party candidate for the 1911 and 1914 elections, later a senator, were frequent visitors. In fact, Owens's law firm handled the incorporation papers for the club. Two years previously, Owens had commissioned Serafino Castrucci, later the secretary of the Italian National Club, to publish a Conservative party-funded Italian newspaper in Toronto. In 1908, Castrucci's friend, Harry Corti, initiated the Italian weekly, *La Tribuna Canadiana*.[32]

By organizing such Italian community institutions these men gave their leadership roles a stamp of legitimacy, and a character of *noblesse oblige* to their recognized élite status. This is not to say, however, that they formed such societies intentionally for that purpose, although of course there were exceptions. They established societies out of a sense of obligation to their fellow immigrants with the likely understanding that their position within the ethnic community could be translated into status, that they could profit through their role as intermediaries, and gain respect in the larger society and polity.[33]

The societies also legitimized other leaders who sought offices in associations that they had not helped found. Indeed, many of the leaders of the postwar community, including those of the *fascio*, began their ascent to notability in the prewar mutual aid societies. Some men, like sculptor, Harry Castrucci, or ethnic entrepreneurs, Francesco Nicoletti or Abramo Puccini, could automatically attain the highest offices without serving in the lower orders of a society. Money and occupational status could buy one's way to notability.

Others gained status by their participation in voluntary associations. Giacomo Altilia, a cobbler, was secretary to the Umberto Primo society in 1912, vice-president in 1914, president in 1918, and president of the *Società Italo-Canadese* (an amalgamation of the Umberto Primo, Vittorio Emanuele, and the Italian Workingmen's

Circle of Ontario) in 1920, 1921, and 1929. Marco Missori was secretary of the Italian Workingmen's Circle in 1917 and 1918 and a founder of the *Circolo Italo-Canadese* (later *Circolo Colombo*) in 1916. During those years he was a clerk with two steamship agencies. He opened his own agency in the 1930s and became one of the more active members of the *fascio*. Angelo Petti served as treasurer of the Vittorio Emanuele III Society from 1913 to 1918. At the same time, he operated an important steamship agency and became an Italian language teacher for the Dante society's evening classes in the early 1920s. Francesco Napolitano was elected president of the Vittorio Emanuele III Society in 1916. In 1926 he became an accountant for the *Società Italo-Canadese*. In the 1930s he was elected a RCSSB trustee. Vincent Piccinnini, who would become a significant figure in the *Circolo Colombo* and then in the *fascio* in the 1920s and 1930s, began his career as a secretary of the Umberto Primo society in 1910. Aspirants to wealth, power, and prestige, as well as immigrants dedicated to the welfare of the community, used the executive positions in the benevolent associations as rungs to the top of the Italian community's social ladder.

Few of the officers had been educated beyond the primary grades, and few if any of them came from the ranks of unskilled labour. Around the turn of the century most officials had been artisans and in Toronto, as in the hometown in Italy, they were respected by the less-skilled peasants. Moveover, they had been exposed in the hometown to organizational life, such as mutual benefit societies.[34] The artisans were either barbers, tailors, or shoemakers. Except for the tailors, who were mostly from the towns surrounding Cerisano, the artisans gradually drifted out of the élite. As the number of clerks, professionals, merchants, and proprietors in the community grew, so did their representation among the notables – over 60 percent in 1910, and 70 percent by 1918.

By the First World War, small merchants and other business proprietors had replaced gradually the artisans as mutual aid society officers. Because many more such entrepreneurs existed in the community in 1915 than in 1900, they changed the profiles of the notables. By the First World War, merchants and proprietors commanded more respect from the community and were represented more than artisans as directors of voluntary associations (see table 18).

The increase in the numbers of merchants, proprietors, and professionals was paralleled by a decline in the number of directorships

Table 18
Occupations of Officers in Toronto's Italian Mutual Aid Societies, 1904, 1910, 1918

Occupation / *Year*	1904	%	1910	%	1918	%
Artisans or Skilled Labourers	11	84.6	5	26.3	3	30.0
Merchants/Proprietors	1	7.7	7	36.8	5	50.0
Clerks/Professionals	1	7.7	5	26.3	2	20.0
Unskilled Labourers	0	0	2	10.6	0	0
No. of Occupations Traced	13	100.0	19	100.0	10	100.0
Total No. of Officers	16		23		17	

Sources: *Might's Toronto Directory* and "Annual Report of the Registrar of Friendly Societies," *Sessional Papers*, Toronto, 1904, 1910, 1918.

controlled by one hometown group. At the turn of the century some hometown groups had ensured that they had a strong representation on the boards of at least one mutual aid society. Thus, the Umberto Primo society was headed by immigrants from Laurenzana; at least four of the five directors of the Italian Workingmen's Circle in 1902 – its founding year – were from the Cerisano area (the towns of San Sisto and Cerisano). The founders and original directors of the Italian National Club in 1909 were from Laurenzana, the Cerisano area, and Lucca. Many of the early members of the *Circolo Italo-Canadese* in 1916 were from Modugno di Bari. By 1915, however, as a Toronto-Italian community emerged, immigrants elected officers to their boards for their status or merit, and not for subethnic loyalties. A candidate seeking election had to appeal to the Italian community as a whole and not to particular townsgroups. As a result, by 1915 none of the mutual aid societies was controlled by any one townsgroup with the exception of the Trinacria Mutual Benefit Society, whose members were almost exclusively from Termini Imerese.

It must be stressed that the officials of the mutual aid societies were not in general connivers, calculating men who sought power and status for their own sake. They genuinely felt they were performing necessary duties beneficial to other Italian immigrants – as in fact they were. They were not, however, naïve and were aware of the status they achieved through their contributions to the community. As the thrust of this chapter and chapter four on the ethnic entrepreneurs suggests, the development of an élite, of a group of leaders or notables was unavoidable because people of the colony needed intermediaries who in turn had to be compensated with status and respect. Certainly these middlemen were in an advantageous position to exploit the rank and file for their own ends. Despite the occasional scandal or bank default, such notables were less likely to be exploiters than their *padroni* predecessors, if for no other reason than that the clientele was not transient and therefore helpless. And while they understood that wealth and power could accrue to them from their offices, they seem often to have been motivated more by a desire for personal respect or family honour than greed.

Although probably aware that their affirmations of Italian patriotism disposed the rank and file to favour them, the patriotism of the notables was neither show nor functional, but reflected real sentiments. If the ambience of Italian patriotism and colony-wide solidarity at the expense of regional loyalties helped create larger markets for their goods and services, it seemed to them only a natural part of the consolidation of the colony.

The constitutions of most of the large mutual aid societies were replete with patriotic incantations which reflected the leaders' concern for the well-being of the immigrants, the probity of the colony, and its reputation in Toronto's anglophone society and in the eyes of visiting officials from Italy. They called for group solidarity and ethnic pride, in the words of the Umberto Primo society's constitution (1888), to "promote reciprocal love among [Italians]" and "to honour the distant fatherland." The Italian National Club's charter included the following objectives:

> To promote the social educational and general welfare of its members.
> To encourage good fellowship and fraternal feeling.
> To conduct and carry on a social club, having for its objects the social and educational betterment of its members, and the augmenting from time to time of the mutual advantages and benefits flowing from the fact of association.[35]

Another club, very closely tied to Our Lady of Mount Carmel, was the *Circolo Colombo*. It resembled the parish confraternities in many Italian hometowns. Its founding members were all young, and a large number of them were from Modugno di Bari or Ghivizzano, Lucca. It seems that the *Circolo* was instituted because new arrivals (1900–10) from hometowns with more recent migration chains to

Toronto did not feel welcome in the old Italian clubs of the city. They had difficulty acquiring official positions in the voluntary associations controlled by the old order. The constitution of the new *Circolo Colombo* paid more lip service to patriotism than did any other society's charter. The objectives of this club were:

> To bind together such men of Italian birth, or origin, professing the Catholic faith ...
> To keep alive among them the profession and practice of the Catholic faith and to render them ever proud of the glorious traditions of their land of birth or origin – ITALY.
> To foster and develop in them and among them the mutual esteem and confidence, and to promote their spiritual, moral, social, physical and intellectual betterment.
> To promote the knowledge and speaking of the Italian language and the love for the Italian art and literature.
> To make of them good, and the good better citizens of this great and beloved country of adoption, or birth – CANADA.[36]

The objectives of the constitutions of the Italian National Club and the *Circolo* called for the moral and patriotic uplifting – the phrase was "betterment" – of its members. Such phrases became more and more common in new mutual aid society charters. One of the four objectives of the *Società Italo-Canadese*, formed in 1919, was "to diffuse learning among its members and to morally uplift them."[37]

The constitutions were only part of the patriotic program of the mutual aid societies. In 1897, for example, the Umberto Primo society petitioned Toronto City Council to raise both the Italian and English flags at city hall on the anniversary of Italy's unification. The Umberto Primo, like other mutual aid societies, organized a corps of uniformed guards who dressed as *bersaglieri*. According to one Socialist in the colony, they "call themselves militants and each has a uniform, and have all the military ranks up to colonel, the commander of the 'military company of the armed forces.'" In a summer 1909 article in *La Tribuna Canadiana*, the president of the *bersaglieri* attacked a Socialist who in an open air assembly had accused his society of existing for the sole purpose "of wearing the uniform which reminds us of our fatherland which refused us bread." In his closing comments the president asserted that "socialism would create true anarchy ... and that he with his soldiers would be ready for the holy mission [of defending themselves and the community against anarchy]." The Toronto correspondent to the Buffalo socialist weekly, *La Fiaccola*, wondered at the kind of association "that would align itself with the capitalists, ready to run its swords through its brothers."[38]

The Umberto Primo society and its *bersaglieri* apparently attempted to present themselves as protectors of respectable *italianità* in Toronto. In doing so they portrayed themselves to the host society as representatives of the Italian colony; at the same time they tried to assume that role in the colony itself. In fact, despite socialist dissidence, the Umberto Primo society did enjoy the support of most of the community – rural, religious, or monarchist. At that time, committed Socialists in the community probably did not number more than fifty.[39]

By the first decade of this century most Italian immigrants in Toronto, although they came from many different hometowns, believed that they had a common national origin with the other immigrants from the Italian peninsula. The notables constantly reminded them of this fact and rarely by deed or word – except among Sicilians – did they endorse regionalism. When Father Pisani was in Toronto in 1908 to set up the first Italian National Parish, he wrote an open letter to the colony, "My dear co-nationals residing in Toronto."[40] The Italians in Toronto did not only have a common origin, they also, in the view of the notables, had a common destiny. In the earlier-cited review of the play "Musolino," Serafino Castrucci preceded his critique with a general comment on the colony: "No stimulating force or moral agency has yet penetrated through the thriving colony of Italians in this portion of the globe nor have they individually or ensemble given any signs of direct coherence with their historic traditions." The implication was that the city's Italians had a duty to propagate their mother country's long lineage of high culture: "The Italians are to be congratulated in their work. They have shown that their destiny in America is not only that of the 'pick and cart,' but for higher professions."[41]

The point of patriotism, though, was not only to build up personal power. Rather it reflected concern for the polity. Patriotism was used as a means of promoting in the colony a political response to its problems. The responses were varied and they represented old and contemporary political viewpoints from the hometowns in Italy as well as political perspectives from the adopted country. The Catholic program of the *Circolo Colombo*, the monarchist stance of Harry Corti or the Umberto Primo members, or the streetcorner invectives of the Italian socialists' spokesman, Primo Giovanelli, directed at the bankers, the stress on education by all parties, all reflected political programs from the old world hometown. The Christian socialism of Giuseppe Merlino, the embracement of Methodism by some of the bankers, the involvement of immigrants in the Liberal and Conservative political machines in the Ward reflected encounters with new world political viewpoints and opportunities.

As the colony developed its Italian consciousness, and as immigrants continued to arrive in Toronto from an Italy intent on colonial expansion, the notables increasingly couched their ambitions in patriotic terms. As we have seen, in 1905 "Prof." Sacco organized the city's local of the Dante society. He reported to the head office of the society in Rome that when the membership would increase "I shall be satisfied for having been successful in having honoured my fatherland in this distant country." To establish a rapport with the new president of the Dante society in 1908, Sacco predicted that the Dante society would "prosper and propagate, so as to assure the glory of Italy, mother and cradle of science and civilization." The next person to head the Dante society was the publisher and publicist, Vanni Oranova. In 1913, when he was reorganizing the society after a three-year lull, Oranova tried to ingratiate himself with Dante society officials in Rome. He described himself to them as "an old and enthusiastic militant of the Dante Society, and in each country that I have visited I have always made a moderate contribution of good, healthy propaganda." References to Italy's "glory," its role as the "cradle of civilization," and to the disinterested commitment of individuals willing to disseminate the precepts of an Italian cultural institution perhaps were heartfelt, but they also helped the notables achieve personal goals.[42]

It was Italy's entry into the First World War that galvanized the Italian community in Toronto. The calls to patriotism, both Italian and Canadian, deflected the socialist critique of capitalism in the colony. For the first time, Italians in the city were not viewed with suspicion or condescension, but rather were accepted as partners with other Canadians in the war. And it was easier to respond to patriotism as new job opportunities opened up in war industries for Italians and other immigrants.

The Italian community's response to the war is best captured in the parade to celebrate Italy's entry on the side of Britain and France. On the evening of 26 May 1915, 4,000 Italians marched from the Italian National Club on D'Arcy Street along a route that included Spadina Avenue, Queen Street, York Street (where many Italian boardinghouses were located), King, Victoria, Shuter, and Yonge streets, and back to D'Arcy Street *via* the Ward. Two brass bands, the orderly march of uniformed members of the three mutual aid societies, and "the glowing of countless torches borne in the hands of the processionists" all enhanced the pomp and circumstance of the occasion. As the crowds waved the 800 Italian flags purchased for the event and cried out "Viva l'Italia, Viva il Canadà," and "Abbassa l'Austria" (down with Austria), the organizers of the demonstration blended solemnity with sentimentality as they halted their horses to salute the South African monument at University Avenue and Queen Street. Returning to D'Arcy Street, Glionna's band played the Garibaldi hymn – "L'Inno di Mameli" (later the Italian national anthem). A lawyer, Luigi Mollo, addressed the crowd from the club's decorated balcony. He "stirred his audience to its depth" as he told of how "out of the dark blue sea the red archangel had appeared, calling with her powerful voice to the Italian people that the time had come to take the Adriatic from the oppressor, and the Italian people would answer in one voice that they were willing even to die for the glory and for the sacred name of their country." *The Toronto Star* described it as "altogether one of the most striking demonstrations Toronto has ever seen, not excepting even the labour and twelfth of July [Orange Day] parades." Indeed, the demonstration was extremely successful. The 4,000 participants, representing about 40 percent of the city's Italian community, were a testimony to the leadership's ability to rally the different groups of patriotic townspeople into a unified assembly. The torches, 800 flags, horses, and spontaneous cheers attested to the Italian National Club's success in seizing the opportunity of war to fuel the nationalistic sentiments of the Italian immigrants.[43]

The orderly structure of the march provides insight into the nature of ethnic loyalties in the community. Antonio Gatto (president of the Trinacria and a prominent member of the large Sicilian community from Termini Imerese), John Glionna (member of the wealthy *laurenzanese* family), and Harry Corti (publisher of the *Tribuna Canadiana*) headed the march on horseback. Following a number of footmen carrying banners, and the band of *bersaglieri*, marched the members of the Italian societies – Umberto Primo, Italian Workingmen's Circle of Ontario, Vittorio Emanuele III, and the Trinacria. The Italian National Club members marched in front of the "unattached" rank and file, while Glionna's band tailed the entire procession. The various clusters of mutual aid society members in the parade suggest that the voluntary associations and their leadership had become for the immigrants emblems of Italian ethnic consciousness. The common crowd at the back of the parade identified Toronto *italianità* with the three major mutual aid societies, with the Italian National Club, the *Tribuna Canadiana*, the élite of ethnic entrepreneurs, educated men, professionals, with Our Lady of Mount Carmel, or the civic band.

Despite the immigrant's perceptions of patriotism and his adherence to the cause of the homeland, the nature of his *italianità* was a far cry from its counterpart in wartime Italy. Toronto's Italian ethnic community strove to form part of the Italian nation. However, as Anthony D. Smith has observed, "unlike the ethnic community ... the nation ... possesses a dynamic character expressed in an institutional program, and a sense of ideological destiny."[44] Toronto's Italian immigrants and their leaders had formed a social and cultural fragment which they saw as Italian. This confused their true identity for they belonged neither in Italy nor in Canada – they had no real country. Their institutional program, though nationalist in rhetoric, was locally specific in reality, comprising a handful of self-help and recreational clubs. Their sense of ideological destiny, although more complex, was easily reduced to Mollo's quaint, sentimental allusions to the "archangel," "glory," and "sacred name of country."[45] The national consciousness of the community, then, was in an odd state – more than an ethnic community – many Italian reservists would return to Italy to fight for the home country – yet not quite a nation. In the postwar period, the élite and especially the fascist Italian consulate would attempt to swing the pendulum towards the homeland. The method would involve an expanded élite, the multiplication of legitimizing institutions, and much more patriotic, sentimental speechifying.

CHAPTER SEVEN

The Fascist Period

Toronto's Italian population increased rapidly during the twenty years before the First World War. The small community of 750 immigrants in 1897 swelled to 6,000 by 1908 and to 10,000 by 1913. During the war many Italians left either to serve in the Italian army or to search for work elsewhere because the large capital projects in Canada had been replaced by the war effort. However, during the 1920s many other Italians arrived in the city. As a result, at the start of the depression the Italian population in Toronto remained at about 10,000. With the postwar immigrants a new vitality erupted in Italian Toronto as the arrivals called for a more representative voice in the community.

A few recreational clubs were initiated during and after the Great War, and throughout the 1920s self-help clubs mushroomed in the community. These voluntary associations were either local, regional, or national in character; that is, their members were from one town or one region, or from all over the peninsula, depending on the type of club. The expansion of institutions in the community required a larger leadership, and by the early 1920s about thirty men – mostly skilled tradesmen, businessmen, or professionals – directed the institutional life and politics of the community. They commanded respect because of their high-status occupations and their official positions in the voluntary associations of the ethnic group. However, beginning in the late 1920s, the prestige of some of these men suffered. As the Italian government permeated the community with fascist propaganda, the old notables lost influence over the Italian population of Toronto, or at best, could not maintain influence without claiming loyalty to the Italian representative. This chapter

Table 19
Membership in Mutual Aid Societies, 1913–18

Year	*Vit. Eman. III*	*It. Workmen's*	*Umberto P.*	*Totals*
1913	32	120	76	228
1914	32	110	50	192
1915	29	75	26	130
1916	18	75	25	118
1917	20	47	22	89
1918	18	47	16	81

Source: "Annual Report of the Registrar of Friendly Societies," *Sessional Papers*, Toronto, 1913–18.

examines the infiltration of the community by the fascist vice-consul and his aides, and its effect on the institutional life and old leadership of Italian Toronto.

One sign of the new vitality was the increased activity in voluntary associations in the colony. The war period had proved particularly troublesome for mutual aid societies because a large part of the population, probably about 2,000, returned to Italy (see table 19). With drastically declining memberships, the three most important mutual benefit societies, the Vittorio Emanuele III, the Italian Workingmen's Circle of Ontario, and the Umberto Primo Benefit Society consolidated in 1919 and formed the *Società Italo-Canadese* which came under the strong influence of the Bagnato family. That same year, the Italian National Club was dissolved.

The first of the noteworthy associations founded by "new blood" was the *Circolo Colombo* in 1916. All sixteen founding members were young Catholics, and except for a Glionna, were born in Italy. Beginning in 1920, mutual benefit societies and associations of all kinds found themselves in more propitious circumstances. As the number of associations grew, so did the roster of notables. In 1920 D.A.G. Glionna, with the help of a *laurenzanese* and two men from San Sisto (Calabria), organized the Italian Aid and Protective Society of Ontario. By 1925 this organization directed four lodges. During the 1920s two more significant mutual aid societies were organized. The Fratellanza (Brotherhood) members were mostly from either the regions of Venetia or Abruzzi and almost all lived in the Dufferin Street and Davenport Road district. The *Circolo Stella Alpina* comprised members almost exclusively from the small towns outside Susa (Piedmont), primarily Gravere and Meana, although a few *friulani* also joined the club. In addition, numerous organizations were formed in the three Catholic national parishes and the three Methodist and

Evangelical churches.[1] The most important association in the colony was the *Comitato Intersociale* (Intersocial Committee, i.e., *Comitato*) which served as an umbrella organization for all the Italian clubs in Toronto. (This club, which became a takeover target of the consulate in the 1930s, will be discussed in greater detail below.) New associations mushroomed in the community after 1927. They included the *Fascio Principe Umberto*, the *Fascio Femminile*, the National Association of War Veterans (Ex-Combattenti), lodges of the Sons of Italy, the Assistance and Repatriation Society. All these clubs would be either controlled or strongly influenced by the Italian vice-consulate in the city.

The evolution of the vice-consulate's power in the community during the fascist era (1928–40) was the most important development in this period in Italian Toronto and deserves particular attention. By the early 1930s the vice-consul controlled the general sentiments of the colony and also defined the terms under which an individual could join the élite. In order to understand how he acquired hegemony over the ethnic community, the general program of fascist propaganda in North America must be examined.[2]

Mussolini's program of "exporting fascism" to Italian immigrants abroad began with the institution of *Fasci all'Estero* (Fascists Abroad) in 1923. This propaganda agency of the Italian Fascist party, and, beginning in 1927, of the Italian Foreign Office, was to organize and oversee the activities of hundreds of *fasci* (fascist clubs) in Little Italies around the world. That same year, the secretariat entrusted the *fascio* in New York with organizing and directing other such clubs in North America. Later in the year, the New York *fascio* was dissolved and a central council replaced it as the governing body for North American Italian fascist organizations. In July 1925 this council was superceded by the Fascist League of North America (FLNA) and Count Ignazio Thaon de Revel was flown to New York to direct the new organization. The FLNA's mandate was to form local *fasci*, keep a tab on directorates, and if necessary, choose local directors. Locals in Canada came under the jurisdiction of the FLNA.[3]

Late in December 1929 the FLNA was replaced by the Lictor Foundation and the local *fasci* were more strongly controlled by the *Fasci all'Estero* agency in Rome. That same year, Mussolini and Pius XI signed the Lateran Treaty. By 1929 the Italian dictator had silenced opposition to his propaganda efforts from Italian consuls of the old diplomatic tradition. In 1928 and 1929 the Italian government opened about seventy new consulates and appointed 120 new fascist career consuls. It was, in fact, in 1929 that Toronto was raised from a consular agency to the level of vice-consulate and that *Cavaliere* (Knight) Giovanni Ambrosi, an injured war veteran, was sent from Italy to become the city's first Italian vice-consul. In the ensuing years, Ambrosi, more than any other official, made the vice-consulate the focus of the community's activities.[4]

John P. Diggins has written that in the 1920s Italian Americans were "ripe for fascism." A "nascent inferiority complex," a nostalgic nationalism, and a fear for family solidarity and community caused them to adhere to the patriotic programs of their local *fasci*.[5] North American Italian immigrants were prepared for fascism and were imbued with a "nostalgic nationalism" because, by 1920, the élite had already prepared them to think in nationalistic terms, to equate God with country, to respect law and order. When Ambrosi arrived in 1929, Toronto's Italians upheld all these attitudes and beliefs. Ambrosi simply needed to consolidate these principles behind one spokesman or organization.

A few important developments prepared the city's immigrants for fascism. The war instilled a strong patriotism in the colony. Flags, nationalistic exclamations, and speeches reflected the heightened loyalties of the people. The formation of the *Circolo Colombo* was a significant milestone for it was the first association in the postwar community to draw a distinct link between church and nation. In fact, the motto of the club was *Dio e Patria* (God and Fatherland). The members were young and upwardly mobile and grew increasingly influential in the community, not only within the *Circolo* itself, but also in other associations. *Circolo Colombo* emerged as *the* spokesgroup for law and order in society, for allegiance to nation, family, and the Catholic church, as the defender against the threat of socialism. In 1919, when, as the *Circolo* described it, "some Italians instigated by enemies of the Church and quasi-subversive societies [i.e., Socialists]" staged a confrontation with Padre Scafuro of St Clement's Parish, the *Circolo* came to the defense of the pastor, even though the club was affiliated with Mount Carmel. Describing themselves as a club of "young Italians, the cream of the Colony," the *Circolo* sent a notice to the archbishop advising him to disregard the attack on Padre Scafuro.[6]

Toronto's Italian immigrants were also steered towards fascism by the city's, and Canadian society's, general acceptance of Mussolini's political philosophy during his early rule. Toronto, like the rest of North America, was generally sympathetic towards *Il Duce* and his policies in the 1920s and early 1930s. A number of public figures in the city spoke favourably of the dictator before the Ethiopian crisis turned public opinion against him. For example, in a November 1928 editorial in *The Globe*, Toronto publicist and world traveller, Thomas O'Hagan, referred to Mussolini as Italy's "saviour." He spoke in highly laudatory terms of the dictator in a *Toronto Star* interview four years later, after a five-month European trip.[7]

In January 1929 Alfred E. Lowell, chief administrator of the Ontario Parole Board, speaking to the Club of Young Canadians at the Walker House Hotel in Toronto, asserted that Italians obeyed laws habitually and that more than any other people they resembled the English. Lowell credited Mussolini with having instilled this discipline into the new Italy. The Italians' proclivity for law and order was also the theme discussed by Police Chief Brig. Gen. D.C. Draper later that year. He praised "the Italian colony because no Italian had taken part in communist meetings which had recently caused disturbances in Queen's Park." Professor James Eustace Shaw, Italian language professor at the University of Toronto, was one of the moving forces behind the Dante society local and very much in contact with the Italian community. In the spring of 1923, he delivered an alumni lecture on "Fascism and the Fascisti." His favourable report perceived Mussolini as one who restored order in a chaotic country, for altruistic reasons: "The essence and moving force was a great love of Italy.... To him morality is love of country, and he trusts in the people's patriotism as a moving power." The city's Italian population certainly would have clung to aspects of Italian life viewed favourably by Toronto's mainstream society.[8]

The postwar period brought a number of Italian immigrants to the city who had lived through the war in Europe or had fought at the front. A number of them would become prominent in the community and serve as models of *italianità*. One of these was F.M. Gualtieri, a disabled war veteran, who organized the War Veterans Association in the city in 1927. Another was Ruggero Bacci who had arrived in 1921 to escape the battles between the Left and Right in his hometown. He was an avid early Fascist – a *fascista di prima ora* – that is, a member of the Fascist party in Italy before Mussolini's October 1922 March on Rome. Bacci became the last, and most intractable political secretary of Toronto's *Fascio Principe Umberto* in the late 1930s.[9]

Two other eager Fascists arrived in this period: the physicians Pasquale Fontanella and Rosario Invidiata. The first settled in Toronto in 1924 and from the start inserted himself into the leadership of the community. Fontanella's oratorical skill was his greatest asset. In the early 1930s he became Ambrosi's right-hand man and acted as representative for the vice-consul on various occasions. The second newcomer, Rosario Invidiata, was described as "a son of strong Sicily and an ardent Fascist." He was one of the organizers of the *fascio* in his hometown of Polizzi Generosa, Sicily, in 1923. When the Italian community held a banquet in Invidiata's honour in 1927, he received a telegram from Eugenio Bonardelli, the Italian consul-general in Ottawa, thanking him for his "manifest patriotic sentiments and attachment to the Duce, the renewer of the Italian conscience."[10]

Another Italian who came to Toronto at this time, but only for a very brief visit, in 1923, was Italia Garibaldi, the hero's granddaughter. She toured Canada to promote an Italian agricultural colonization scheme in Manitoba, and was able to organize fascist locals in Toronto, Winnipeg, and Montreal.[11] It seems, however, that public enthusiasm waned and that the Toronto *fascio* had a short life span. A second attempt at forming one was made in 1926. In August of that year Nicola Selvaggio, one of the *fascio*'s organizers, had an audience with Mussolini. He returned with an autographed photograph of the dictator "addressed to 'the Blackshirts of Toronto.' " At least two of the other three officials of the *fascio* at that time were from the Sicilian town of Termini Imerese.[12]

In 1929 as *Fasci all'Estero* in Rome sought to centralize fascist locals around the world and bring these locals under the control of new career consuls, the council, which was formed in 1926 and directed the *fascio*, was abolished and the the general secretary of *Fasci all'Estero*, Piero Parini, appointed Ettore Fattori, a local artist, extraordinary commissioner of the Toronto *fascio*. In 1931, the local was reorganized with a new council, presumably because it had grown large enough to warrant an executive. Massimo Jacopo Magi, a wealthy proprietor of a statuary firm, the Florentine Company on King Street West, was appointed political secretary. The directorate comprised Marco Missori (a steamship agent whom we have already encountered), Orlando Eliseo (a foreman at the W.R. Johnston Company, clothing contractors), Pasquale Palange (president of the Dante society in the early 1920s), and Teodoro Zambri (also a director of the Dante society in the 1920s). In 1932, Giuseppe Angelo Carboni, a teacher at Toronto's Conservatory of Music, became secretary. Magi continued as an assistant secretary, a post he had held under Fattori. From 1929 the council was directly responsible to the Italian vice-consul, Giovanni Battista Ambrosi.[13]

Besides the *fascio*, Vice-Consul Ambrosi also relied on the War Veterans Association to bring the colony within his grasp. The association was organized in Italy in 1919 but it was not until 1925, after much resistance, that the Fascists acquired control of it. The Toronto local was established in March 1927 by two former officers, F.M. Gualtieri and Donato Sansone, M.D. Both were well educated, and Gualtieri had been badly wounded in the war. The Toronto local originally came under the jurisdiction of the American Federation of Italian War Veterans in New York, but later was administered by a directorate general in Rome. Another veteran officer, Alfredo Bassanese, was elected the first president of the association.[14]

The *fascio* and the War Veterans Association were both a product of, and also enhanced the patriotism of the city's Italian community. The patriotic fervour of the colony had developed significantly during the war and before Ambrosi began his tenure in Toronto in 1929, the commemoration of patriotic events – many of them connected with the war – had become commonplace, especially after 1928. In February 1927 the women's club, *Società Duchessa D'Aosta*, sponsored an evening of entertainment to raise proceeds for the Italian Soldiers' Orphans' Institute. In March, the Alhambra Hall on Spadina Avenue was the site of the institution of the Italian War Veterans Association. The following month the *Fascio Principe Umberto* observed the "Birth of Rome" in the Italian Hall at St Agnes Church. The following year (March 1928) the *Comitato* organized a memorial Mass at Our Lady of Mount Carmel for the recently deceased Italian General Diaz, and a *Te Deum* Mass at St Agnes for the recovery of the Italian king. The *Fascio Principe Umberto* invited FLNA president, Count Thaon de Revel, and Toto Giurato, publisher of the FLNA organ *Giovinezza*, to the baptism of the *fascio*'s coat of arms, in April 1928, but neither was able to attend the event. The following October the *fascio* celebrated the sixth anniversary of the fascist March on Rome; this time, Giurato attended the function in

Massey Hall. A few weeks later, the War Veterans Association began their annual 4 November pilgrimage to city hall to lay a wreath on the Tomb of the Unknown Soldier.[15]

Many of the Italian societies and lodges participated officially in the events, which usually had a relatively large Italian audience. At the Diaz ceremony, representatives from at least nine societies attended, and apparently "all clubs" were present at the Italian monarch's *Te Deum* Mass. *Circolo Colombo* and the Ontario Lodge of the Sons of Italy, "patriotic Italian societies," sent delegates to the *Fascio Principe Umberto*'s banner-blessing ceremony. The 4 November 1928 memorial function was attended by officials from the Trinacria Mutual Benefit Society, the *Società Italo-Canadese*, Ontario Lodge of Sons of Italy, the *Società Stella Alpina*, and the Fratellanza Society. By the time of Ambrosi's arrival in 1929, the presence of these associations at any patriotic event was taken for granted: not to attend was tantamount to showing irreverence for the homeland.[16]

A solemn air pervaded all the assemblies. Michel Angelo's band, or students of Maestro Ferrari-Fontana, a well-known voice teacher, or Maestro Carboni performed *Giovinezza*, the fascist anthem, the Italian and Canadian national anthems, and selections from Italian opera.[17] The gatherings included speeches which became increasingly patriotic and profascist. The discourses usually alluded to Italy in vague but grandiose terms, and also centred on the Toronto colony's achievements and duties. That way the city's Italian immigrants felt they had an integral part to play in the *Grande Italia*. At the *Duchessa D'Aosta* fundraising entertainment of March 1927, Dr Fontanella "spoke of the Italian emigrant, colonial life, the distant homeland, weaving a hymn of glory to those who gave their lives for the grandeur of Italy where one sees the marks of the Great War, which touched our hearts – those are especially the wounded and the orphaned." When F.M. Gualtieri initiated the War Veterans Association local, he distinguished the advantages of such an organization over others: "unlike other Italian societies in Toronto, which are especially admirable, we better assure the goals, esteem, and respect to which we have a right as representatives of a great people, virtuous and strong."[18]

Dr Fontanella was fast becoming the fascist bard of the colony and in the 1930s was the keynote speaker at all nationalistic functions not addressed by Ambrosi himself. As early as 1927, Pasquale Molinaro, Toronto correspondent to New York's *Progresso Italo-Americano*, described him as "first in all manifestations of Italianity." The physician's address to the audience commemorating the "Birth of Rome" that year was "erudite and patriotic ... a true hymn to the great and sound work of Duce Mussolini."[19]

In 1928 the patriotic fervour had become self-perpetuating. No society dared oppose any of the nationalistic assemblies operated by the *fascio*. To do so was to spite the homeland. Much to the contrary, the colony's organizations paid more than just lip service to the fascist regime. At the 4 November memorial of 1928, the *Circolo Colombo*, "forerunner of Italianity in Canada," telegraphed King Vittorio Emanuele and *il Duce* himself with "kindest regards wishing continuing success for the good and grandeur of Italy." Feeding the general patriotic frenzy in the colony were prominent personalities both from within and outside Toronto. Giuseppe Angelo Carboni, the vocal instructor of some note at the Royal Conservatory, asserted that "it was the duty of all Italians to be fascists" when he was initiated into the Toronto fascist local. At the Toronto celebrations of the tenth anniversary of the founding of Italian Fascist party, Cesare Maccari, a prominent New York Fascist closely connected to the former FLNA, gave an "erudite speech ... a hymn to Fascism, the Duce, and the Italian race."[20]

The approval of the clergy for the *fascio* was not negligible either. They were ignorant of the nature of fascism yet were encouraged by the better relations between church and state in Italy, and by the law and order regime of Mussolini. Thus the clergy in Toronto gave their support to the political movement. Father Truffa, pastor of St Agnes, attended the blessing of the *Fascio Principe Umberto*'s coat of arms in April 1928. He informed the audience that "when one says Italian, he also means Catholic, and because Catholicism has for the first time assumed its place as state religion, I give my approval and augur Fascism well; Fascism, which is composed of, and directed by, men of an upright Catholic faith." After the 1929 Lateran Treaty, when the pastor of an Italian national parish emphasized the ties between *italianità* and Catholicism, he justified for his parishioners their allegiances to Italian fascism, the local *fascio*, the vice-consul, and the pious platitudes of any nationalist member of the élite.[21]

Father Truffa and his partner, Father Volontè, supported the vice-consul and *fascio* throughout their tenure at St Agnes. When the Salesians' superiors decided to withdraw their two confrères from the parish in 1934, the fascist leaders protested, backed by Ambrosi.

The vice-consul obviously feared losing the allies he had at St Agnes Church. The Salesians had always encouraged their parishioners to obey the Italian representative. Tommaso Mari, Pasquale Fontanella, Rosario Invidiata, and Prof. Emilio Goggio (appointed by Ambrosi as director of the Dante society, an organization which had come under fascist control in Italy and the colonies) pleaded with the archbishop "in their capacity as exponents of their Italian colony" that the Salesians remain in the city. Citing the clerics' work among youth, their fundraising capabilities for the diocese, and their anti-communist campaign, the quartet advised the archbishop to place the other two Italian national parishes in the Salesians' care.[22]

Although Goggio and his colleagues claimed that they interpreted the sentiments of the entire community from "Ambrosi down to the poor labourers," it was clear that the vice-consul was behind the effort to persuade the church hierarchy. In March 1934 the secretary of the *Fascio Principe Umberto* wrote the superior of the Salesian order in Turin praising the "religious and patriotic" work of their two disciples in Toronto. He requested on behalf of the *fascio*, the War Veterans Association, and the Retired Officers that Truffa and Volontè be allowed to remain at St Agnes. All three of these associations came under Ambrosi's jurisdiction. The vice-consul informed Luigi Petrucci, the Italian consul-general in Ottawa, of the "great damage that would derive to our Colony" should the Salesians leave.[23] Petrucci wrote to his superiors in Rome (the Directorate of Italians Abroad) indicating the need for Italian clergy in North America, because "more than any other official, the pastor can keep [our colonies] united, keep alive their Catholic and Italian spirit, and prevent their absorption into the Anglo-Saxon world by the Irish Church." As tangible proof he pointed to the Salesians at St Agnes who administered the parish "to the great satisfaction of our co-nationals and to the great benefit of the Italianity of this Colony of ours."[24]

By the late 1920s support for the *fascio* came from among the notables of the colony and the clergy. The rank and file were certainly patriotic but had not completely associated fascism with patriotism: the fascist local was not yet well organized nor had it set itself up as the central organizing force of the community. In 1929, acting on instructions from his superiors, Giovanni Battista Ambrosi came to Toronto from Italy planning to change that.

The decisive year for Italian fascist activities in the Toronto colony as well as in many Little Italies around the world was 1929. It was in the spring of that year that the consular agency in the city was upgraded to a vice-consulate. Many other such agencies in North America experienced a similar change. Years later, Libero Sauro, minister of St Paul's Italian United Church, correctly observed that "the raising of the Italian agency to a vice-consulate was just a means used by the Italian government to exploit its people here in the interests of Fascism."[25] The *fascio* was restructured and sent an extraordinary commissioner by the *Fasci all'Estero* commissariat in Rome. Tommaso Mari and Attilio Perilli journeyed respectively from Hamilton, Ontario and New York to operate the Italian Publishing Company and Italian Information Bureau on Elm Street. It seems that the Italian government's propaganda wing commissioned the publisher and news reporter to publish the fascist weekly, *Bollettino Italo-Canadese*, and later, an annual Toronto-Italian directory. The *Fasci all'Estero* subsidized the tabloid at sixty dollars per month. (When Italy declared war on Great Britain in June 1940, the two entrepreneurs left for New York under diplomatic immunity.)[26]

From his arrival in 1929, Ambrosi made his presence strongly felt in the Italian community. Solid support from the War Veterans Association was not forthcoming until the early 1930s but the *fascio* expressed its loyalty to him from the start. Ambrosi's approach was to use his office and the *fascio* to play on the patriotic sentiments of the rank and file. In his exhaustive study, *Mussolini and Fascism: The View from America*, John P. Diggins observed that in the United States it was crucial for "propagandists not only to exploit the anxieties of Italian Americans but to identify Fascism with Italian Nationalism itself. In effect, the Blackshirts had stolen the thunder of patriotism, using a rhetoric that enabled them to parade as Italy's historic heir and the only genuine Italophiles." Ambrosi and the *fascio* also succeeded in making fascism synonymous with Italian nationalism.[27]

Ambrosi astutely perceived that Italian patriotism in Toronto was strongly influenced by the political leaders of the colony through the institutions they headed. The vice-consul also sensed that those institutions – mutual aid societies and sociorecreational clubs – had to be brought under his influence if not taken over by him and the *fascio*. In this way he could maintain a close check on the élite to ensure it remained loyal to him. What is significant here is that Ambrosi did not have to indoctrinate the community with patriotism and nationalism, for the city's Italian immigrants had already developed a sense of nationalism in the preceding thirty years. He had only to convince immigrants that the consulate and institutions loyal to fascism were the sole legitimate sources of patriotism in the colony.

One way Ambrosi chose to accomplish this was by attending all patriotic manifestations in the colony, and by visiting most of the mutual aid societies. In his first public appearance in the city on 8 April 1929, Giovanni Battista Ambrosi entered the hall of *Circolo Colombo* with a flourish, accompanied by a "hurricane of applause," the fascist anthem, *Giovinezza*, and the colours of the Italian flag decorating the room. The vice-consul, who had arrived from Italy only one week previously, had come to attend a special lecture by Mgr Ernesto Coppo of Kimberly, Australia. The lecture dealt with the 1929 church-state accords in Italy – one of the principal issues Ambrosi wished to stress at the start of his appointment. A few days later he received a solid show of support from St Agnes Parish's Salesian fathers, "heralds of Italianity who in Canada exercise a true apostolate for religion and fatherland." St Agnes's pastor, Father Truffa, informed the *Progresso Italo-Americano* correspondent that "the Salesians will cooperate fully with the new Vice-Consul Cavaliere G.B. Ambrosi, destined by the Duce, his eminence Benito Mussolini, to direct the high offices of the Toronto vice-consulate."[28]

From April 1929, all organizations began to feel the presence of the new vice-consul, and one by one, they voiced their allegiances. Ambrosi surrounded himself with patriotic professionals at all public events, especially the physicians, Invidiata and Fontanella, or the newspaperman, Tommaso Mari. He attended the public functions of all mutual aid societies during his first two years in the city. At all these events, either he, Fontanella, or Mari waxed sentimental over Italy's grandeur and *il Duce*'s heroic feats. In mid-May 1929, accompanied by Dr Invidiata, Ambrosi visited a social at the Trinacria society. The members, almost all of whom were from the town of Termini Imerese, "cheered him enthusiastically." For his part, Invidiata turned to Ambrosi during a speech and observed that "as usual, the Sicilians had responded eagerly to the appeals of the beloved, distant fatherland; so will they respond to the appeals of the Vice-Consul."[29]

Ambrosi continued to maintain a high profile the following year.

In one month alone he addressed three important functions – the blessing of the coat of arms of the Fratellanza Society, the Columbus Day celebrations, and the eighth anniversary observance of the fascist March on Rome. By that time (late 1930), Ambrosi had won the allegiances of the Trinacria and *Stella Alpina* mutual aid societies. It seems, from newspaper reports, that he limited his public appearances to only the most patriotic and ostentatious events in the colony.[30]

In order to ensure a successful propaganda campaign, Ambrosi depended upon two resources – public speeches and the press. From the start the vice-consul established more than amicable relations with the Italian immigrant press. The *Bollettino Italo-Canadese*, of course, was fascist and its editor, Tommaso Mari, extended his full support to the Italian representative. The publisher of the short-lived *Progresso Italo-Canadese*, banker and steamship agent, Francesco Tomaiuolo, was only too happy to please the vice-consul because much of his work involved Italian documents handled by the consulate – passports, military leaves, etc. Thus the complete text of Ambrosi's speeches appeared in the *Progresso* with obliging statements such as "acting on his [i.e., Ambrosi's] kind concession" For his part, Ambrosi promoted his press coverage as much as possible. After delivering his address at the blessing of the Fratellanza Society's coat of arms, Ambrosi handed the text to Frank Marrocco, president of the mutual aid society, "asking that he circulate it to directors of the Italian press that they might publish it." Although Ambrosi's speeches did not appear in New York's *Progresso Italo-Americano* because the Toronto news had only limited space allotment, the correspondent, Pasquale Molinaro, gave the vice-consul ample and favourable coverage. In one article he exhorted "our colonies in Ontario [to bless] always the name of Benito Mussolini, Duce of Italy, who has sent to this peninsula of Ontario a representative who has conquered the sympathies of all our colonies which are very fond of him." By reporting all events concerning the *fascio* and the vice-consulate and by writing so favourably about the latter, the Italian press in the city made Ambrosi appear as *the* patriotic leader of Italian Toronto, just as he had hoped.[31]

The events Ambrosi patronized and at which he often delivered addresses were usually well attended – 100 to 400 people – given the size of halls and the population of the colony. The vice-consul's approach was to play on the sentiments of the people by linking their everyday lives and the values of their upbringing with a "brotherhood" of Italians, their personal memories with a great Italian legacy. To explain fascism as a movement of the people at a ceremony commemorating the March on Rome, Ambrosi began with the individual and the family: "The individual lives in the family, the family in the state, the supreme realization of the collective and individual weal."[32]

In the same address Ambrosi referred to the "colonial family." The vice-consul once more relied on sentimentality to discuss the labour laws and work projects under the Italian fascist state: "Work must not be considered punishment but part of the joy of living, the means of production of the nation [and again], the family, the individual ..." In his discourse to the Trinacria society soon after his arrival, Ambrosi exhorted the Sicilians to "work always from the good of Toronto's Italian colony, trusting that each Italian should be seen as a father, a brother."[33]

The following year, at the blessing of the Fratellanza coat of arms, he alluded to the royal Savoyard cross on the flag, "the symbol of Rome, of the land of your forefathers which encompasses for you the highest sentiments and the dearest memories." The immigrant audience, overwhelmed by a sequence of emotionally charged words, unconsciously selected and associated key terms: family and state, colony in Toronto and Italian brotherhood, memories of the hometown and Rome, land of their forefathers. The term *patria* (homeland) was just as effective in seducing Ambrosi's listeners. After introducing the "god and country" connection at a Columbus Day celebration, Ambrosi defined *patria* as "the synthesis of moral, cultural, and economic sentiments of a determined group [which] completes and perfects man." This was certainly not a definition, but it sufficed to touch the sentiments of the immigrant group. With his trite references to family and *patria*, Ambrosi attempted to evoke a sentimental response from his audience.[34] It is interesting to observe the correlation between the ever-increasing sentimentality in public addresses and the growing centralization of the community as the vice-consulate came to dominate the colony.

The speeches ultimately did have a structure, the literary equivalent of music's modified binary form (ABA – modified): sentimental gestures about the Fatherland (A), followed by a summary of Italy's artistic and scientific legacy – usually covering Rome, the Renaissance, and the nineteenth century (B), with a return to other affected blurbs on the *patria* (modified A). Effective features included the rhetorical question ("Our fatherland in Italy – and pronouncing that word "Italy" are our hearts not moved; does it not strike a lively and profound chord in one's very depths"), and odd metaphors ("The blood running in our veins is the purest to have been produced in Nature's laboratories.").[35]

Fontanella's speech of 24 April 1930 at the Italian Hall for the celebration of the "Birth of Rome" and May Day (sponsored by the *fascio* and the War Veterans Association) illustrates most clearly his propagandist intention. After a brief introduction he plunged into a eulogy of Rome: "What memories does the birth of Rome strike in us? Its long history ... Rome, known by the wise as *caput mundi* ... it almost seems that the air which surrounds our beautiful Italy smacks of the divine ... [followed by a foray into Italian explorers] ... and if anyone out of ignorance or jealousy does not like this state of affairs, the divine poet [Dante] would say 'do not consider them but look at once and pass and speak no more of them.' " Fontanella then alluded to the present Rome as a continuation of the old empire: "The 2683 years of Rome ... almost signifies that with her children's hands and brains Rome is always destined to be *caput mundi*." The doctor proceeded to list Italian inventions and to toast the War Veterans Association and Ambrosi. He defined the Fascists for his audience as those who stamped out bolshevism, as 101 percent Italians because they placed Italy's grandeur before their party. A toast to *il Duce* and a short encomium of Ambrosi as a war victim and perfect man for the vice-consulate, ended the address. All of Fontanella's speeches were hackneyed variations of the same themes – the grandeur of Imperial Rome and the new Rome, Italy's discoveries – interspersed with sentimental evocations and quotations.[36]

From 1930, Ambrosi restricted his appearances to the most nationalistic events sponsored by the *fascio* and War Veterans Association. Almost all societies in the colony had a group of members loyal to him; in this way the societies came under the vice-consul's influence. By manipulating the clubs, the vice-consul was able to organize events embracing the entire community. That in turn allowed him to emerge as the central figure within the Italian colony, and appear as leader of Italian Toronto to mainstream society. Ambrosi was concerned with permeating those associations which exercised authority in Italian Toronto, yet remained independent of the vice-consulate. Resistance on the part of the community to

Ambrosi's intrusions was certainly greater than the Italian official could have expected. An examination of Ambrosi's dealings with two such organizations will help assess the impact of his takeover attempts.

The *Comitato* and the Italian War Veterans Association both existed before Ambrosi appeared in the colony in 1929. As mentioned earlier, the *Comitato* was an umbrella organization of all associations in the colony. Little is known about its inception but it clearly was in existence as early as 1916 and directed the successful Italian Red Cross fundraising efforts during the First World War. The *Comitato* came to prominence in the late 1920s with its attempts to establish an after-school Italian class for immigrant children. One page in Francesco Tomaiuolo's weekly, *Il progresso Italo-Canadese*, was devoted to the *Comitato*'s news bulletin and was edited by Dante Colussi, and later, Luigi Galli.

The *Comitato* posed two significant problems for Ambrosi. First, as an umbrella organization, it served as the focus of the Italian community's social life. The bulletin in the *Progresso* described the events in the community clubs and invited members of all clubs to attend particular social events. Second, the *Comitato* was responsible for organizing after-school Italian language classes for Italian children in the city, or what the committee and the colony called *La Scuola Italiana* (Italian School), a *cause célèbre*. If Ambrosi wished to be the central organizing force in the colony, he either had to dominate the *Comitato* or do away with it.

Courses in Italian language for children in the colony had been organized a number of times over the years. Methodist minister Nestor Cacciapuoti, Michael Basso (1900–10), and Father Viglianti (1913–18), were among the early instructors. The Dante society had instituted a short-lived course between 1920 and 1923. The *Comitato* was reviving an old dream when in early 1930 it requested after-school classroom facilities at St Patrick's, St Francis's, and St Clement's schools – one in each Little Italy – to instruct children of the colony in the Italian language. Trustee Francesco Napolitano made the request on behalf of Tommaso Mari. Evidently Ambrosi already had infiltrated the *Comitato*.[37]

Over the next couple of years the *Comitato* drew much publicity in its attempts to raise money for *La Scuola Italiana*. Scarcely an issue of the *Progresso* was printed without mention of the drive. All mutual aid societies were enlisted in the effort and almost all held a benefit dance or banquet to raise funds. Articles and editorials praised the drive and *La Scuola Italiana* as "noble and patriotic ... our Italian spring in the colony." The teacher's advertisement advised parents to "leave your children the patrimony of your language." Ambrosi, however, was conspicuously reticent about the work of the executive of the *Comitato* and the topic of language schools (even though he had written one open congratulatory letter regarding the school and despite the fact that the movement was popular in the colony) because he planned to take over the *Comitato*.[38]

President Antonio Gatto, Vice-President Zaccaria Leone, and bulletin editor, Dante Colussi, published the most important antifascist paper in the colony, *Il Messaggero*. Though the facts are not documented, in about 1934 or 1935, members of the *fascio* underhandedly convinced Gatto to sell them *Il Messaggero*. This action simplified Ambrosi and the *fascio*'s task of infiltrating the *Comitato* because they had eliminated potential opposition.[39] An Italian teacher sought by the *Comitato* would be used for teaching the language but now also for indoctrinating the children with fascist ideology. In order to import such a teacher, Consul-General Luigi Petrucci in Ottawa in 1934 brought Arnaldo Michelet into Canada as a consular employee under the pretence that as secretaries and clerks in the country's Italian consulates had no command of the Italian language, he would instruct them. In fact, Consul-General Pettrucci had complained to his superiors in Rome about the clerks in Ottawa, Montreal, and Toronto but had not expected quick action on the part of his government. The Royal Italian Emigration's commissioner in Ottawa, Eugenio Bonardelli, had arranged for the arrival of Michelet and one other teacher destined for Ottawa. Petrucci informed the Canadian assistant deputy minister of Immigration that Michelet would also teach Italian part-time outside the consulate "as opportunity offers." Michelet was expected to teach clerks in the vice-consulate in Toronto; in fact, he had been enrolled to teach and diffuse propaganda in the Italian-language classes.[40]

By 1935 the vice-consulate felt itself enough in control of *La Scuola Italiana* to show its official support for the project. In June, the acting vice-consul forwarded a communication to the Roman Catholic Separate School Board (RCSSB) expressing thanks on behalf of the Italian people for the use of its classrooms during the previous year. *La Scuola Italiana* was now directed by the Italian School Committee whose chairman was Antonio Gatto. Gatto had been won over completely to the fascist side and, indeed, was soon to become Tommaso Mari's father-in-law. The school met with more success under the wing of the vice-consulate. By autumn 1936, Italian language classes were also conducted at St Mary's and St Paul's schools three times a week. In 1938 the board allowed increased classroom facilities at St Clement's and St Paul's. The board granted the requests despite a written protest three years earlier from the Italian Canadian Cooperative Commonwealth Federation (CCF) Club. Carlo Lamberti and Joe Giovanetti, respectively president and secretary of the club, were important anti-Fascists in the community. When Father Balò, pastor of St Agnes, informed the board that Lamberti was an official of one of the Italian Orange Lodges, it was "recommended that no further attention be paid to the communication."[41]

More serious were the claims of Toronto Alderman Stewart Smith in March 1939 before the Legislation Committee of city council. Referring to the Italian classes, Smith declared that fascism was being taught in separate schools. Chairman E.T. Duggan of the RCSSB, diocesan clergy, and Vice-Consul Guido Colonna denied the charges. The latter explained that "Italian language schools operate here solely for the purpose of fostering the mother tongue of new Canadians, and teaching Italian history and literature."[42] He denied that fascist propaganda was being fed to the students. However, Colonna admitted that an employee of the Italian consulate, Arnaldo Michelet, conducted one of the "schools." He also acknowledged that in the past some books supplied for the class carried pictures of King Victor Emanuele and Mussolini marked "this is our king," and "this is Il Duce." Such books were discontinued and pictures were removed from books still in use when people took exception to them. In fact, the 1938 permits for classroom use had been renewed "on the assurance of Italian representatives" that fascism not be taught in the course.

The Committee of Supervision at the RCSSB attempted to taint Alderman Smith's claims by indicating he was a Communist. Nevertheless, at least one member, J.G. Culnan, took the matter seriously and recommended an investigation. Antonio Gatto was asked to provide copies of all textbooks that had been used by *La Scuola Italiana*. He also signed an affidavit testifying that they were the only books used since 1938 and that no political doctrines had been or were being taught. Despite the denials, *La Scuola Italiana* was suddenly dissolved. A letter accompanying the books and affidavit explained that since "this matter was causing the board some embarrassment ... rather than cause further embarrassment it was decided to discontinue these classes in the schools.[43]

Much of the opposition to *La Scuola Italiana* and especially to Ambrosi's takeover of the *Comitato* unfortunately has not been recorded. Only scattered references to individuals criticizing the teaching of fascist ideology in the classroom could be found. However, one may easily conclude that anti-Fascists would view the takeover of the *Comitato* as yet another step by the vice-consulate to assume direction of the Italian community. Perhaps the most careless incident in Ambrosi's program occurred earlier in March 1932 involving the Italian War Veterans Association.

The Toronto chapter of the National Association of War Veterans was initiated in 1927, that is, two years before Ambrosi's arrival in Toronto. From 1927, the War Veterans Association conducted 4 November Memorial Day (actually Victory Day, *Giornata della Vittoria*) observances annually. In 1931 they suddenly became much more active. It seems that Ambrosi was tightening his grip on the association. As a fascist vice-consul he was following his duties, because Italian Ministry of External Affairs's regulations placed war veterans' associations under the jurisdiction of consular officials. In November 1931, the veterans laid a wreath on the Tomb of the Unknown Soldier at city hall in front of 400 onlookers. They also telegraphed Dino Grandi, Italian Ministry of External Affairs at the Italian Consulate in New York to wish him luck during his American tour. In July 1931, the veterans requested seven military uniforms of the Italian Ministry of External Affairs, although the Ministry of War, which handled such matters, could not comply with the request for legal reasons.[44]

In the flurry of activity a group of war veterans who had never attended any of the Toronto local's meetings were present at its assembly in early February 1932. They insisted that the word "National" be deleted from the association's title. It seems that the intruders were protesting the vice-consul's increasing intervention among the war veterans. One month later a more serious confrontation split the organization. The president, vice-president, and corresponding secretary developed hostile relations with Ambrosi and either retired from their posts or were asked to step down. The three former officials then proceeded to form a rival organization of Italian war veterans.[45]

In March of that year a dance was sponsored by the *Società Italo-Canadese*. The vice-consul was unable to attend and in his stead sent his reliable retainer, Pasquale Fontanella. The doctor carelessly forgot his official position that evening when he encountered Messrs Ferrari and Laudadio, two of the three war veteran renegades. Fontanella chided them and warned that "Italian associations abroad, which depend on Italian consular authorities ... should obey the Consul, who is their recognized head." Ferrari and Laudadio retorted that "the dissident association would never obey the deliberations of Vice-Consul G.B. Ambrosi." Not to be outdone in public, Fontanella advised the pair "to beware, for should their disposition towards the National Association of War Veterans continue, their families or relatives in Italy might undergo unpleasant consequences."[46]

The antifascist newspaper, *L'Emigrato*, published by Joseph Bagnato, president of the *Società Italo-Canadese*, expressed shock that such words should emanate from the mouth of the vice-consul's representative: "If this is truly the method used by the government and Italian authorities abroad, we cannot but blush with shame and shudder with disdain at the thought that innocents ... must pay for wrongs committed not by them but by others. The strong are generous but similar acts, if true, denote only aberration and weakness." Fontanella responded to the charges in Tomaiuolo's *Progresso Italo-Canadese*, while Ambrosi wisely kept clear of the matter. The doctor offered the lame excuse that he had argued with Romolo Laudadio and Giuseppe Ferrari in his capacity as a physician and not as vice-consular representative.[47]

It was obvious by the 1930s that the vice-consulate would not approve of any colonial association or individuals who refused to come under its influence. The Italian-Canadian Economic Committee, Sons of Italy locals, the Italian Aid and Protective Society, or the *Dopolavoro* (a recreational club instituted by *fascio* locals) all maintained pious relations with the vice-consul, and he, in turn, accepted invitations to their socials.

It is clear that although many of the community leaders gave allegiance to the vice-consul and the *fascio* in the late 1920s, others resented Ambrosi's and his successors' attempts to control the colony. For example, by the mid-1930s the city was the centre of a small but active core of Communists and Anarchists who were carefully watched by the vice-consulate. The most influential antifascist union leader was a Calabrian, Nicola Giancotti, a presser at Tip Top Tailors, and affiliated with the Communist party of Canada. The anarchist group was comprised almost exclusively of men from Codroipo (Friuli) and Pesaro (Marche). Most influential were Arturo Pittana, Ruggero Benvenuti, Ernesto Gava, and Attilio Bortolotti, all four from the Dufferin and Davenport neighbourhood. Augusto Ongaro was from New Toronto. The Toronto group had important connections with Chicago and Detroit anarchist cells. In fact, during June 1932, the elusive Italian anarchist subversive, Armando Borghi, always one step ahead of American immigration agents and Italian consular and embassy officials, sojourned at the home of Pittana and Benvenuti for a few weeks.[48] Despite sporadic demonstrations, organizing a Mazzini Society cell, a Matteotti Club, and publishing a number of bulletins and newspapers (*Il Libertario* was printed occasionally by the Anarchists; *La Voce Operaia* by Giancotti), the radical anti-Fascists did not exert a particularly strong influence on the colony.[49]

Some of the opposition to the consulate in the colony was organized within mutual aid societies in the city. However, many of the societies supported the vice-consul and invited him to their socials until at least the early 1930s. Much of the opposition and resentment stemmed from the frustrations of the members of the old élite, many of whom were officials in mutual aid societies and now faced new conditions – adherence to a new political philosophy and obedience to an official not indigenous to Toronto. These men were losing their places among the notables. By the early 1930s, Ambrosi had effectively undermined the élite structure that had evolved in the community over the previous forty years.

The bitterness of older, prominent men was aimed at the young, newly arrived officials who instantly ensconced themselves in the élite. Pasquale Fontanella, for example, had arrived only in 1927; Arnaldo Michelet in 1934; Tommaso Mari and Ambrosi in 1929. In 1931, in his fascist *Bollettino Italo-Canadese* weekly, Mari published a series of critical articles discussing the development of an Italian Day at the Canadian National Exhibition (CNE). Giuseppe Tomasicchio, a *modugnese* salesman for City Dairy who had been active in the community since the First World War, penned a strident response to the article, directing much of his venom at the fact that Mari was a greenhorn: "He who writes this article [i.e. Tomasicchio] is not the last [Italian] to arrive in Toronto nor the last of the Fascists ... and believe me Mr Mari, that in Toronto, those who have established themselves for more than twenty years, living and suffering the saga of their emigration always worked loyally for their distant fatherland." Tomasicchio advised Mari that he was not the appropriate person to write the history of the initiative to set up an Italian Day in the city.[50]

More poignant were the comments of the antifascist *L'Emigrato* by ITROC (CORTI spelled backwards; most certainly Harry Corti, former publisher of the *Tribuna Canadiana*) in March 1932. The year-old newspaper published by *Società Italo-Canadese* president, Joseph Bagnato, headlined an issue with an editorial asking whether "an Italian-Canadian citizen can be a fascist?" The editor stated:

If the Fascio under that name wishes, like any other society, to continue its program of good works and charity in the colony, then that is fine and acceptable, but without any rights superior to the older colonial associations, which in the past have shown their ability to look after their own needs and those of the needy of the fatherland. In 1916–17 and 1918 the colony, with the help of her societies united at that time under the Intersocial Committee, and the poor and humble *Tribuna* [*Canadiana*, Corti's former paper] was able to collect in three or four campaigns over 100,000 dollars for the Red Cross. There was no Fascism nor were there instructions from Rome but simply the conscience of the Colony which knew how to carry out its proper duty towards the fatherland and her brothers who offered their lives for the fortune of a greater Italy.[51]

It was certainly the most eloquent antifascist statement published in the colony. Clearly, then, the antifascist older leaders of Italian Toronto – Joseph Bagnato, Harry Corti, Dante Colussi, Zaccaria Leone, and others – were not adherents to radical politics. They were long-standing members and leaders of the Italian community who resented the interference of the Italian government's representative and of other new arrivals seeking leadership in the colony.

The downgrading of the *prominenti*'s status did not shake up the élite structure. The representation of proprietors and professionals on boards of directors of mutual aid societies in 1935 was almost identical to their representation in 1910 and 1918 (see table 18), and is shown in table 20.

Table 20
Occupations of Officers in Italian Mutual Aid Societies, Toronto, 1935

Occupations	1935	%
Proprietors	19	32.8
Professionals, Clerical, Foremen	15	25.9
Skilled Labour	14	24.2
Unskilled Labour	6	10.2
Labour, Unspecified	4	6.9
Total	58	100.0
Total no. of Offices	71	

Sources: *Might's Toronto Directory*, and "Annual Report of the Registrar of Friendly Societies," *Sessional Papers*, Toronto, 1935. The occupations of 13 officers could not be traced.

What *had* changed was the addition of a suprastructure of notables on top of the old élite structure by the vice-consul and *fascio*. Even though the steamship agents, Giuseppe Gatto, Francesco Tomaiuolo, or Carmine Petti continued to enjoy prestige until bankruptcy, the most prominent individuals in the colony were those professionals or wealthy men who pledged strong allegiance to the vice-consul.[52]

The last chapter examined the career of D.A.G. Glionna to 1920. An extension of that biography to 1935 will illustrate how a notable had to change tactics in order to remain in the Italian-Canadian immigrant élite during the fascist era. In the immediate postwar period, when he was in his midfifties, Glionna made another attempt at setting himself up as *the* spokesman for Italian Toronto to the country's government agencies. Soon after the return of the Liberal party to federal power, Glionna instituted a new grand lodge of Italian mutual benefit societies, the Italian Aid and Protective Society. The impressive list of honourary members on the society's letterhead was a testimony to Glionna's ability to establish connections in the Canadian and Italian governments. Dignitaries on the list in the early 1930s included (Conservative!) Prime Minister Richard Bennett, seven cabinet ministers, one senator, two Toronto aldermen, three members of provincial Parliament, the Canadian High Commissioner to London, and all of Toronto's Italian doctors, among others.[53]

Glionna followed his old scheme of appearing as intermediary between the colony and government, and as one attending to the best interests of the community. In the few months following the founding of the association, a resolution was sent to the under-secretary of state, Thomas Mulvey, calling for an inspection of immigrants at embarkation points in Italy rather than at Ellis Island. A draft accompanied the note adding that "the said Society would be greatly honoured if you would deem it fit for us to lend you any assistance with regards to immigrants in the neighbourhood of Toronto or elsewhere within the province of Ontario."[54]

When Prime Minister W.L. Mackenzie King visited Toronto in January 1925, Glionna, as president of the Italian Aid and Protective Society, represented the Italian community at the King Edward Hotel handshaking ceremony. The same year, he sent a letter to Ontario premier, Howard Ferguson, with a copy of his society's resolution accusing the township of East York of discrimination in hiring and granting contracts to naturalized Italian Canadians.[55]

Until the mid-1920s, Glionna depended upon the Liberal party to maintain his power in the community. Some men were not convinced of his motives and saw him as an opportunist. In December 1926 Glionna wrote to Montreal M.P., Sam W. Jacobs, the country's first Jewish member of Parliament, requesting support for his plans to bring Italian immigrants to Canada. Perhaps with a touch of cynicism, Jacobs advised Glionna to contact Superintendent W.J. Egan or the honourary officers of his society. Jacobs wrote Egan that Glionna was an opportunist; the superintendent need simply connect the society's vague and lofty objectives with the list of honourary officers, mostly federal and provincial politicians. Egan informed the member of Parliament that he knew of Glionna's schemes and would expand on the matter in the near future. The exchange occurred one and one-half years after Glionna had been appointed an official for the Royal Italian Emigration Society. That organization secured entry permits for Italian labourers to work with specific contractors and farmers in Canada.[56]

Indeed, Glionna was involved in a plan to settle Italians in northern Ontario. The source of this information was Sidney Wise, an elderly Toronto importer who in 1927 was charged with forging entry permits for Italian immigrants. He turned to forgery when his contacts with government officials could no longer provide authentic permits. One of his suppliers of authentic permits had been D.A.G. Glionna, whose contact was Sam Bilsky, Sam Jacobs's brother-in-law. Wise accused Glionna of voting "all around the parties, having been mainly a Grit but supporting [Horatio C.] Hocken [Conservative, Toronto West Centre] in the last election." He claimed that the Aid and Protective Society with its impressive letterhead was formed to advance the scheme to settle Italians in the northlands. Mr MacDowell of the Colonization Department at Queen's Park told Wise that "the Ontario Government [will not] stand for anyone, even [a] so-called Benevolent Society dumping Italians into the Northern bush to freeze to death the first winter.[57]

Glionna was under strong pressure in 1925 and 1926 to perform for the minority Liberal government. It was perhaps for that reason that he decided to don the patriotic cloak at that time. In early 1926, his Italian Aid and Protective Society organized a funeral memorial Mass for Italian Queen Mother Margherita. The Toronto archbishop and Italian consular agent were invited to the ceremony. When Marshal Diaz died in March 1928, Glionna, as president of the society, sent a telegram of condolence to the duchess. However, Glionna knew enough not to infringe on the territory of Ambrosi when the new career vice-consul commenced his duties in Toronto. When in late 1930 the Aid and Protective society blessed its coat of arms, Ambrosi's protegé, Fontanella, delivered the keynote address; Ambrosi had been invited but because of illness sent a letter instead. The presence of English and Italian journalists, municipal politicians, and all Italian professionals in the city at the ceremony testified to Glionna's unique place in the community: he derived his power in the colony from his contacts in Canadian political circles, maintained his prestige and *italianità* by allying himself with the professionals in the élite, and secured his position by deferring to the leadership of the vice-consul.[58]

Except for an annual *Scuola Italiana* children's picnic, Glionna organized no nationalistic events in the colony after 1929. Instead, the Aid and Protective society officially attended the affairs sponsored by the *fascio* or the War Veterans Association.[59] That way Glionna preserved his place among the notables and did not appear overly political in the community. In 1935 when Canadian opinion turned more hostile towards Italy because of the Ethiopian crisis, Glionna withdrew from the colonial scene untainted, not accused of favouring fascism. By the 1930s Glionna probably was no longer interested in enhancing his prestige in the Italian community. His duty was to win votes for the Liberal party and that required a sympathetic profile on his part.

However, as we have seen, other older notables lost status during the period of fascist infiltration in the colony. These individuals brought about their own downfall. From the turn of the century, through the First World War, and into the postwar period, the prominent individuals of Italian Toronto played on the national and patriotic sentiments of the immigrants from the peninsula and strongly influenced the creation of a unified Italian community. The notables were responsible for most of the mutual benefit societies, and the offices of those organizations gave their leadership a stamp of legitimacy. That way the élite contributed to developing the ethnic boundaries of the city's Italian community. When the fascist vice-consul, Ambrosi, arrived in 1929, he had only to continue the old élite's patriotic program. If his cronies were unable to control any of the old voluntary organizations, they had only to create new ones. Thus by 1935 the community no longer orbited around the old élite but rather around the vice-consul, the *fascio*, and their adherents. The old élite members had prepared the groundwork for Ambrosi and the *fascio*.

The final years of the *fascio*'s and the vice-consulate's tenure in Toronto continued the program of centralizing the Italian community, including the worn tactics of creating public events with Italian emblems to draw the attention of the entire community. In July 1934, for example, nineteen Toronto-Italian girls, along with six girls from other Ontario cities, were chosen to represent Ontario fascist clubs in a meeting of world-wide fascist youth in Italy. Dressed in black fascist garb, they assembled in front of Mari and Perilli's Italian Publishing Company on Elm Street for final official farewells before proceeding to Union Station.[60]

That same year, Giorgio Tiberi, Ambrosi's successor, announced plans to build an Italian cultural centre. The fundraising was difficult in depression times, but the community did eventually purchase Chudleigh House at Beverly and Dundas streets. *Casa d'Italia* (House of Italy) housed the vice-consulate, the *fascio*, the *Dopolavoro*, and the Colonial Office (the latter replaced the *Comitato*). Tommaso Mari declared that "there was no political significance in the formation of an Italian cultural centre," and he also hastened to add that the *fascio* was not connected to British or Canadian Fascists.[61]

On 10 June 1940 the *fascio*'s and the vice-consulate's control of

Italian Toronto came to an end. When Mussolini declared war on Britain, the Royal Canadian Mounted Police (RCMP) seized the *fascio*'s guestbook and arrested over 200 Torontonians and shipped them to Camp Petawawa with 500 other Italian Canadians. Some arrests were justified. However, most internees were not involved actively in fascist propaganda or fifth-column activities. The *Casa d'Italia* was sequestered by the RCMP and not returned to the Italian community until 1956. Along with the *fascio* and the consulate, the entire élite structure of the Italian community collapsed. No one wished to lead a community whose members were being arrested, fired from their jobs, or whose businesses were being vandalized. Even the staunch anti-Fascist, Dante Colussi, burned all back issues of his antifascist newspaper, *Il Messaggero*, in his landlord's fireplace on the night of 10 June. A new Italian immigrant leadership did not emerge in Toronto until the 1950s when young hopefuls who had come of age, and new immigrants from Italy began the process of rebuilding institutions and re-activating the community. One of the early projects of the new leadership was an attempt to restore the *Casa d'Italia* to the Italians of the city but the building reverted to the Italian Ministry of External Affairs in 1956. Today it houses the Italian Consulate.

Although some Italians began turning their backs on fascism with the Ethiopian crisis, most of the immigrants renounced Mussolini's government when Italy declared war on England in June 1940. Virtually no Italians in the city had been disloyal to Canada, but they repledged their allegiance to reassure other Canadians. Very few of them had understood fascist ideology but they had supported the Italian government, whose representative in Toronto, Ambrosi, had been able to capture the sympathies of various voluntary associations, hometown groups, and families. In May 1940, the president of the Italian Independent Fruit Merchants Association, comprising *termitani* almost exclusively, sent a telegram to Mackenzie King pledging loyalty to Canada and king. The association promised that it would fight against Mussolini and his armies just the same as any other Canadian." Ultimately, the immigrants' true loyalties remained with their *paesani* and families and to their land of adoption.[62]

Conclusion

When the peasants, tinkers, and tradesmen of Termini, Vita, Gravere, Fanna, Terracina, and a host of other towns took ship's passage, they went to "make America" (*a fare l'America*), that is, to make their fortune abroad. Yet, going there they discovered a sense of belonging to an Italian nation. If one were to take the simple view that one's nationality is "in one's blood," then this phenomenon would not be problematic. But certainly there is something fascinating in the fact that these immigrants should have continued to identify themselves as Italians, that, in fact, they became even more conscious of their *italianità* while in Toronto. They no longer resided within the Italian state; they were not really part of the Italian nation except as in that loose definition of the Italian foreign ministry, "Italian workers living abroad." Why then did they come to feel more Italian?

It is difficult to understand ethnic sentiments. Ethnicity is an elusive concept encompassing so many varied aspects of a community, a people, subcommunities, individuals – beyond their work, commerce, settlement, psychology, religion, origins – that any attempt to explain it will appear trite.

To begin, it is clear that the immigrants from the various hometown groups in Toronto before the Second World War had a sense of belonging to a nation. Yet they were also people of their hometowns. They identified with their *paesani*. The immigrant travelled to Toronto with his townspeople as part of the migration chain of his townspeople to the new world. In Toronto, as noted, he worked with his fellow townsmen, launched small enterprises with them, lived with them, celebrated with them, married one of them. The immigrant therefore lived his life on two planes, as a man of his town, and as an Italian in Toronto. In other words, although he lived in a Canadian city, might feel part of the labour force, though he might even identify himself as a Torontonian, he was also *other* by virtue of his accent, by virtue of belonging to a minority.

It would seem logical, almost obvious to accept Caroline Ware's argument, as presented in the introduction, that immigrants developed their ethnicity as a defence mechanism against rejection by, or discrimination on the part of the host society; a litany of instances of discrimination against the Italian population or, for that matter, against any ethnic group in Toronto, are easily attainable. Yet Ware's argument seems simplistic.

The Italian ethnicity of the immigrants did not begin in Canada but in the hometown. Certain conditions in Toronto, however, heightened the ethnic consciousness of the immigrant. This study suggests that it was not the discrimination against Italian immigrants but rather their isolation which increased their sense of being Italian. The travelling Italian immigration inspectors and other officials from Italy who wrote about the Italian "colony" in Toronto might have used that word indiscriminately, but the term "colony" was apposite. The writings by Amy Bernardy and Adolfo Rossi on Italian immigrants in the Americas portrayed, not without affection, a marginal people, too foreign to be American or Canadian, yet too parochial to be Italian.

Very often we read that the immigrant belonged neither in the old world nor in the new. This argument, too, is appealing and it seems to make sense. Yet how did the immigrant realize that something was lacking, that he did not belong to one nation or the other? Or did he? Or did it matter to him? Did the immigrant not already have a sense of belonging? Was he not already part of a community?

This study has accompanied the immigrant along his continuum from old world village peasant or craftsman to new world urban labourer or entrepreneur, attempting to examine how each step of the process impinged on his sense of community and nationality. Chapter 1 observed that at his departure from the hometown, and upon his arrival in the new world, the immigrant was who he was, a man of his hometown or his hometown group in Toronto. His fellow townsmen, however, could not provide all his necessities.

The immigrant had come to Toronto to meet particular goals and the short-run method of achieving these was to build a nest-egg.

Thus everything became directed towards this immediate end. A job and a residence were of course the most elementary prerequisites for accumulating savings. The priest would continue to provide the spiritual care to which the migrant and his family had had access in the hometown. Ethnic brokers and politicians could establish useful contacts with even more influential officials of the Italian and Canadian federal, provincial, or municipal governments. The *padrone* was indispensable to the migrant's search for work in the outdoor construction industry, and to his search for room and board, banking, insurance, or letter-writing.

The intermediaries were willing to help the immigrants but they also realized that they could profit from the services they offered, especially if they had a sizeable clientele composed of "Italian" ethnics. This is not to suggest that they acted with cunning or malice – although some did – but rather that they were astute. The *padrone*, for example, as a middleman, found it convenient to categorize the sojourners as Italians rather than as people of their towns. The effect, as suggested in chapter 6, was to consolidate the community, to make the members of the various hometown groups become more aware of belonging to an "Italian" ethnic group in the city. This was especially apparent with the notables who represented political parties. The Liberal and Conservative parties, for example, preferred to isolate the Italian community because politically it was easier to manage that way. The Italians, as a single group, could be handled by a few ethnic brokers such as Donato Glionna for the Liberals and Harry Corti and Joseph Bagnato for the Conservatives.

Chapter 3 noted that the isolation of the Italian immigrants was also manifested in their occupational profile in Toronto. Although they performed a wide variety of occupations, Italians in general were relegated to a few general occupational sectors. Throughout the period of this study, the immigrants from the peninsula were involved in numerous service trades, from providing street music to bootblacking, from catering to barbering. The Ministry of the Interior, in the 1900s, had sought rural rather than urban immigrants, and had singled out Italians as one of the unwanted nationalities. Italian immigrants in Toronto sought a variety of opportunities, but, through a combination of skills, stereotyping, and the needs of the economy, were destined to work in three major sections: service, construction, and the garment industry.

Chapter 2 examined the settlements of the various Italian hometown groups and concluded that although people from the same town tended to live near each other, they also lived near other Italians. The effect of living among other Italians also helped the immigrants to develop a sense of belonging to a larger Italian ethnic group in the city. Italians were dispersed throughout the city, but they tended to concentrate in three main neighbourhoods. The neighbourhoods grew out of historical factors. The three Little Italies were also economical and conveniently located near places of employment and streetcar routes. Thus for a number of reasons, the Italians became isolated even in their settlements, more specifically in the Ward, at College and Grace streets, and at Dufferin Street and Davenport Road.

The migrants were in Canada but they were still Italian subjects, at least before acquiring citizenship papers. And even if they became British subjects (Canadian citizenship was introduced after the Second World War), they would still require the services of the Italian consular agent and, later, the vice-consul, from time to time. This official, like most of the Italian government officials and visitors encountered in chapter one, viewed the Italians as a people apart from Canadian society, yet not as Italians, but as members of the Italian "colony" in Toronto. Chapter 7 indicated that this was even more apparent in the 1930s as the vice-consul tried to strengthen the bonds of the colony by bringing it within the program of the *Fascio all'Estero*.

The church hierarchy and priests also isolated the Italians. Chapter 5 argued that the bishops, although concerned for their flock, were also interested in good management and efficiency. They recognized the problems associated with an ethnic group in the diocese and sought to address these problems. Their remedy, however, was simplistic; the bishops felt they could resolve the issue with expert priests or religious orders. They usually realized when it was too late that many of the clerics they received had been misfits in their original dioceses or orders and had come to Canada less out of a sense of mission than out of a desire to begin their lives anew. The letters of these priests reveal a lack of affection both for their parishioners and their vocation. An unfortunate result of this "efficient" approach was the relegation of the Italians as well as of other immigrants to a peripheral place in the archdiocese. The church was Irish in character and its ethnics were "taken care of" by special delegates.

The immigrants, as noted, sensed that they were a people apart, that they were "other," and as they were recognized and addressed as Italians by Torontonians and intermediaries, their Italian ethnic consciousness, which had been with them from childhood, grew. Their sense of Italy, of nation, as one writer stressed in 1916, "did not rise to a high idealism of country," but rather could be reduced "to the indelible recollections of youth, or family, of home, the confused deeds of our history, or our illustrious men."[1] Their sense of nation was always filtered through the familial and local experience. Thus, in Toronto, Vice-Consul Ambrosi had wisely made a point of visiting all the local and regional-based mutual aid societies in his efforts to bring the community within the fascist program. He referred time and again to the interdependence of God, Family and Nation, less out of religious conviction than a desire for good management.

Toronto's Italians were ultimately more loyal to their hometown groups than to an Italian nation, were more aware of belonging to a community of *paesani* than to an Italian ethnic group. Indeed, the clubs which survived the Second World War, such as the *Vitese*, the Trinacria, the Fratellanza, or the *Famee Furlane* were all local or regional in nature. With the collapse of the *fascio* and the wartime internment of Italians, the immigrants turned their backs on the "Italian" organizations that had been controlled by the vice-consul. They continued, however, to associate with those who had always been their kin, their coregionalists, or fellow townsmen.

All along, of course, some members of the Italian community opposed the Fascists. The old world Liberals and Monarchists who had become intermediaries of the colony to Canada's Conservative and Liberal parties had already faced opposition from the Socialists from before the Great War. After the war, both groups, though not together, opposed the Fascists. It was not a simple question of fighting old world feuds in the new world, but rather a struggle for direction of the polity in the city with the additional element of the old élite's resentment towards the newly arrived Fascists for having upset the old order.

Except for very few individuals, Italian immigrants in Toronto did not embrace fascism even though they supported the vice-consul and his colleagues. Political ideology was never an issue for the vast majority of the immigrants. Patriotism was. During the Great Depression, immigrants, like native Canadians, looked to charismatic leaders. If it appeared that the *fascio*'s leaders honoured and represented Italy best in the adopted land, then they should be followed as the legitimate leaders of the colony.

The "chiaroscuro," or the contrast between the immigrants' two loyalties, can be distinguished, but there are always certain fleeting images in the picture which cannot be captured. Given the limits of the sources and our sensibility, it is difficult to state with unwavering confidence exactly what the immigrant perceived as his ethnic identity. This study does suggest that his notions of *italianità* were superficial, that he remained, above all, a man of his hometown's community in Toronto.

This is not to say that the immigrants studied in this book were divorced from Canadian society. At the same time that they developed an old world national consciousness, they were also introduced into mainstream Canadian society and politics. The ethnic intermediaries were crucial, for as they struck a public discourse within an Italian *qua* Italian colony, they also drew the community into the larger Canadian polity. Perhaps the federal government had learned an important historical lesson when it adopted the program of multiculturalism in the late 1960s.

The immigrants after the Second World War remained loyal to their hometowns. However, their children, and those of the immigrants studied in this book, became more integrated into the Canadian nation – they remained Italians in the national sense (even though they often spoke only the hometown dialect), while the hometown receded into the background as part of their parents' memories and world.

The Italian community which exists today is a product of all the forces mentioned in this book. Waves of immigrants benefitted from and settled into a world created by their forbears – a world resembling the old, yet part of the new – thus encouraging more immigration and leading to the populous and clearly defined community of Italian-Canadians in contemporary Toronto.

Notes

ABBREVIATIONS

Archives

ABPR	Archives of the Baltimore Province of the Redemptorists, Brooklyn, N.Y.
AFPIC	Archives of the Franciscan Province of the Immaculate Conception, New York
ARCAT	Archives of the Roman Catholic Archdiocese of Toronto
AS	Archivio dello Stato, Rome
CTA	City of Toronto Archives
MAE	Archivio Storico del Ministero degli Affari Esteri, Rome
MHSO	Multicultural History Society of Ontario, Toronto
MSSBA	Metropolitan Separate School Board Archives
PAC	Public Archives of Canada, Ottawa
SDA	*Società Nazionale Dante Alighieri*, Rome
UCA	United Church Archives, Toronto

Journals and Newspapers

Boll. Cons.	*Bollettino consolare*
Boll. Emig.	*Bollettino dell'emigrazione*
PIA	*Progresso Italo-Americano*
PIC	*Progresso Italo-Canadese*
RC	*Rivista coloniale*
RE	*Rivista di emigrazione*
RISS	*Rivista internazionale di scienze sociali e discipline ausiliari*

INTRODUCTION

1 The Canadian census for 1981 lists 297,205 residents of Italian origin in the metropolitan area of Toronto. Unofficial estimates are usually around 400,000 and up to 500,000. The same census recorded 166,510 Italian-born residents in Toronto. See *Census of Canada* 2.3, Provincial Series II, tables 7 and 8.
2 Harney, "Entwined Fortunes." Ramirez, "Ethnic Studies," 45-48.
3 Thistlethwaite, "Migration from Europe," 77.
4 For a good review of the state of immigration history see R. Perin, "Clio as an Ethnic: The Third Force in Canadian historiography," *Canadian Historial Review* 64, no. 4 (1983): 441-67.
5 A. Rossi, "Per la tutela" 20-1. All Italian quotations have been translated into English by the author unless otherwise indicated.
6 Bernardy, *America vissuta*, 331.
7 Park and Miller, *Old World Traits*, 145-9, 152.
8 Ware, *Greenwich Village*, 158, 169, 63. See also her "Cultural Groups," 165.
9 For example, see Schafer, *Faces of Nationalism*, 221; Hayes, *Nationalism*, 9; Dobb, *Patriotism and Nationalism*, 48-9; A.D. Smith, *Nationalism in the Twentieth Century*, 112; and Deutsch, *Nationalism and Social Communication*, 104.
10 See Freye, "Socialization to National Identification" and Harney, "Chiaroscuro."

CHAPTER ONE

1 Ciuffoletti and Degl'Innocenti, *L'emigrazione d'Italia*; Briani, *Il lavoro italiano all'estero*; Foerster, *Italian Emigration*; Rosoli, ed., *Secolo di emigrazione*.
2 Levi, *Cristo si è fermato*.
3 Azimonte, *Colonizzazione in Basilicata*, 91. A. Rossi, "Vantaggi e danni," 13, 15. Memo from N. Borrelli, township secretary of Laurenzana to Zanardelli, 3 Sept. 1902, in *Presidenza Zanardelli, 1902–3*, Basilicata: b. 1-3 (Potenza): Min. dell'Interno, A.S. Also in the same collection, see Finance Minister Mazziotto to Zanardelli, 8 Oct. 1908.
4 Manzotti, *Polemica sull'emigrazione*, chap. 8 and Bosworth, *Least of Great Powers*.
5 A. Rossi, "Vantaggi e danni," 15. Also, Min. di agricoltura, Industria e Commercio, *Statistica della emigrazione 1887*, 135.

6 Quoted in Manzotti, *La polemica sull'emigrazione*, 22. By 1887 Italian emigration had surpassed 200,000 people. Between 1895 and 1900 annual emigration hovered at the 300,000 level and then jumped dramatically. Statistics are from Favero and Tassello, "Cent'anni dei emigrazione." Also see appendices in same volume.
7 Dore, *La democrazia italiana*, 25.
8 Prato, "L'emigrazione della fame," 43. See responses to questionnaires sent to the prefects of each province in *Statistica della emigrazione* during the 1880s. Prefects and mayors were asked whether immigration from the various towns was natural or whether it was induced by transportation companies. Prefects usually saw the influence of agents as one of the many factors and not the predominant one. See esp. the 1880 and 1882 editions.
9 Quoted in Bosworth, *Least of Great Powers*, 89.
10 Ibid, 50.
11 "Un Piemontese," "Risorgimento italiano," 725; Preziosi, "Il problema politico-intelletuale," 6. For similar tracts, see "XXX," "L'italianità all'estero"; Cianfarra, "La conservazione dell'italianità"; Caretta, "Italiani all'estero," 34-6; Pertusio, "L'amor patria."
12 Manzotti, *Polemica sull'emigrazione*, 103-5.
13 *Boll. Emig.* was the bulletin of the *Commissariato Generale dell'Emigrazione*, the national agency responsible for overseeing Italian emigration and its related problems. Other scholarly journals included *Rassegna Nazionale* and *RISS*.
14 Bosworth, *Least of Great Powers*, 57ff. and 49. The representative was E.J. Sacco; Pisani, *Il Canadà presente*, 42. Papers of the Toronto local SDA.
15 "James A. Smart, Montreal, restricting undesirable Italian immigration," W.D. Scott to G.L. Stewart (Toronto Dominion Immigration Agent), 14 March 1908, Immigration Branch Records, RG76, vol. 491, file 76 1900, PAC. The best general history of the period is Brown and Cook, *Canada, 1896–1921*. On immigration policy during that period of liberal government, see Timlin, "Canada's Immigration Policy."
16 See Chapman, "Commerce et navigation." His private reports to superiors can be found in Serie seconda, Divisione "delle legazioni" e divisione "consolare" 1861–1869, MAE. Gianelli, "Sulle presenti condizioni." Also see Gianelli's report on Newfoundland, "L'Isola di Terranuova," *Boll. Cons.* 14, no. 8 (Aug. 1878): 145-55. Mention should be made of Cavalieri's "Il dominio del Canadà." These are notes of a trip through the Maritimes, Central Canada, and Manitoba in 1876.

17 Min. di Agricoltura, Industria e Commercio, *Statistica della emigrazione* 1884–5, 286-7. E. Rossi, *Patronato degli emigranti*.
18 De Luca, *Della emigrazione europea*, 186-8. The unfortunate enterprise is alluded to in a review by "m.b." of Pisani's *Il Canadà presente*, 44-5.
19 Pisani, "L'emigrazione italiana," 327. Also *Il Canadà presente* and "L'agricoltura nel Canadà Centrale."
20 Under "Notiziario," "Di alcune notizie," 155.
21 Review of Pisani in *RE*, see n. 25. See also, "Il presente e l'avvenire del Canadà," *Domenica del Corriere* 40, no. 48 (28 Nov.–5 Dec. 1909): 7, and "Italia e Canadà," *RC* anno 5, vol. 1, fasc. 4 (10 May 1910): 110.
22 De Stefani, *Canadà e l'emigrazione*, 12. See for example, "Di alcune notizie" and "Italia e Canadà"; "Avvertenze per gli emigrati," 4; "L'emigrazione italiana"; "Canada," 13; "L'educazione tecnico-professionale,"; "Emigrazione nel Canadà." The latter five articles, aimed at nonagricultural urban labourers, give advice to emigrants going to Canada.
23 See chap. 2, "L'emigrazione per il Canadà," in *L'emigrazione italiana*.
24 Bonardelli, "Dominio del Canadà," 311. *Revised Statutes of Canada*, Immigration Act, 9 & 10 Edw. 7, c. 27, sec. 38, par. c, 1910. Section 43A begins: "No immigrant shall bring into Canada any pistol, sheath knife, dagger, stiletto, weapon or other offensive weapon that can be concealed upon the person."
25 Bonardelli, "Dominio del Canadà," 296, 319-20, 323. On Canadian environmentalists, see Berger, *Sense of Power*, 128-33. On Italian consular service in North America see "O.B.C.," "La circoscrizione consolare," 48-50. At that time, Toronto and Vancouver were consular agencies; the author of this article called for upgrading them to vice-consulates.
26 Bonardelli, "Dominio del Canadà," 317.
27 Villari, "L'emigrazione e le sue conseguenze in Italia," *Nuova Antologia* 40 (1 Jan. 1907): 53, quoted in Foerster, *Italian Emigration*, 27. See also Emile de Laveleye, *Lettres d'Italie: 1878–1879* (Paris: n.p. 1880), 350. He writes of the Lombard peasants' reply to the government minister who was asking them not to emigrate: "What do you mean by a nation ... is it the crowd of the unhappy? Ah, then indeed we are a nation ... We seed and harvest grain but never eat white bread. We cultivate the vines but drink no wine. We raise cattle but eat no meat. We are dressed in rags ... and despite this you counsel us, min-

ister, not to abandon the fatherland. But is the country in which one cannot live by the sweat of one's brow a fatherland?" Quoted in Sereni, *Il capitalismo*, 402.

28 Denis Mack Smith's *Italy*, 133-262, 43-50; Clough, *Economic History*, 57-210; and Sereni, *Il capitalismo*.

29 "Giunta parlamentare" (henceforth giunt. parl.), Archivi Parlamentari, AS, b. 5, fasc. 4. *Atti della giunta* (henceforth Jacini Comm.): 322, AS.

30 Giunt. parl., b. 3, fasc. 1, s.f. 365, Casacalenda, 1908.

31 Giunt. parl, b. 5, fasc. 4, s.f. 20, Termini: 355; b. 3, fasc. 1, s.f. 397, Isernia, 1908. In 1895 in Vita the tax on some animals was doubled and even tripled. Petition to Codronchi from townspeople, 25 May 1896; Vincenzo Catalfo et al. to Codronchi, 25 Sept. 1896. Commissariato civile per la Sicilia, serie 3, b. 357, fasc. 129, 1896, AS.

32 di Marco, "L'emigrazione siciliana," 61-9. See also, giunt. parl., b. 5, fasc. 4, s.f. 20, Termini Imerese: reports on Aliminusa and Alia.

33 di Marco, "L'emigrazione siciliana," 65. Giunt. parl., b. 4, fasc. 4, s.f. 2, Trapani: 14; b. 3, fasc. 1, s.f. 381, Boiano (sanitation official, 3 June 1908); and b. 3, fasc. 1, s.f. 358, Vasto (Chieti); b. 4, fasc. 4, s.f. 2, Trapani; Castelvetrano: 17 and in the same fasc., s.f. 5, Salemi and Partanna: 24, 28. "L'emigrazione temporanea," *Boll. Emig.* 3 (1904): 3-94.

34 Giunt. par., b. 3, fasc. 4, s.f. 15, Siracusa, 14 Jan. 1908.

35 Min. di Agricoltura, Industria e Commercio, *Statistica della emigrazione 1884–85*, 157-8, 170. *Statistica della emigrazione 1887*, 148-72.

36 Giunt. parl., b. 5, fasc. 4, s.f. 21, Alcamo: Gibellina: 1, 3; s.f. 22, Cefalù: Pollina: 21-2; Termini: Caccamo: 20.

37 Giunt. parl., b. 5, fasc. 4, s.f. 20, Termini; b. 3, fasc. 1, s.f. 358, Vasto (Chieti), 1908; b. 5, fasc. 4, s.f. 21, Alcamo: Camporeale, 1908.

38 Positano, "L'emigrazione femminile," 66.

39 Regarding Susa, see Jacini Comm., 1883, vol. VIII, tome II: 67. Interview with Mr Attilio Bonavero, 8 Feb. 1982. Regarding Termini and Vita, see Jacini Comm., 1885, fasc. V, *Statistiche agrarie*, table 12. For immigrants from Cosenza (including San Vincenzo la Costa) in Chicago and Toronto, see Sturino, "Inside the Chain."

40 Cinel, "Seasonal Emigration," 43-68, esp. 61.

41 Giunt. parl., b. 5, fasc. 4, s.f. 20, Termini: Alia: 5; in same s.f. Montemaggiore Belsito, b. 3, fasc. 1, s.f. 365, Casacalenda, 1908; and b. 3, fasc. 1, s.f. 381, Boiano, 1908; Positano, "L'emigrazione femminile," 67-9; Prato, "L'emigrazione della fame," 30-1, 32.

42 On the knife-grinders from Val Rendena, see Bolognani, *A Courageous People*. On emigration from Trentino, see Pedrotti, *L'emigrazione del Trentino* and Briani, *Dalle valli trentine*. On the *laurenzanesi* and *viggianesi* as street musicians, see Bremner, "Children with the Organ Man"; Vecoli, "Chicago's Italians," 53ff. and 101ff. Also see Schiro, *Americans by Choice*, 127. As well, in the 1880s, *laurenzanesi* fruit vendors, hotel-keepers, and labourers were to be found in Buenos Aires and Rosario di S.F. See Min. di Agricoltura, Industria e Commercio, *Statistica dell'emigrazione 1887*, 135. On the diaspora of the *termitani*, see Briggs, *Italian Passage*, 70-2. On the immigrants from Termini Imerese in Chicago see Vecoli, "Chicago's Italians," 107ff.

43 Min. di Agricoltura, Industria e Commercio, *Statistica dell'emigrazione 1887*, 104-42, 49. Albonico, *Saggio di una inchiesta*, 3.

44 Regarding Boiano, see Min. di Agricoltura, Industria e Commercio, *Statistica dell'emigrazione 1887*, 112 and interview with Michael Chivitti, 2 Oct. 1981. For *boianesi* in Duluth, Minn., see Jacqueline Rochio Moran, "Little Italy: A Casualty of Time in Duluth," in *Italian Immigrants in Rural and Small Town America*, edited by R.J. Vecoli (New York: American Italian Historical Association 1987), 126-34. For Fossacesia see *Statistica dell'emigrazione 1887*, 115. For Pisticci, *Statistica dell'emigrazione 1887*, 133; Prato, "L'emigrazione della fame," 44; Spani, *Pisticci di ieri*, 355. The best studies on temporary emigration from Friuli remain Cosattini's "L'emigrazione temporanea" and Zanini's *Friuli migrante*. The only major studies of *friulani* in North America are Ridolfi's *I friulani* and *Quadri e cuori*. Albonico, *Saggio di una inchiesta*, 148. On *modugnesi* in Chicago see Vecoli, "Chicago's Italians," 166. Regarding Zompicchia, interview with Mr Luigi Piccoli, 23 May 1980.

45 Giunt. parl., b. 4, fasc. 4, s.f. 2, Trapani: 3. Between 1862 and 1881 Vita's population increased dramatically from 3,913 to 5,255. Figures are taken from Possenti, *Relazione al Sig. Min. Del Lavoro*, 161; and Jacini Comm., fasc. 5, *Statistiche agrarie* table 12. In all the hometowns, emigrants who intended to return home sent transcripts of their children's births to the town registrar. That way, when they came back their children would be considered citizens of the town. Until 1915 almost all the transcripts sent back to Vita came from Tunisia, although some were also sent from New York. See *trascrizioni* in *Registro delle nascite*, Archivio Comunale di Vita. Regarding Marsala, see giunt. parl., b. 4, s.f. 3, Marsala: 4.

CHAPTER TWO

1 Lynch, *Image of the City*, chap. 3, esp. 72-7.
2 Harney, *Italians in Canada*. Philip De Grassi's papers are in the University of Toronto Archives. On James Forneri see King, *McCaul; Croft; Forneri*. Also, Molinaro, "Giacomo Forneri."
3 *Directory of the Town of York*, 1832 and 1833, CTA. There is one existing invoice in ARCAT from Rossi to Bishop Michael Power, 1847. By that time Rossi had moved to Queen Street.
4 King, "Foreigners in Toronto," 10.
5 Kealey, "Workers Respond," 3-34. Goheen, *Victorian Toronto*.
6 Mulvaney, *Toronto*, 44. Bureau of Municipal Research, *What is the "Ward" to Do?*, 32.
7 King, "Foreigners in Toronto," 10.
8 Bridle, "Drama of the Ward," 6. Weaver, "Italians in Toronto," 2. At the time Weaver's article was published (1910), Toronto and Montreal had been swept by a wave of Italian Black Hand murders involving revolvers and stilettos.
9 *Toronto News*, 29 Nov. 1906, 8.
10 On the Irish, see, for example, "Poverty Stricken Immigrants," *The Globe*, 17 Nov. 1883, 8. Turano's fellow townsman, Luigi Spizziri, was the banker-*padrone* responsible for bringing many Calabrian immigrants to Chicago during the 1880s. Vecoli's "Chicago's Italians," 90.
11 "A Day in the Works of the Canada Foundry Company," *Globe and Mail*, 2 March 1907, 10. Roberts, "Toronto's Metal Workers." Information on the Terracina moulders was obtained by cross-referencing city directories with marriage registers (which give the hometowns) from Our Lady of Mount Carmel Italian National Parish.
12 E. Rossi, "Delle condizioni italiana," 9; "Notiziario": "Informazioni sulle condizioni," 74; *Census of Canada*, 1911. For an excellent study of the immigrant boardinghouse see Harney, "Boarding and Belonging." "Forced to Live with Crime and City Lands are Vacant," *The Globe*, 21 Dec. 1906, 10.
13 King, "Foreigners in Toronto." E. Weaver, "Italians in Toronto," 2.
14 James Mavor Papers, Coll. 119, Box 70, Arc 19, Thomas Fisher Rare Book Room, University of Toronto Library.
15 Ibid.
16 "Messina Earthquake," *Evening Telegram*, 30 Dec. 1908, 1.
17 Harney, "King of Labour," 69.
18 *Might's Toronto Directory* is indispensable for recreating the neigh-

bourhoods and tracing the labour agents and grocers.

19 J.S. and L.D. Macdonald, "Chain Migration"; Thistlethwaite, "Migration from Europe."

20 *Catholic Register*, 27 Aug. 1908, 1; Sturino, "Inside the Chain," 440; Ridolfi, *I friulani*, 119.

21 Information on settlement patterns was obtained by cross-referencing data in marriage registers with addresses in city directories and oral testimony.

22 On the *laurenzanesi* in Toronto before 1905 see Zucchi, "*Paesani*," chap. 1. On Glionna, see Florenzano, *Emigrazione italiana*, 167n.

23 In addition to city directories and church registers, some oral interviews with immigrants or their children were helpful in analyzing the settlement of townsgroups: for the *laurenzanesi*, Mr Michael Glionna (15 Nov. 1978); the *modugnesi*, Mr Jim Farano (18 Dec. 1978); the *boianesi*, Mr Michael Chiovitti (2 Oct. 1981); the *friulani*, Mrs Albina De Clare (9 March 1980) and Mr Luigi Piccoli (23 May 1980); for the *vitesi* and *pachinesi*, Mrs Rose Catalano (31 Jan. 1982). Similarly, the immigrants from Sora and the towns surrounding Susa had their own centres; those from Sora lived along Claremont Street and Manning Avenue, while those from Gravere and Meana di Susa lived mostly on Beatrice and Grace streets. For the latter group, interviews with Mr and Mts Attilio Bonavero (8 Feb. 1982) and Mr Fred Peirolo (18 Dec. 1981) were very helpful.

24 De Marco, *Ethnics and Enclaves*, 35-44 and Briggs, *Italian Passage*, 73-94. For Slovaks, see Alexander, "Immigrant Church and Community," 158-208.

25 See *trascrizioni* in *Registro delle nascite*, Archivio Comunale di Pisticci.

26 Information on all the mutual aid societies can be found in the "Annual Reports of the Registrar of Friendly Societies," in the "Annual Report of the Inspector of Insurance," *Sessional Papers*, Toronto, 1896–1940. The incorporation papers and charters of the Vittorio Emanuele III, Italian National Club, and later, for the Vitese Mutual Benefit Society can be found in the Business and Partnership Registry, Department of Consumer and Commercial Relations, Toronto. On the grand Lodge of Sicilian Mutual Benefit Societies, see Giovanni Oranova to Bonomelli, SDA President, 7 July 1913, SDA.

27 Toronto's first Italian newspaper, *Lo Stendardo*, was published by Joseph Saporita between 1898 and 1900. Saporita was also president of the Italian Workingmen's Circle Mutual Benefit Society in 1902

and financial secretary from 1903 to 1905. See McLaren, ed, *Ontario Newspapers*, 107-10; also "Annual Reports of the Registrar of Friendly Societies," *Sessional Papers*, Toronto, 1900–1905. Interview with Mrs Iglesias, daughter of Harry Corti, 9 May 1978, MHSO.

28 Father A Scafuro, pastor of St Clement's Church in the Dufferin/Davenport neighbourhood noted in 1924 that "years ago it was not safe to pass by Beaver Avenue and Dufferin Street." Scafuro to Archbishop McNeil, October 1924, "National Parishes," McNeil Papers, ARCAT.

29 Harney, "Chiaroscuro."

CHAPTER THREE

1 Thistlethwaite, "Migration from Europe"; Foerster, *Italian Emigration*. Thistlethwaite has written an interesting article on the migration of one skill. See "Atlantic Migration." Vecoli, "*Contadini*" and Gutman, "Work, Culture, and Society." Douglass has provided fascinating insights into the migration of Basque sheepherders in North America. See *Echalar and Murelaga*, 114-15, 121-6 and Douglass and Bilbao, *Amerikanuak*. On the relationship between kin and enterprise see Watson, *Emigration and the Chinese*.

2 Pisani, *Il Canadà presente*, 39-40. There is one inaccuracy in Pisani's report regarding the Sicilian fruit trade. Toronto's fruiterers were from the Sicilian towns of Termini Imerese, Vita, and Pachino, and not from Valledolmo. Immigrants from the latter town settled in large numbers in Buffalo and Fredonia which Pisani also visited in 1908, and he may have confused the two towns with Toronto.

3 Ibid.

4 Moroni, "Provincia dell'Ontario," 75.

5 "Canadà gli italiani," 63.

6 "Notiziaro": "Informazioni sulle condizioni," 74; Moroni, "La provincia dell'Ontario," 75.

7 Bell, "Toronto's Melting-Pot," 234.

8 Quoted in Gibbon, "Foreign Born," 332. W.G. Smith, *Canadian Immigration*, 195; Gibbon, *Canadian Mosaic*, 386.

9 Woodsworth, *Strangers*, 132. Bell, "Toronto's Melting-Pot," 242. Gibbon, *Canadian Mosaic*, 386.

10 D. Gualtieri, "Methodist Mission," 355. See also W.G. Smith, *Canadian Immigration*, 196. Gualtieri's statement is almost identical to Smith's and was probably copied from him. J.M. Gibbon suggested

that "if a fruit store looks particularly attractive, the probability is that it is run by an Italian," *Canadian Mosaic*, 391. See also James Robertson Memorial Committee, *Non-English Speaking Canadians*, 26.

11 W.G. Smith, *Building the Nation*, 68–9.

12 Sherwood, "Italian Fruit Vendor," 60.

13 The figure appears in "Report of the Bureau of Labour," *Sessional Papers*, Toronto, 1907:184.

14 Kealey, *Workers Respond*, 3–34.

15 Robert Barber, a factory inspector for Ontario's Western District and Toronto's West End, reported in 1899 that "the Transvaal War ... necessitated a large amount of supplies being hurriedly got together, some of which were obtained in Canada for the regular troops. But in addition, the British Government accepted two contingents of volunteers from Canada, and they had to be fully equipped before setting out on their long journey. Clothing, saddlery, harness, wagons and other articles being needed, it was necessary to work some factories overtime to prepare the necessaries in time. The effect of this stimulation extended into this year to a certain extent." See "Annual Report of the Inspector of Factories," *Sessional Papers*, Toronto, 1900.

16 Roberts, "Toronto Metal Workers," 64. Also on the 1903 strike see *Toronto Star*, 19 July 1903, 1. On the Canada Foundry operation in Dovercourt, see "A Day in the Works of the Canada Foundry Co.," *Globe*, 2 March 1907, 10. "Notiziario": "Informazioni sulle condizioni," 75.

17 *Daily Mail and Empire*, 27 June 1896, 6; and "An Italian Fracas," *Daily Mail and Empire*, 7 July 1898, 7.

18 "Notiziario," "Informazioni sulle condizione," 75.

19 Carbone, *Fonti per la storia del Risorgimento*, 16–23, 86–7; Cerruti, "Alcune notizie," 580. References to the statuette makers from Lucca and the street musicians from Basilicata in towns and cities abroad are replete in Italian government statistics. See Leone Carpi's works which allude to many of those statistics, especially *Delle colonie e dell'emigrazione*. Marriage registers and city directories were used to trace the different occupations and the towns of origin of the immigrants. In addition, oral testimony of immigrants or their children was useful.

20 On the *viggianesi* see G. Regaldi, "I viggianesi," in *Usi e costumi di Napoli e contorni*, edited by F. de Bouchard (Milan: Longanesi 1970),

215–23. On Pelletieri, see Schiro, *Americans by Choice*.

21 Robert Foerster makes numerous references to the child street musicians in *Italian Emigration*. Very useful on the problem in general is Florenzano, *Emigrazione italiana*, chap. 7, 151–67 and Bremner, "Children with the Organ Man." Bixio, et al., *Rapport fait au nom du conseil d'administration de la Société Italienne de Bienfaisance de Paris sur la situation des petits italiens* (Paris: Société Italienne de Bienfaisance de Paris 1868); *Report of the Committee of the Charity Organisation Society Appointed to Inquire into the Employment of Italian Children for Mendicant and Immoral Purposes* (London: Charity Organization Society 1877). Camera dei Deputati, *Relazione della Giunta sul progetto di legge ... Probizione dell'impiego di fanciulli in professioni girovaghe* (Città di Castello: S. Lapi 1873). For the problem in England see de'Calboli, *Girovaghi italiani*. For the problem in Chicago, see Vecoli, "Chicago's Italians," 53ff and 101ff.

22 "La prima procedura legale contro la tratta dei fanciulli italiani," *L'Eco d'Italia*, 26 July 1873, 1–2; "The Italian Slaves: Arrest of a Padrone," *New York Times*, 22 July 1873, 5; "Selling Italian Children," *New York Times*, 24 July 1873, 5. The author is presently writing a book on "The Little Slaves of the Harp."

23 Interview with Mr Michael Glionna, 15 Nov. 1978.

24 Advertisement in *Torontonensis*, (University of Toronto yearbook), 1898.

25 Glazebrook, *Story of Toronto*, 219.

26 Bolognani, *A Courageous People*, 283; Briani, *Dalle valli trentine*, 87.

27 Interviews with Mr Attilio Bonavero, 8 Feb. 1982 and Mr Fred Peirolo, 18 Dec. 1981.

28 Interview with Mr Jim Farano, 18 Dec. 1978.

29 Favero and Tassello, "Cent'anni di emigrazione," 25.

30 Ridolfi, *I friulani*, 17–19.

31 *The Marble Worker*, 10, no. 10 (Nov. 1914): 238.

32 Interviews with Mr Gid De Spirt, 1 Oct. 1980 and Mrs Mary Forbes, daughter of Albino Pedron, 27 March 1979.

33 Interviews with Mr Luigi Piccoli, 23 May 1980 and Mrs Albina De Clare, 9 March 1980.

34 Interview with Mrs Maria De Zorzi, 4 May 1978, MHSO. On the housing crisis of the 1900s see James Mavor Papers, coll. 119, Box 70, Arc. 19, Thomas Fisher Rare Book Library, University of Toronto Library. An Ontario Housing Act and a Municipal Housing Act were passed in 1919 and 1920 to provide loans and to ease the erection of

"dwelling houses of a class suitable for the accommodation of persons who have been on active service during the present war ... and working men and working women and men and women of moderate means." See *Statutes of Ontario*, 1919, c. 54 and 1920, c. 84.

35 Interview with Mr Paul Bertoia, 23 May 1978.

36 Interviews with Mr Gid De Spirt, 1 Oct. 1980 and Mr Paul Bertoia, 23 May 1978.

37 See "Annual Report of the City Treasurer of the City of Toronto for the Year Ending December 31, 1884," *City Council Minutes*, Toronto, 1885 and Books of Account, 1870–1886, CTA. Names from these lists were cross-referenced with marriage registers to determine hometowns of the pedlars. *Telegram*, 22 Sept. 1888, 5.

38 Interview with Mr Michael Chiovitti, 2 Oct. 1981. During the 1930s and the 1940s the *boianesi* played a significant role in banana wholesaling and jobbing in Toronto. Families included the Chiovittis, Pitoscias, Riccis, and Pietrangelos.

39 Most information and data in the following section was compiled from *Might's Toronto Directories*, 1885, 1895, 1905, 1915, 1925, 1935; from the *Annuario Italiano*, 1935; and the marriage registers of the three Italian national parishes.

40 Moroni, "Provincia dell'Ontario," 76.

41 On the *genovesi*, telephone interview with Miss M. Deferrari, 13 Jan. 1982. On the *vitesi*, interview with Mrs Rose Catalano, 31 Jan. 1982.

42 On the emigration of the *termitani* see Briggs, *Italian Passage*, 70–2. Between 1901 and 1921, Toronto received about 5 per cent of Termini's annual emigration. On the immigrants from Termini in Chicago, see Vecoli, "Chicago's Italians," 106ff.

43 Granata, "L'avvenire dell'importazione," 7–9.

44 *Mercantile Reference Book*.

45 The Vitese Mutual Benefit Society charter and incorporation papers are in the Business and Partnerships Registry, Department of Consumer and Commercial Relations, Toronto.

46 Financial statements of the Trinacria and Italo-Canadese mutual benefit societies are found in the "Annual Report of the Registrar of Friendly Societies," in "Reports of the Inspector of Insurance," *Sessional Papers*, Toronto, 1915–1930. "... the sources of immigrant social mobility and economic activity are to be found within the cultural and historical traditions of particular ethnic groups and embodied in the collective self-help institutions created by the group." Cummings, introduction to *Self-Help in America*, 9.

47 Goody, "Strategies of Heirship."

48 Apparently the Black Hand or "Banana Society" problem among Sicilians, especially those from Termini Imerese, was serious in various cities in Ohio and Pennsylvania. See report of the Italian consul in Chicago to the Minister of the Interior in Rome, 28 July 1909, Polizia Giudiziaria, b. 60, fasc. 10900.2.31 – 10900.40.57, Malfattori all'estero, AS. On the Black Hand in America, see Thomas M. Pitkin and Francesco Cordasco, *The Black Hand: A Chapter in Ethnic Crime* (Totawa, N.J.: Littlefield, Adams & Co. 1977).

49 I culled this information from a sample of 438 families or bachelors (612 individuals) in 1935. I cross-referenced names beginning with A, B, C, and P with occupations listed in the city directory. For further information, see Zucchi, "Italians in Toronto: Development of a National Identity 1875–1935" (Ph.D. diss., Univ. of Toronto 1983), 164ff.

CHAPTER FOUR

1 On the Italian *padrone* system see Koren, "The Padrone System"; Vecoli, "Italian American Workers"; Iorizzo, "Padrone and Immigrant Distribution"; Harney, "The Padrone and Immigrant."

2 *Globe*, 25 Jan. 1904, 1.

3 See Harney, "King of Labour." On the Veltri agency see Potestio, "Navvies to Builders."

4 "Italian Laborers," *Globe*, 14 Nov. 1883, 1. The Buffalo agent paid one dollar to each foreman for each man he obtained. "Those Deluded Italians," *Toronto Empire*, 9 Aug. 1888, 8. "How Crow's Nest Workmen are Got," *Globe*, 4 June 1898, 6. The report examined complaints regarding low wages, excessive boarding fees, and dishonest practices by railroad contractors towards railway labourers. "Report of the Commissioner Respecting Treatment of Labourers," *Sessional Papers*, Ottawa, 1898.

5 "The Trades Council," *Daily Mail*, 2 June 1888, 13.

6 U.S. Senate, *Reports of the Immigration Commission* (henceforth Dillingham Comm.), vol. 37: 203–350, 61st Cong., 3rd sess., Doc. 662 is a report on "Immigrant Banks."

7 Dillingham Comm., vol. 37: 219–20.

8 See Memorandum from M.B. Scarth (travelling immigration inspector) to W.D. Scott, Dept. of Interior, 9 Dec. 1913; and W.D. Scott (supt. of immigration), to Bryce M. Stewart, Dept. of Labour, 10

Feb. 1916, Immigration Branch Records, RG 76 vol. 579, file 785 496, PAC. Also, *Might's Toronto Directory*, 1900–1915. By 1903 Alberto Dini had set up a branch of his Montreal labour agency in Toronto; his brothers ran the new office. The Glionna family's townsmen in New York, Chicago, and Utica also operated saloons and labour agencies and probably provided their Toronto counterparts with labourers.

9 "Nostre Corrispondenze," *La Fiaccola*, 21 Aug. 1903, 3 and 24 Dec. 1910, 4. *Bersaglieri* clubs were to be found in Montreal and New York, and other American cities at that time.

10 "Le credenziali di un ministro di fede cr ... na ai compagni di Boston Mass.," *Il Proletario* 4 (March 1910): 3–4.

11 *La Fiaccola*, 19 March 1910, 2. The Socialists of course were not the only critics of the bankers. On the poor reputation of Italian immigrant bankers in Montreal, Toronto, and the rest of North America, see Pisani, *Il Canadà presente*, 34–5. See also Vinci, "Banche e banchieri italiani." Vinci was aware of the dishonest practices of many bankers, but he argued that these men were indispensable to the community because of the services they provided. Vinci estimated that about 1,000 Italian immigrant bankers operated in the United States.

12 "An Act Respecting Private, Voluntary and Municipal Employment Bureaux," *Statutes of Ontario*, 1917, c. 37.

13 Information on the agents was obtained from city directories and bankruptcy proceedings and oral testimony of Mr Gatto's relatives.

14 Dillingham Comm., vol. 37: 214–18. Napolitano, *Troppo grano*, 24.

15 Dillingham Comm., vol. 37: 203, 241.

16 See Bonachich, "Middleman Minorities," 588-9.

17 Examination of Giuseppe Gatto, "In the Matter of Giuseppe Gatto", 1933, Bankruptcy Office, Supreme Court of Ontario (henceforth Gatto Bankruptcy Proceedings). On Eugenio D'Angelo, interviews with Mr Rocco D'Angelo, 1 March 1979.

18 Memorandum for registrar and evidence taken before the Honourable Mr Justice Sedgewick at Osgoode Hall, "In the Matter of Francesco Tomaiuolo," 1931, Bankruptcy Office, Supreme Court of Ontario (henceforth Tomaiuolo Bankruptcy Proceedings). Details of the bankruptcy can also be found in the later issues of Tomaiuolo's newspaper, *Il Progresso Italo-Canadese*.

19 Gatto Bankruptcy Proceedings.

20 Tomaiuolo Bankruptcy Proceedings

21 Dillingham Comm., vol. 37: 301–15; Gatto Bankruptcy Proceedings,

evidence, p. 65. On Giannetti, see "Italians are in Great Despair over Loss of their Deposits: Pitiful Scenes in Colony," *Toronto Daily News*, 21 Aug. 1907, 1–2.

22 Dillingham Comm. vol. 37: 215–19; 230–1.

23 Memorandum for Registrar from David Goldstick, Solicitor to the Trustees, Tomaiuolo Bankruptcy Proceedings.

24 Ibid.

25 This and the following data come from the "Statement of Affairs" of the bankruptcy proceedings of Tomaiuolo and Gatto.

26 Affidavit of Maria Giunta, Gatto Bankruptcy Proceedings, 20 Sept. 1933. Comparisons are made to cases in Dillingham Comm., vol. 37: 239; the commission examined thirty-one banks among eight ethnic groups.

27 Obtained by cross-referencing names from the list of deposit creditors in the Tomaiuolo Bankruptcy Proceedings with marriage registers at the three Italian national parishes.

28 Dillingham Comm., vol. 37: 231.

29 "In the Matter of Frank Joseph Glionna," 1928, Bankruptcy Office, Supreme Court of Ontario. Statements of affairs of Tomaiuolo Bankruptcy Proceedings and Gatto Bankruptcy Proceedings.

30 Regarding Puccini and Ciceri memberships see *La Rivista Commerciale* 7, no. 10 (Oct. 1917): 3–4. Ciceri's advertisement appears, for example, in the same magazine 7, no. 12 (Dec. 1917). Paul Ciceri was also the only Italian member of the Toronto Board of Trade, Board of Trade of the City of Toronto, Canada, *Yearbook 1910*.

31 The study of the networks of ethnic economies in North America will require a larger base of sources. From these one could understand more completely the intricacies of the ethnic economy, the manner in which the immigrants' tastes were moulded, and the effect these had on their ethnic identity. Finally, one could also study the influence of the ethnic economy on mainstream society's tastes and the mechanisms by which the ethnic brokers found a niche in the economies of towns and cities (e.g. by selling pasta, olives, or olive oil). See Wilson and Martin, "Ethnic Enclaves."

CHAPTER FIVE

1 Pasteris, "Religione e Clero."

2 Quoted in Bosworth, *Least of Great Powers*, 114.

3 An extremely useful reference on the Holy See's documents regard-

ing the migrant is *Chiesa e mobilità umana: documenti della Santa Sede dal 1883 al 1983* (Rome: Centro Studi Emigrazione 1985). Helpful in formulating this chapter were T. Smith, "Religion and Ethnicity"; Dolan, *Immigrant Church*; Tomasi, *Piety and Power*. On the attitude of anglophone priests in the archdiocese in the 1910s and 1920s, see Scafuro to Archbishop McNeil, October 1924, "National Parishes," Neil McNeil Papers, Box 13, ARCAT.

4 Byrne, *Redemptorist Centenaries*, 374; "Priests," McEvay Papers, ARCAT.

5 McEvay to Sbarretti, 6 July 1908, McEvay Papers; McEvay to Brick (rector of St Patrick's Church), 3 Aug. 1908, McEvay Papers. On national parishes and for an explanation between territoria vs. personal (including national) parishes, see Ciesluk, *National Parishes*.

6 Lawrence Jung Papers, ABPR; Joseph Basso to Thomas Manley, Chancellor, 7 Dec. 1922, "National Parishes," McNeil Papers. See also Archbishop McNeil to the Pastor of St Agnes, 25 July 1923, St Agnes Papers, ARCAT. Crowley to Parziale, 6 Oct. 1934, Parziale Papers, AFPIC. The temporary nature of these parishes must have been a common assumption among the clergy. In a 1920 letter to Archbishop McNeil, Father Scafuro wrote: "The Italian Churches of the city, as it is evident, are only a temporary affair." Scafuro to McNeil, 20 Jan. 1920, "National Parishes," McNeil Papers.

7 McEvay to Brick, 3 Aug. 1908 and Licking to McEvay, 12 Aug. 1908; Licking to McEvay, 12 Aug. 1908, McEvay Papers.

8 Scafuro to McNeil, 13 Jan. 1920 Scafuro Papers, ARCAT; Scafuro to Archbishop McNeil, October 1924, "National Parishes," McNeil Papers.

9 Scafuro to Treacy, 20 Jan. 1920. Longo to McGuigan, 13 April 1936, Longo Papers, ARCAT. Coughlan to Joseph Schneider (Redemptorist Provincial), 17 March 1913, Schneider Papers, ABPR.

10 Various letters, pamphlets, and reports on Italian Methodist missions are available in the United Church Archives, Toronto. See Italian Missions file, *Annual Report of the Missionary Society Methodist Church*, *The Missionary Outlook*, *The Christian Guardian*, *Annual Report of the Home Department*. More specifically, see *The Italian Methodist House of Toronto*, (N.p: n.p. ca. 1910) and "Dufferin Street United Church," both in Toronto-Italian church file, UCA. UCA also contains many issues of *La Favilla*, a bimonthly Italian Methodist magazine published in Toronto by the Methodist minister D.R. Gualtieri. The success of the Methodist missions was from the very

start an incentive for the Catholic archbishop to form an Italian national parish. McEvay wrote to the pastor of St Patrick's Church in 1908 regarding "the Italian people some of whom are being led away by non Catholic money and their children do not attend the Catholic Schools." McEvay to Brick, 3 Aug. 1908, McEvay Papers.

11 Church of England, *First Annual Report*.

12 Unsigned note, n.d., "National Parishes," McNeil Papers; Scafuro to McNeil, 30 Jan. 1920, Scafuro Papers.

13 Report to Neil McNeil for May-June 1913, Papers of the Carmelite Sisters of the Divine Heart, ARCAT.

14 Biographical notes on Fathers Dodsworth, Viglianti, and Bonomo are available in ABPR in their respective files. Biographical information on the other priests assigned to Toronto can be found in their respective files in ARCAT.

15 Scafuro to McNeil, 17 May 1919, Scafuro Papers.

16 Scafuro to McNeil, 30 Jan. "National Parishes," McNeil Papers.

17 Scafuro to Treacy, 20 Jan. 1920, Scafuro Papers.

18 Scafuro to Manley, 10 May 1925, 17 Jan. 1925, Scafuro Papers.

19 Longo to Mgr Kidd, 24 Jan. 1910, Longo Papers.

20 Coughlan to Redemptorist Provincial Joseph Schneider, 17 March 1913, Schneider Papers. Longo sent the archbishop a five-page letter in 1913 when he was transferred to St Agnes Church. He summed up his grievances against the Redemptorists in fifteen points and demanded that amends be made. See Longo to McNeil, 13 March 1913, "National Parishes," McNeil Papers. Also Byrne, *Redemptorist Centenaries*, 375.

21 Longo to McNeil, 11 April 1922, Longo Papers; Cassullo to McNeil, 4 Jan. 1930, McNeil Papers.

22 Longo to Cassullo, 7 Sept. 1930, Longo Papers.

23 Longo to McGuigan, 14 July 1936, Longo Papers; Scafuro to Archbishop McNeil, October 1924, "National Parishes," McNeil Papers.

24 McEvay to Bishop Hickey (of Rochester), 27 April and 13 May 1910. McEvay to Apostolic Delegate, 5 Nov. 1909, Longo Papers. Doglio had been sent to Toronto by the bishop of Buffalo in 1908; the bishop did not want him back in 1910. McEvay to Apostolic Delegate, 28 May 1910; Doglio to McEvay, 13 June 1910; Charles Colton (bishop of Buffalo) to McEvay, 29 Oct. 1908, McEvay Papers. Pisani was aware of Longo's background when he recommended him to McEvay. In a 1908 article he devoted a page to discussing the plight of the poor cleric. See Pisani, "Problemi dell'emigrazione," 516.

25 Curley, *Provincial Story*, 252, 431 n. 126; Byrne, Redemptorist Centenaries, 374.
26 Coughlan to Schneider, 17 March 1913, Schneider Papers.
27 Richard Sittini to Neil McNeil, 11 Aug. and 10 Dec. 1932, Salesian Papers, ARCAT.
28 Alfonso Parziale to James McGuigan, 1 Jan. 1935, "Religious Orders," Franciscan Papers, ARCAT.
29 Parziale to Procurator General of Franciscan Order, Rome, 20 June 1935, Parziale Papers. Also, a copy of the agreement can be found in the Franciscan Papers.
30 Parziale to Archbishop McGuigan (memorandum), 21 June 1937, McGuigan Papers, ARCAT.
31 Sbarretti to McEvay, 3 July 1908, McEvay Papers. Apparently the Glionna family had made attempts earlier to purchase a Methodist chapel for Roman Catholic services for the Italian population.
32 W.G. Licking to McEvay, 12 Aug. 1908, "Priests," McEvay Papers.
33 J. Kidd to Charles Doglio, n.d., (c.a. 1909); McEvay to Apostolic Delegate, 28 May 1910, McEvay Papers.
34 McEvay to Apostolic Delegate, 5 Nov. 1909, Longo Papers.
35 "ARGO" in *La Fiaccola*, 19 March 1910, 3.
36 Unsigned letter by pastor of St Agnes Church (Fr Basso), "Egregi Signori del Comitato e Cari Parocchiani di S. Agnese" ("To Parish Committee and Parishioners"), n.d.; letters of resignation of F.A. Miceli et al. and A. Teolis, 21 March 1923, "Religious Orders," Salesian Papers.
37 Our Lady of Mount Carmel Parish Committee to McNeil, n.d. (ca. 1930), Stephen Auad Papers, ARCAT.
38 Doglio to McEvay, 13 June 1910, McEvay Papers. In fact, Doglio began the letter by complaining that the bishop of Buffalo, to whom he had been recommended by McEvay, had not accepted him and that he might have no job. Ironically, the bishop of Buffalo originally had highly recommended Doglio to the archbishop of Toronto.
39 Byrne, *Redemptorist Centenaries*, 376.
40 Coughlan to Schneider, 17 March 1913, Schneider Papers. In the same way a parishioner at St Agnes complained to the archbishop about the departure of the Salesians in 1934: "Your Excellency will remember that Your church, St Agnes, had virtually no faithful before the Salesians arrived." M.J. Volpone to Neil McNeil, n.d., Salesian Papers. Coughlan to Schneider, 17 March 1913, Schneider Papers.
41 Scafuro to McNeil, 17 May 1919, Scafuro Papers; Longo to Cassullo,

8 Jan. 1930, Longo Papers; Scafuro to Treacy, 20 Jan. 1920, Scafuro Papers.

42 R.F. Kehoe to J.C. McGuigan, 15 March 1939, St Clare Parish Papers, ARCAT.

43 *Progresso Italo-Canadese*: "Per la festa di Villa S. Lucia," 11 June 1931, 3; "Sottoscrizione per la festa di S. Rocco," 27 Aug. 1932, 3; "Un bel gesto," 17 Sept. 1931, 3; "Zelante Michele Pucacco," 25 Sept. 1930, 3; "Ai Pisticcessi [*sic*] di Toronto," 18 June 1931, 3; "Sottoscrizioni pro chiesa," 17 Sept. 1931, 3.

44 "Venerdì Santo," *Progresso Italo-Canadese*, 20 March 1930, 3.

45 Rev. James Frannan to Chancellor, 8 Sept. 1938, Our Lady of Mount Carmel Papers, ARCAT. *Progresso Italo-Canadese*, 17 July 1930, 3.

46 On the problems between the *monteleonesi* and *modugnesi* see Our Lady of Mount Carmel Papers.

47 "Inauguration of Italian Parish," *Catholic Register*, 12 Nov. 1908, 1.

CHAPTER SIX

1 Park and Miller, *Old World Traits*; Warner and Srole, *Social Systems*, 156–219; for the "defensive" view see also Ware, *Greenwich Village* and "Cultural Groups." T. Smith, "Lay Initiative"; "Religious Denominations"; "Religion and Ethnicity"; Greene, *God and Country*.

2 See Higham's introduction, "Ethnic Leadership," in *Ethnic Leadership* and Glazer, "Jews," in *Ethnic Leadership*, 1–18 and 20–35. Also, Greene, " 'Becoming American'."

3 On the "politics of reputation" in the old world see Bailey's "*Signori?*" and "Management of Reputation," both in Bailey, *Gifts and Poison*.

4 Virtually all the major townsgroups in Toronto came from towns which had at least one mutual aid society by the 1880s. The largest such society in Laurenzana was named the *Operaia M.S. Beniamino Franklin*, which, of course, speaks of the influence of the *americani*. See Min. di Agricoltura, Industria e Commercia, *Statistica delle Società*. Population estimate for 1897 is from "Foreigners in Toronto," *Daily Mail and Empire*, 2 Oct. 1897, 10.

5 The board of directors for each society is listed in Annual Report of the Registrars of Friendly Societies, in the "Annual Registrar of Friendly Societies," in the "Annual Report of the Inspector of Insurance," *Sessional Papers*, Toronto, 1893–1913.

6 Pisani, *Il Canadà presente*, 40.
7 See esp. vol. 5 of the Dillingham Comm., *Dictionary of the Races*. The dictionary distinguishes northern and southern Italians as two distinct races.
8 Roman Catholic Separate School Board of Toronto (RCSSB), "Board Minutes," 14 Jan. 1885–4 Aug. 1891, 7 Jan. 1889, MSSBA: 320–21.
9 RCSSB, "Board Minutes," 5 Feb. 1889, MSSBA: 338-39.
10 Regarding the internal colony thesis applied to Afro-American studies, see Michel S. Laguerre, "Internal Dependency: The Structural Position of the Black Ghetto in American Society," *Journal of Ethnic Studies* 6, no. 4 (Winter 1979): 29–44.
11 *Catholic Register*, 23 July 1908, 3.
12 Individuals were traced in *Might's Toronto Directory*.
13 On social status in the old world agrotowns, see Cronin, *Sting of Change* and Lopreato, *Peasants No More*. On the transfer of status from old world towns to the new world ethnic community, see Alex Simirenko, *Pilgrims, Colonists, and Frontiersmen* (London: The Free Press of Glencoe 1964), 5–7.
14 *Catholic Register*, 27 Aug. 1908, 1.
15 Memo for the establishment book, Dept. of Interior, Immigration Branch Records, RG 76 vol. 509, file 785, 496, PAC.
16 A.E. Hacken to Hon. Frank Oliver, 12 May 1910, Immigration Branch Records, RG 76, vol. 509, file 785 496.
17 *Ottawa Free Press*, 15 May 1908. See articles in all Toronto newspapers on four separate murders involving Italians in early 1911: 21 Jan., 31 March, 15 April, and 24 April. Follow-up reports continued for a few days after each murder.
18 W.D. Scott to Frank Oliver, 3 April 1911, Immigration Branch Records, RG 76, vol. 509, file 785 496.
19 F.W. Ungaro to Sir Richard Cartwright, 3 May 1911, Immigration Branch Records, RG 76, vol. 509, file 785 496.
20 Ungaro to Laurier, 29 June 1911, Wilfrid Laurier Papers, MG 260, vol. 688, file 188 263, PAC.
21 Berardo to Oliver, 27 July 1911, Immigration Branch Records, RG 76, vol. 509, file 785 496.
22 Scott to Berardo, 5 Aug. 1911; Deputy Minister to Scott, 10 Aug. 1911; and Supt. of Immigration to D.A.G. Glionna, 12 Aug. 1911, all in Immigration Branch Records, RG 76, vol. 509, file 785 496.
23 Edmund Bristol to Scott, 9 Sept. 1911; Thomas W. Anktell for G.L. Stewart, Dom. Immig. Agent, to W.D. Scott, 14 Sept. 1911, in Immi-

gration Branch Records, RG 76, vol. 509, file 785 496.

24 Sacco to Boselli, 8 June 1908, SDA. The Methodist meeting-hall probably gave Merlino some leverage in the community. For example 14 May 1908, Michael Basso held a meeting for the city's unemployed Italians at the hall (1,200 to 1,500 Italians in the city were unemployed during that depression), *Ottawa Free Press*, 15 May 1908, clipping found in Immigration Branch Records, RG 76, vol. 310, file 286 736. Especially before 1908, Italians had no meeting-places for large groups. Socialists met in the Finnish or Ukrainian halls. When Pietro Pisani held a meeting of the colony regarding the formation of a national parish, he used St George's Hall on Elm Street near Yonge Street. Merlino also sent a letter to Toronto's City Council thanking the council for a grant made by the city for the relief of the sufferers from the Messina earthquake. See *City Council Minutes*, Toronto, 6 Jan. 1909: 369 (#694).

25 "Le credenziali di un ministro di fede Cr ... na – Ai compagni di Boston, Mass., *Il Proletario*, 4 March 1910, 3–4.

26 *Might's Toronto Directory, 1897–1915*; Sacco to Sec-Gen. of the SDA, 18 March 1905, SDA; "Board Minutes," 9 March 1899, 1 April and 4 July 1902, 4 Oct. 1904.

27 *Evening Telegram*, 31 March 1911, 12; Sacco to Sec.-Gen. of SDA, 18 March and 25 May 1905, SDA.

28 Sacco described the plight of the Italians who had come up from the United States during the 1907 depression to work on northern Ontario railroads; see Pisani, *Il Canadà presente*, 43. Sacco to Sec-Gen. of SDA, 15 Jan. 1909; Sacco to Sen. Paolo Boselli, 11 Nov. 1910; Sacco to Boselli, 22 Feb. 1911, SDA.

29 "Italians are in great Despair over loss of their Deposits; Pitiful Scenes in Colony," *Toronto Daily News*, 21 Aug. 1907, 1–2.

30 Pisani, *Il Canadà presente*, 43–5.

31 Ibid., 43.

32 See incorporation papers and charters of Vittorio Emanuele III Society and Italian National Club, files C 401367 and C 6553, Business and Partnerships Registry, Department of Consumer and Commercial Relations, Toronto. On the Sicilian lodges, see Vanni Oranova (Giovanni Danovaro) to Boselli, SDA President, 7 July 1913, SDA.

33 An analogy can be made to Allan H. Spear's discussion of the middle class black leaders who gradually replaced the old blacke élite in Chicago after the turn of the century: "The new leaders ... stood to

benefit from separate Negro development ... their ideas influenced the subsequent course of community development." See *Black Chicago*, 83 and chap. 4, "New Leadership," 71–89.

34 See Barton, *Peasants and Strangers*, 64–90; Briggs, *Italian Passage*, 15–36, 136–82.

35 Incorporation papers, Italian National Club, Business and Partnerships Registry.

36 Constitution of the *Circolo Colombo*, "Committees," McNeil Papers, ARCAT.

37 *Statuto della Società di Mutuo Soccorso*, MHSO.

38 Pisani, *Il Canadà presente*, 40; *La Fiaccola*, 28 Aug. 1909, 6.

39 *City Council Minutes*, Toronto, 31 May 1897: 147. Pisani, *Il Canadà presente*, 40. Estimate of size of the socialist group comes from a letter in the Buffalo Italian socialist newspaper in 1910 regarding a request from a Toronto Socialist for fifty copies of one issues to distribute in Toronto. See *La Fiaccola*, 26 March 1910, 5. Although a small group, Toronto's Socialists were extremely active, holding outdoor assemblies and indoor lectures frequently. They also corresponded regularly with New York's *Il Proletario*, Chicago's *La Parola dei Socialisti*, and Buffalo's *La Fiaccola*. All these papers are available in microform in the Immigration History Research Center, University of Minnesota.

40 Open letter by Pisani to the Italian community of the city, 30 Sept. 1908, Our Lady of Mount Carmel Papers, ARCAT.

41 *Catholic Register*, 23 July 1908, 3.

42 Sacco to Sec-Gen. of SDA, 25 May 1905; Sacco to Boselli, 1 Feb. 1908; Oranova to Boselli, 7 July 1913, SDA.

43 *Globe*, 27 May 1915, 5; *Toronto Daily News*, 27 May 1915, 3; *Toronto Star*, 27 May 1915, 7.

44 A. Smith, "War and Ethnicity," 380.

45 Mollo, a lawyer, was also publisher of *La Tribuna Canadiana* for a short period.

CHAPTER SEVEN

1 Marco Missori, one of the founders, stated that the *Circolo* "should be the base of young men, well-educated in moral, intellectual, civic, and religious senses, that they might occupy the higher positions in the [Italian] public offices of Toronto." *Bolletino Italo-Canadese* 30 (Nov. 1931), clipping in Marco Missori Papers, MG 30 C99, PAC. Mem-

bership lists were obtained from occasional reports in the *PIC* (1929–32). They were cross-referenced with city directories and marriage registers to obtain birthplace and residence of members.

2 The most helpful works for studying Mussolini's program of "exporting fascism" are Diggins, *Mussolini and Fascism*; Cassels, "Fascism for Export"; Salvemini, *Fascist Activities*; Cannistraro, "Fascism and Italian Americans."

3 Salvemini, *Fascist Activities*, 14–16.

4 Cannistraro in Salvemini, *Fascist Activities*, 37n. 152.

5 Diggins, *Mussolini and Fascism*, 80.

6 See *Lease of St Patrick's Hall to Circolo Colombo*, 1 Jan. 1924; *Circolo Cattolico Italo-Canadese* to McNeil, 3 June 1919, "National Parishes," McNeil Papers, ARCAT. The *Circolo* was also responsible for many of the colony's patriotic celebrations. For example, Columbus Day was celebrated annually at their headquarters, St Patrick's Hall on McCaul Street. In 1928 the *Circolo* sponsored Armistice Day commemoration services at Mount Carmel Church, which had probably been an annual event under their auspices until the War Veterans Association assumed control. *PIA*, 16 Oct. 1924, 7; 10 Nov. 1928, 7.

7 For American public opinion in the 1920s and 1930s regarding Mussolini and fascism see Diggins, *Mussolini and Fascism*; for Canadian see Betcherman, *Swastika and Maple Leaf*; Luigi Bruti Liberati, *Il Canada, l'Italia e il fascismo 1919–1945* (Rome: Bonacci 1984). *Globe* article quoted in *PIA*, 24 Nov. 1928, 8. "Traveller Likes 'Il Duce' Dr Thomas O'Hagan, World Traveller," *Toronto Star*, 25 Nov. 1932, 1. Regarding knighting of Goggio and Carboni, *PIC*, 29 Oct. 1931, 3.

8 *PIA*, 31 Jan. 1929, 7 and 31 Aug. 1929, 5. On Chief Draper, see chap. 1 of Betcherman's *The Little Band*; Shaw, "Fascismo and the Fascisti." See also, "Duce's Energy Given Praise, W.A. Mackintosh of Queen's University Addressed Canadian Club and Praised Duce for Seeking Prestige for Italy," *The Globe*, 5 Nov. 1935, 11.

9 Interviews with Mr Ruggero Bacci, 1 and 9 Aug. 1978, MHSO.

10 *PIA*, 15 Nov. 1924, 8 and 4 Jan. 1928, 7. Invidiata was the medical doctor for the Sicilian Trinacria Mutual Benefit Society, and in 1927 the "Sicilian colony" purchased an automobile for him. Those who donated funds were mostly from Termini Imerese.

11 Garibaldi to Mussolini, n.d. (early 1923). "Viaggi di propaganda," Records of the Commissariato Generale dell'Emigrazione, b. 29, fasc. 4, MAE. The niece of the war hero also spoke to the Canadian Club, the Knights of Columbus, the League of Women, the Local Council

of Women, the Jewish Association, Sons of Italy, and the Daughters of the Empire. A summer 1923 report on North American *fasci* by the Italian consul in Boston, Silvano Vitiliani, indicated that a Giuseppe Parosi had organized a *fascio* in Toronto. It is unclear whether the club came under the direction of New York's Central Fascist Council. "Special Report #71," in "Reports of the Psychological Warfare Branch," RG 59, box #5, National Archives, Washington.

12 "Blackshirts Here are Presented with Mussolini's Picture," *Toronto Star*, 24 Aug. 1927, 1.

13 "Le Attività del Prof Ettore Fattori," *PIC*, 6 March 1930, 3. *Bollettino Italo-Canadese*, 23 Oct. 1931, n.p. from Missori Collection, MG30 C99. Also *PIC*, 28 Jan. 1932, 3.

14 On War Veterans Association in Italy see Salvemini, *Fascist Activities*, 118 and Cannistraro's footnote in same, 152. *PIA*, 1 April 1927, 7 and "Camerati," *PIC*, 24 Feb. 1932, 3.

15 As early as, and probably earlier than, October 1924, the colony celebrated Columbus Day at St Patrick's Auditorium; *PIA*, 16 Oct. 1924, 7. Also see *PIA*, 1 March 1927, 7; 1 April 1927, 7; 29 April 1927, 7; 15 March 1928, 7; 19 April 1928, 7; 26 April 1928, 7; 12 Oct. 1928, 9; 22 Oct. 1928, 9; 10 Nov. 1928, 7.

16 *PIA*, 15 March 1928, 7; 26 April 1928, 7; 22 Oct. 1928, 9.

17 See for example, *PIA*, 19 April 1928, 7.

18 *PIA*, 1 March 1927, 7.

19 *PIA*, 29 April 1927, 7.

20 *PIA*, 10 Nov. 1928, 7; *PIA*, 29 March 1929, 7; 29 April 1927, 7. On Maccari see Salvemini, *Fascist Activities*, 19, 33, 112, 193.

21 *PIA*, 19 April 1928, 7.

22 Tommaso Mari et al. to Neil McNeil, n.d., Salesian Papers, ARCAT.

23 Petrucci to Direzione degli Italiani all'Estero (DIE), 12 May 1934. Serie Politiche, 1934, b. 2, fasc. 3, "Miscellaneous," MAE.

24 Ibid.

25 "New Canadian Minister Claims People Fooled into Aiding Fascists – Most Loyal," *Evening Telegram*, 17 June 1940, 17. At the same time (30 June 1929) the Hamilton and Niagara Falls consular offices were closed and replaced by the Toronto vice-consulate. *PIA*, 27 Aug. 1929, 8.

26 Interviews with Ruggero Bacci, 1 and 9 Aug 1978, MHSO. Scattered issues or clippings of the *Bollettino Italo-Canadese* can be found in various collections. The annual Italian city directory, *Annuario Italiano*, is available in the Central Library, Toronto, for the years 1929–

35. No documents have verified the newspaper subsidy; documents in MAE, however, reveal that Montreal's *L'Italia* received an annual subsidy of $2,500 beginning in 1934. See Italian Consul Brigidi (Montreal) to Pol. DIE (telegram), 8 April 1936, in "giornali e giornalisti," b. 4, fasc. 4, Affari Politici Canadà, 1936, Serie Politiche, Canadà, 1934–40 MAE.

27 Diggins, *Mussolini and Fascism*, 116–17.

28 *PIA*, 12 April 1929, 7; 17 April 1929, 7.

29 *PIA*, 23 May 1929, 7; See also, 8 June 1929, 7; 29 June 1929, 8; 27 Aug. 1919, 8.

30 Apparently, at one 4 November Armistice Day commemoration, the Fascists tried to win Fratellanza president, Frank Marrocco, to their side. He almost gave in but was later chided by the mainly antifascist membership of the society. See Principe, "Anti-Fascist Press," 124.

31 *PIC*, 16 Oct. 1930, 3; 20 Oct. 1930, 3; *PIA*, 27 Aug. 1929, 8.

32 *PIC*, 30 Oct. 1930, 3; 23 May 1929, 2.

33 Ibid.

34 *PIC*, 2 Oct. 1930, 3; *PIA*, 16 Oct. 1939, 3.

35 *PIC*, 4 Dec. 1930, 1,3; 26 May 1932, 3,6.

36 *PIC*, 1 May 1930, 1,6.

37 Italy's Ministry of External Affairs published a census of Italian schools abroad in 1927. The census indicated that 112 boys and 120 girls attended Mount Carmel Elementary School; 92 male students and 38 female students attended the Italian Methodist Evening School. The report also noted that an Italian evening school had been formed recently by the *Circolo Colombo*. The numbers of Mount Carmel seem large; it could be that the report gave the total number of Italian children attending St Patrick's School. The Methodist school was operated by the Methodist pastor, Nestor Cacciapuoti. Lieutenant Montanari, an official in the War Veterans Association, taught two Italian classes weekly in 1928–9 at St Agnes Hall (the Italian Hall). Classes were organized by the Salesian fathers. See *PIA*, 18 Oct. 1928, 7; *PIC*, 8 Oct. 1931, 6; *Censimento degli italiani*, appendix, MAE.

38 *PIC*, 4 Feb. 1932, 3; 20 March 1930, 3. Regarding participation by the various social organizations in fundraising see "Ballo Loggia #4 della Società di Aiuto e Protezione," *PIC*, 7 April 1931, 3. "Fratellanza," *PIC*, 7 April 1932, 3; "Stella Alpina," 24 Sept. 1931. The *Circolo Filodramatico C. Goldoni* held a benefit performance in the Ukrainian Hall on 3 March 1932; *PIC*, 10 March 1932, 6. *PIC*, 26 Feb. 1931, 3.

39 Interviews with Mr Ruggero Bacci, 1 and 9 Aug. 1978, MHSO.
40 Assistant Deputy Minister of Immigration, F.C. Blair, memo for file, 19 Sept. 1934, Immigration Branch Records, RG 76, vol. 130, file 28885, part 9, PAC.
41 G. Sabino, Acting Vice-Consul, Toronto, to Mr Henderson, 27 June 1935, RCSSB, "Board Minutes," 1932–35, 9 July 1935; "Board Minutes," 1932–35, 12 March 1935; "Management Committee Minutes," 3 March 1936, MSSBA. The advertisement for the parochial school of St Mary of the Angels in 1937 indicated that an Italian teacher "nominated by the Royal Consul," taught Italian. *Programma ricordo della chiesa italiana di S. Maria degli Angeli* (Toronto, June 1937), St Mary of the Angel's Parish Papers, ARCAT. RCSSB, "Board Minutes," 1932–35, 12 March 1935, MSSBA.
42 *Toronto Star*, 28 March 193, 2.
43 *Toronto Star*, 28 March 1939, 2; RCSSB, "Minutes of the Committee of Supervision," 5 May 1939, MSSBA. See Committee on Legislation Meeting in Board of Control Report No. 5, Appendix "A", *City Council Minutes*, Toronto, 1939: 475, 657–8, 732–3.
44 Diggins, *Mussolini and Fascism*, 123–5; Salvemini, *Fascist Activities*, 118–23. *PIC*, 29 Oct. 1931, 8; 12 Nov. 1931, 1,3; 26 Nov. 1931, 3; 7 Jan. 1932, 4. Regarding the uniforms, see MAE to Con. Gen., Ottawa, 14 April and 22 June 1932, Affari Politici, Canadà, Serie Politiche, Canadà, 1934–40, MAE. The issue is discussed in Pautasso, "Cinquantesimo anniversario," 9.
45 *PIC*, 24 Feb. 1932, 3. *PIC* berated the renegades stating that it was "Benito Mussolini who gave veterans their true value."
46 "Minacce di ricatto," *L'Emigrato*, 30 March 1932, 2. "Nessune minacce di ricatto," *PIC*, 7 April 1932, 3.
47 "Nessune minacce di ricatto," 3.
48 The *Casellario Politico Centrale* (CPC) files at the national archives in Rome have dossiers on eight Italian Toronto anti-Fascists and Anarchists. Information was collected on them by the Italian vice-consulate in the city and the consulate-general in Ottawa and sent back to Rome. See files of Arturo Pittana, Augusto Ongaro, Nicola Giancotti, Ernesto Gava, Attilio Bortolotti, Armando Borghi, and Ruggiero Benvenuti in CPC, AS. One of the more memorable antifascist demonstrations occurred in August 1935. Outside the Oddfellows Temple at College Street and Spadina Avenue 150 demonstrators marched, while indoors, lawyer Nicholas F.A. Scandiffio and Dr Rosario Invidiata tried to explain the Italian view in the Italian-Ethi-

opian crisis; a fracas broke out as the two groups clashed. "Toronto Italians Fight in Street Over War Issue," *Toronto Star*, 13 Aug. 1935, 1, 21.

49 *La Voce Operaia* was published from 1933–4; *Il Lavoratore* from 1936–8; and *La Voce degli Italo-Canadesi* from 1938–40. For a review see Principe, "Anti-Fascist Press." Mr Principe describes the newspapers as "very modest" by today's standards, with a circulation of 500 to 700 per issue. He also states that at its apex in 1933–4, the Mozzini club had 150 members.

50 *PIC*, 17 Sept. 1931, 3, 7. See for example, *PIC*, 8 Oct. 1931, 3.

51 *L'Emigrato*, 30 March 1932, 1. In an equally eloquent editorial in *La Voce degli Italo-Canadesi*, an anti-Fascist from Pisticci, Donato Di Giulio, criticized the Jewish racialist decrees of 1938 in Italy. He saw fascism as epitomizing the sunset of a civilization. He called for Italians in Canada to carry on the great civilization of the Italian people: "If great racial problems created by the fascist government exist in Italy we in Canada must be united in one people made up of many races, governed by the same laws ..." n.d. D. Di Giulio Papers, MHSO.

52 Napolitano, *Troppo grano*, 8, 19–27.

53 See Italian Aid and Protective Society, Business and Partnerships Registry, Department of Consumer and Commercial Relations, Toronto. See also, constitution of the society in the same file. The front cover of the constitution states at bottom, centre: "Organized by D.A.G. Glionna." The booklet was printed by Tommaso Mari's Italian Publishing Co.

54 Correspondence on the matter is in Immigration Branch Records, RG 76, vol. 130, file 28885, part 5. Under-Sec. to Thomas Mulvey to Deputy Minister of Immigration, 22 April 1920; copy of resolution received by Mulvey, 22 April 1920; R.T. Rutherford (Canadian Immigration official at Ellis Island) to Commissioner of Immigration, Eastern District, Ottawa, 14 May 1920. Copy of resolution signed by D.A.G. Glionna and F.D. Ungaro, 23 Nov. 1920; Ungaro to Mulvey, 1 Dec. 1920; F.C. Blair to Ungaro, 10 Dec. 1920.

55 *PIA*, 25 Jan. 1925, 6.

56 S.W. Jacobs to D.A.G. Glionna, 28 Dec. 1926; Jacobs to W.G. Egan (Dep. Min. of Immig.), 28 Dec. 1926; Egan to Jacobs, 29 Dec. 1926, Samuel Jacobs Papers, MG 27 III, C3 – vol V, 1612–14, PAC. See also Agriculture and Colonization, *Minutes of Proceedings*, appendix D. The issue of many Italians coming in all at once in 1926 came up at

this committee meeting. Hon. Edwards complained that "we had a case yesterday where in 1926, when things were supposed to be tightened up, and these permits were issued to responsible Members of Parliament, 300 were brought in at one crack, Italians. I do not want to say anything against Italians, but Italians are Italians. Those from the Northern part of Italy are good farmers, I believe, and they are very different from the people in the South of Italy, very different indeed."

57 See "evidence of Sidney Wise," n.d. (ca. 1929), Case of Forgery in Name of Thomas Gelley, Immigration Branch Records, RG 76, vol 340, file 35784, part 1.

58 *PIA*, 14 Jan. 1926, 8; 8 March 1928, 7; *PIC*, 4 Dec. 1930, 3.

59 For example, for 24 May 1932 celebrations see *PIC*, 26 May 1932, 3.

60 "Italian Girls of Ontario Will Tour through Italy," *Globe*, 13 July 1934, 5.

61 "Italians to Build Cultural Centre," *Globe*, 5 Nov. 1934, 5. "Denies Italians Here Linked with Fascists," *Telegram*, 21 Oct. 1936, 2. Petrucci advised his superiors that it was best to keep Italian *fasci* in Canada independent of any indigenous Canadian fascist movements. See, for example, Petrucci to MAE, CGAP and DIE, 7 May 1934, "Rapporti Politici," b. 1, fasci. 1, Aff. Pol. Canadà 1934, Serie Politiche, Canadà, 1934–40, MAE.

62 "Italian Canadian would fight Duce," *Toronto Star*, 27 May 1940, 2.

CONCLUSION

1 Eugenio Bonardelli, *Lo Stato di S. Paolo del Brasile e l'emigrazione italiana* (Turin: Fratelli Bocca 1916), 120; quoted in Foerster, *Italian Emigration*, 431 n.1.

Bibliography

MANUSCRIPTS

Canada

Ottawa

Public Archives of Canada (PAC)
Immigration Branch Records, RG 76
Samuel Jacobs Papers
Wilfrid Laurier Papers
Manuscript Census of Canada, 1861, 1871, and 1881
Marco Missori Papers
Multiculturalism Records

Toronto

Archives of the Metropolitan Separate School Board (MSSBA)
"Board Minutes, 1888–1940."
"Minutes of the Committee of Supervision, 1935–40."
"Standing Committee on Management, Minutes, 1880–1940"

Archives of the Roman Catholic Archdiocese of Toronto (ARCAT)
Parish Files:
Our Lady of Mount Carmel. Parish Papers, Marriage, and Baptismal Registers.
St Agnes. Parish Papers, Marriage, and Baptismal Registers.
St Clare. Parish Papers.

St Clement. (St Mary of the Angels). Parish Papers, Marriage, and Baptismal Registers.
St Mary. Marriage Registers.
St Michael's Cathedral. Marriage Registers.
St Paul. Marriage Registers.

Priest's and Bishop's Files:
Stephen Auad Papers
Joseph Bagnasco Papers
Marco Berardo Papers
Joseph Longo Papers
Fergus McEvay Papers
James McGuigan Papers
Neil McNeil Papers
Aloysius Scafuro Papers

Religious Order Files:
Carmelite Sisters of the Divine Heart Papers
Dominican Order Papers
Franciscan Order Papers
Salesian Order Papers

Bankruptcy Office, Supreme Court of Ontario
In the Matter of the Authorized Assignment of Frank Joseph Olionna carrying on business under the name of GENERAL IMPORT CORPORATION in the city of Toronto, in the Province of Ontario, file 690-28, 1928.
In the Matter of the Bankruptcy of Francesco Tomaiuolo, Carrying on Business in the City of Toronto, in the County of York, file 585-31, 1931.
In the Matter of Giuseppe Gatto trading as G. Gatto and Co. of the City of Toronto in the Province of Ontario, file 503-33, 1933.

City of Toronto Archives (CTA)
Assessment Rolls, 1878–88.
Books of Account: Board of Police Commissioners: Licences – Cash Distribution Journal, 1870–86.
Directory of the Town of York, 1832, 1833.

Multicultural History Society of Ontario (MHSO)
Ruggero Bacci Interviews

Donato Di Giulio Papers
Elena Grittani Papers
Statuto della Società Mutuo Soccorso Italo-Canadese

Ontario Department of Consumer and Commercial Relations, Business and Partnerships Registry. Incorporation Records:
Italian Aid and Protective Society, 1920
Italian National Club, 1907
Vitese Mutual Benefit Society, 1935
Vittorio Emanuele III Mutual Benefit Society, 1902

United Church Archives

University of Toronto Libraries
Thomas Fisher Rare Book Library, James Mavor Papers, Coll. 119.

Italy

Laurenzana
Archivio Comunale di Laurenzana. *Registro delle nascite*, 1870–1900.

Pisticci
Archivio Comunale di Pisticci. *Registro delle nascite*, 1985–1925.

Rome

Archivi Parlamentari (in AS)
Polizia Giudiziaria
Presidenza Zanardelli, 1902–. Ministero dell'Interno.

Archivio dello Stato (AS)
Casellario Politico Centrale
"Giunta parlamentare d'inchiesta sulle condizioni nelle provincie meridionali e nella Sicilia (1904–8)."
Ministero dell'Interno, Commissariato civile per la Sicilia.

Archivio Storico del Ministero degli Affari Esteri (MAE)
"Viaggi di propaganda e studio nel Canadà della Signa Italia Garibaldi (1923–26)." Records of the Commissariato Generale dell'Emigrazione.
Serie Politiche, Canadà, 1934–40.

Serie seconda, Divisione "delle legazioni" e divisione "consolare" 1861–69, III: Pacchi della corrispondenza ricevuta dal ministero, 3[a] serie, pacco 253, "rapporti del consolato, Montréal 1861–69."

Società Nazionale Dante Alighieri (SDA)
Dante Alighieri Society, Toronto, Papers.

Vita
Archivio Comunale di Vita. *Registro delle nascite*, 1900–35.

United States

Brooklyn, N.Y.

Archives of the Baltimore Province of the Redemptorists (ABPR)
Umberto Bonomo Papers
Cyril Dodsworth Papers
Lawrence Jung Papers
Joseph Schneider Papers
Domenico Viglianti Papers

New York, N.Y.

Archives of the Franciscan Province of the Immaculate Conception (AFPIC)
Alfonso Parziale Papers
St Agnes Parish Papers

Washington, D.C.

National Archives
"Special Report #71. "Reports of the Psychological Warfare Branch," RG 59, box 5. (Documents found in the Ministry of Popular Culture, Rome.)

GOVERNMENT DOCUMENTS

Canada

Ottawa
Agriculture and Colonization. Select Standing Committee. *Minutes of*

Proceedings and Evidence and Report. Ottawa 1928.
Canadian Parliamentary Guide. Ottawa 1912, 1936, and 1947.
Department of Labour. *Labour Gazette*. Ottawa 1908.
Dominion Bureau of Statistics. *Census of Canada*. Ottawa 1891, 1901, 1911, 1921, 1931, 1941.
Revised Statutes of Canada. Ottawa 1903 and 1919.
Royal Commission on the Relation of Capital and Labour. Vol. 5: *Evidence Ontario*. Ottawa 1889.
Ottawa. *Sessional Papers*, 1898, no. 90A, "Report of the Commissioner Appointed to Inquire Into Complaints Respecting the Treatment of Labourers on the Crow's Nest Pass Railway."
Ottawa. *Sessional Papers*, 1905, no. 36b, "The Royal Commission Appointed to Inquire into the Immigration of Italian Labourers to Montreal and the Alleged Fraudulent Practices of Employment Agencies."

Ontario

Legislative Assembly of Ontario. *Sessional Papers*. Toronto 1880–1940.
Statutes of Ontario. Toronto 1918–20.

Toronto

Board of Trade of the City of Toronto. *Yearbook 1910*. Toronto 1911.
Bureau of Municipal Research. *What is the "Ward" Going to do with Toronto? A Report on Undesirable Living Conditions in One Section of the City of Toronto*. Toronto 1918.
City of Toronto. *City Council Minutes*, 1880–1940.
Department of Health. *Report of the Medical Health Officer Dealing with the Recent Investigation of Slum Conditions in Toronto*, 1911.
Toronto Home and School Council. *Preliminary Report of Canadian Citizenship Committee*, 1923.

Italy

Atti della giunta per l'inchiesta agraria e sulle condizioni della classe agricola (Jacini Commission), Tome II, fasc. IV & V and vol. VIII, tome II. Rome: Tip. del Senato 1883–85, AS.
Ministero degli Affari Esteri: MAE. *Censimento degli italiani all'estero alla metà dell'anno 1927*. Rome: MAE 1928.
Ministero di Agricoltura, Industria e Commercio, Direzione Generale della Statistica. *Statistica della emigrazione italiana nell'anno 1884–5*. Rome: Tip. di Camera dei Deputati 1886.

Ministero di Agricoltura, Industria e Commercio, Direzione Generale della statistica. *Statistica delle Società di mutuo soccorso e delle istituzioni cooperative annesse alle medesime, anno 1885*. Rome: MAE 1886.

Ministero di Agricoltura, Industria e Commercio, Direzione Generale della Statistica. *Statistica della emigrazione italiana nell'anno 1887*. Rome: Tip. Aldina 1888.

United States

Koren, John. "The Padrone System and Padrone Bankers." *Bulletin of the Dept. of Labor* 9 (March 1897): 112-29.

U.S. Senate. *Reports of the Immigration Commission* (Dillingham Commission). 61st Cong., 3rd sess., Doc. 662, 1911.

INTERVIEWS

Ruggero Bacci, 1 and 9 August 1978
Paul Bertoia, 23 May 1978
Attilio Bonavero, 8 February 1982
Rose Catalano, 31 January 1982
Michael Chiovitti, 2 October 1981
Albina De Clare, 9 March 1980
M. Deferrari (telephone interview), 13 January 1982
Gid De Spirt, 1 October 1980
Maria De Zorzi, 4 May 1978
Jim Farano, 18 December 1978
Mary Forbes, 27 March 1979
Michael Glionna, 15 November 1978
Fred Peirolo, 18 December 1981
Luigi Piccoli, 23 May 1980

NEWSPAPERS AND PERIODICALS
(Published in Toronto unless otherwise indicated)

The Catholic Register (Kingston, Ontario)
The Christian Guardian
The Daily Mail and Empire
L'Emigrato
The Evening Telegram
La Favilla

La Fiaccola (Buffalo, N.Y.)
The Globe
The Globe and Mail
The Marble Worker (New York)
Missionary Bulletin (of the Methodist Church)
Missionary Society of the Methodist Church. *Annual Report*
The New York Times (New York)
Ottawa Free Press
La Parola dei Socialisti (Chicago)
Il Progresso Italo-Americano (New York)
Il Progresso Italo-Canadese
Il Proletario (New York)
The Toronto Daily News
The Toronto Empire
The Toronto Star

THESES

Alexander, S. June. "The Immigrant Church and Community: The Formation of Pittsburgh's Slovak Religious Institutions, 1880–1914." PH.D.diss., University of Minnesota 1980.

Craig, Joyce Carol. "Associations of Persons of Italian Origin in Toronto." Master's thesis, University of Toronto 1957.

Gregg, Marjorie W. "The Housing Problem in a City Block." Master's thesis, University of Toronto 1916.

Potestio, John A. "From Navvies to Railway Builders: the History of Vincenzo and Giovanni Veltri, Founders of R.F. Welch Limited, 1885–1932." Master's thesis, Lakehead University 1982.

Quinn, George Wm. "Impact of European Immigration Upon the Elementary Schools of Central Toronto, 1815–1915." Master's thesis, University of Toronto 1968.

Sidlosky, Samuel. "Post-War Immigrants in the Changing Metropolis with Special Reference to Toronto's Italian Population." PH.D. diss., University of Toronto 1969.

Sturino, Franc. "Inside the Chain: A Case Study in Southern Italian Migration to North America, 1880–1930." PH.D. diss., Ontario Institute for Studies in Education 1981.

Vecoli, Rudolph J. "Chicago's Italians Prior to World War I: A Study of their Social and Economic Adjustment." PH.D. diss., University of Wisconsin 1963.

Zucchi, John E. "*Paesani* in a Toronto Neighbourhood: Italian Immigrants in the 'Ward,' 1870–1940." Master's thesis, University of Toronto 1979.

BOOKS, ARTICLES, AND PAMPHLETS

Albonico, Erminio. *Saggio di una prima inchiesta sulla emigrazione italiana in Europa*. Milan: Opera Bonomelli 1921.

Alexander, June Granatir. "City Directories as 'Idea' Censuses: Slovak Immigrants and Pittsburgh's Early Twentieth-Century Directories as a Test Cast." *Western Pennsylvania Historial Magazine* 65, no. 3 (July 1982): 203-20.

Annuario Italiano: Toronto, Ontario. Toronto: Italian Information Bureau 1929–35.

"Avvertenze per gli emigrati diretti in Canadà." *Bollettino d'Informazione* (of the *Ufficio Italiana sul Lavoro e sull'emigrazione*, New York) II, 49 (18 May 1911):4.

Azimonte, Eugenio. *La colonizzazione in Basilicata*. Rome: Tip. del Senato del Dott. G. Baroli 1929.

Bailey, F.O., ed. *Gifts and Poison: The Politics of Reputation*. London: Basil Blackwell 1971.

Banfield, B.C. *The Moral Basis of a Backward Society*. New York: The Free Press 1958.

Barton, Joseph J. *Peasants and Strangers. Italians, Rumanians, and Slovaks in an American City, 1890–1950*. Cambridge: Harvard University Press 1975.

– "Eastern and Southern Europeans." *Ethnic Leadership in America*. Edited by John Higham. Baltimore: The Johns Hopkins University Press 1978: 150–75.

Bator, Paul Adolphus. "Health and Poverty in Toronto, 1910–1921." *Journal of Canadian Studies* 14, no. 1 (Spring 1979): 36-49.

Bell, Margaret. "Toronto's Melting-Pot." *Canadian Magazine* XLI, no. 3 (July 1913): 3-38.

Berger, Carl C. *A Sense of Power: Studies in the Ideas of Canadian Imperialism 1867–1914*. Toronto: University of Toronto Press 1970.

Bernardy, Amy A. *America vissuta*. Turin: Fratelli Bocca Editori 1911.

Betcherman, Lita Rose. *The Swastika and the Maple Leaf: Fascist Movements in Canada in the 30's*. Toronto: Fitzhenry and Whiteside 1975.

Bianco, Carla. *The Two Rosetos*. Bloomington: Indiana University Press 1974.

Blok, Anton. "South Italian Agro-towns." *Comparative Studies in Society and History* XI (1969): 121-35.

Bolognani, Bonifacio. *A Courageous People from the Dolomites: The Immigrants from Trentino on U.S.A. Trails*. Trento: Edition and Patronage of the Autonomous Province in Trento 1981.

Bonachich, Edna. "A Theory of Middleman Minorities." *American Sociological Review* 38 (1973): 583–94.

Bonardelli, Eugenio. "Il Dominio del Canadà e la nostra emigrazione." *Italia Gens* III, no. 10–11 (Oct.-Nov. 1912): 294–324.

Bossange, Gustave. *La nuova Francia: Il Canada, antica colonia francese. Appello alle classi operaie*. Paris: Gustave Bossange, Allan Lines Agent 1873.

Bosworth, R.J.B. *Italy, The Least of the Great Powers: Italian Foreign Policy before the First World War*. London: Cambridge University Press 1979.

Bremner, Robert. "Children with the Organ Man." *American Quarterly* 8 (Fall 1956): 277–82.

Brenna, Paolo G. *L'Emigrazione italiana nel periodo ante bellico*. Roma: Lib. ed. Manteguzza di Paolo Cremonese 1928.

Breton, Raymond. "Institutional Completeness of Ethnic Communities and the Personal Relations of Immigrants." *American Journal of Sociology* LXX (1964): 193–206.

Briani, Vittorio. *Dalle valli trentine per le vie del mondo*. Trento: Trentini nel Mondo 1980.

– *Il lavoro italiano all'estero negli ultimi cento anni*. Rome: Italiani nel Mondo 1970.

Bridle, Augustus. "The Drama of the Ward." *Canadian Magazine* 34, no. 11 (Nov. 1909): 3–38.

Briggs, John W. *An Italian Passage: Immigrants to Three American Cities, 1890–1930*. New Haven: Yale University Press 1978.

Brown, R.C. and R. Cook. *Canada, 1896–1921. A Nation Transformed*. Toronto: McClelland and Stewart 1974.

Byrne, John F. *Redemptorist Centenaries 1832–1932*. Philadelphia: The Dolphin Press 1932.

"Canadà." *Emigrazione e Lavoro* VII, no. 9 (March 1921): 13.

"Canadà: gli italiani nella provincia dell'Ontario." *Boll. Emig.* 5 (1927): 62–64.

Cannistraro, Philip V. "Fascism and the Italian Americans." *Perspectives in Italian Immigration and Ethnicity*. Edited by S.M. Tomasi. New York: Center for Migration Studies 1977: 51–66.

Carbone, Salvatore. *Fonti per la storia del Risorgimento italiano negli Archivi Nazionali di Parigi: I rifugiati italiani*, 1815–1830. Rome: Institutio per la Storia del Risorgimento Italiano 1962.

Caretta, Edoardo. "Gli italiani all'estero: insegno e patriottismo." *RE* anno III, fasc. 3–4 (Mar.–April, 1910): 34–6.

Carpi, Leone. *Delle colonie e dell'emigrazione d'italiani all'estero sotto l'aspetto dell'industria, commercio, agricoltura con trattazione d'importanti questioni sociali*, 4 vols. Milan: Lombarda 1874.

Cassels, Allen. "Fascism for Export: Italy and the United States in the Twenties." *American Historical Review* 49, no. 3 (April 1964): 707–12.

Cavalieri, Enea. "Il dominio del Canadà: appunti di viaggio." *Nuova Antologia* 12 (1879): 700–47; 14 (1879): 319–53 and 665–92.

Cerruti, Luigi. "Alcune notizie." *Boll. Cons.* (1861): 580.

Chapman, Henry. "Commerce et navigation du Canada." *Boll. Cons.* 1, no. 7 (Aug. 1962): 481–83.

Church of England. Mission to the Italians of Toronto & Canada. *First Annual Report 1899–1900*. Toronto: Church of England 1900.

Cianfarra, Camillo. "La conservazione dell'italianità negli emigranti nell'America del Nord." *RC* anno 6, serie 2, vol. 2, fasc. 6 (10 June 1911): 120–2.

Ciesluk, Joseph. *National Parishes in the U.S.* Washington: Catholic University of America 1944.

Cinel, Dino. *From Italy to San Francisco: The Immigrant Experience*. Stanford: Stanford University Press 1982.

– "The Seasonal Emigration of Italians in the Nineteenth Century: From Internal to International Destinations." *Journal of Ethnic Studies* 10, no. 1 (1982): 43–68.

Ciuffoletti, A. and M. Degl'Innocenti. *L'emigrazione nella storia d'Italia, 1868–1975*. 2 vols. Florence: Vallecchi 1978.

Clark, C.S. *Of Toronto the Good*. 1897. Reprint. Toronto: Coles 1970.

Clough, Shepard B. *The Economic History of Modern Italy*. New York: Columbia University Press 1964.

Cohen, Abner, ed. *Urban Ethnicity*. London: Tavistock Publication 1974.

Conzen, Kathleen Neils. *Immigrant Milwaukee, 1830–1860:* Accommodation and Community in a Frontier City. Cambridge Mass: Harvard University Press 1976.

Cosattini, Giovanni. "L'emigrazione temporanea del Friuli." *Boll. Emig.* 3 (1904): 3–94.

Cronin, Constance. *The Sting of Change: Sicilians in Sicily and Australia.* Chicago: University of Chicago Press 1970.

Cummings, Scott, ed. *Self-Help in Urban America: Patterns of Minority Economic Development.* New York: Kennikat Press 1980.

Curley, Michael J. *The Provincial Story: A History of the Baltimore Province of the Congregation of the Most Holy Redeemer.* New York: The Redemptorist Fathers Baltimore Province 1963.

de'Calboli, R. Paulucci. *I girovaghi italiani in Inghilterra ed i suonatori ambulanti.* Città di Castello: S. Lapi 1893.

De Luca, Paolo Emilio. *Della emigrazione europea: ed in particolare di quella italiana.* Vol. 2. Turin: Fratelli Bocca 1909.

De Marco, William M. *Ethnics and Enclaves: Boston's Italian North End.* Ann Arbor, Mich: UMI Research Press 1981.

De Stefani, Carlo. *Il Canadà e l'emigrazione italiana.* Florence: Mariano Ricci 1914.

Deutsch, Karl. *Nationalism and Social Communication: An Inquiry into the Foundations of Nationality.* 2d ed. Cambridge Mass: The M.I.T. Press 1969.

"Di alcune notizie sulla provincia dell'Ontario." *RE* anno 7, fasc. 5 (May 1914): 146–60, and fasc. 6–7 (June–July 1914): 186–90.

Diggins, John P. *Mussolini and Fascism: The View From America.* Princeton: Princeton University Press 1972.

Di Marco, Luigi Arcuri. "L'emigrazione siciliana all'estero nel cinquantennio 1876–1925." *Studi sul lavoro degli italiani all'estero: con particolare riferimento ai lavoratori siciliani.* N.p: Regione Siciliana n.d.

Di Stasi, Michael. *50 years of Italian Evangelism: The Story of St Paul's United Church Toronto.* Toronto: St Paul's Italian United Church 1955.

Dobb, Lawrence W. *Patriotism and Nationalism: Their Psychological Foundations.* New Haven: Yale University Press 1964.

Dolan, Jay P. *The Immigrant Church: New York's Irish and German Catholics, 1815–1865.* Baltimore: The Johns Hopkins University Press 1975.

Dore, Grazia. *La democrazia italiana e l'emigrazione in America.* Brescia: Morcelliana 1964.

Douglass, William A. *Echalar and Murelaga: Opportunity and Rural Exodus in Two Spanish Basque Villages.* London: C. Hurst and Co. 1975.

Douglass, William A. and Jan Bilbao. *Amerikanuak: Basques in the New World.* Reno, Nevada: University of Nevada Press 1975.

"L'educazione tecnico-professionale delle classi lavoratrici nel Canadà."

Emigrazione e Lavoro 5, no. 9 (Nov. 1921): 1–3.
"L'emigrazione italiana nel Canadà." *Emigrazione e Lavoro* 7, no. 9 (Sept. 1923): 11–15.
"Emigrazione nel Canadà." *Emigrazione e Lavoro* 5, no. 1–2 (Jan.–Feb. 1921): 12.
"L'emigrazione per il Canadà." *L'emigrazione italiana dal 1910 al 1923: relazioni presentate a S.E. il Ministro degli Affari Esteri della CGE.* Roma: CGE 1926: chapter 2.
Favero, Luigi and Graziano Tassello. "Cent'anni di emigrazione italiana (1876–1976). "*Un secolo di emigrazione italiana: 1876–1976.* Edited by Gianfausto Rosoli. Rome: Centro Studi Emigrazione 1978: 9–64.
Florenzano, Giovanni. *Della emigrazione italiana in America comparata alle altre emigrazioni europee.* Naples: Giannini 1874.
Foerster, Robert F. *The Italian Emigration of our Times.* Cambridge: Harvard University Press 1919.
Fontana, Vittorio. *La Dante e l'emigrazione.* Senigallia: Società Dante Alighieri 1906.
Fratellanza Mutual Benefit Society. *Constitution.* Toronto: Fratellanza Society 1924.
Freidl, Ernestine. "Kinship, Class and Selective Migration." *Mediterranean Family Structures.* Edited by J.G. Peristiany. Cambridge: Cambridge University Press 1976: 363–87.
Freye, Fredrick W. "Socialization to National Identification Among Turkish Peasants." *The Journal of Politics* 30, no. 4 (Nov. 1968): 934–65.
Gerber, David. "Ethnics, Enterprise, and Middle Class Formation: Using Dun and Bradstreet Collection for Research in Ethnic History." *The Immigration History Newsletter* 12, no. 1 (May 1980): 1–7.
Gianelli, Angelo. "Sulle presenti condizioni del Canadà." *Bolletino Consolare* 8, part 2, fasc. 7 (July 1872): 87–120.
Gibbon, J. Murray. *The Canadian Mosaic: The Making of a Northern Nation.* Toronto: McClelland and Stewart, 1938.
– "The Foreign Born." *Queen's Quarterly* 27 (April–June 1920): 331–51.
Glazebrook, G.P. de T. *The Story of Toronto.* Toronto: University of Toronto Press 1973.
Goheen, Peter, G. *Victorian Toronto, 1850–1900: Pattern and Process of Growth.* Chicago: University of Chicago Press 1970.
Goody, Jack. "Strategies of Heirship." *Comparative Studies in Society and History* 15 (Jan. 1973): 3–16.
Granata, Genserico. "L'avvenire dell'importazione italiana in America." *La Rivista Commerciale* (8 Aug. 1917): 7–9.

Greene, V. "Becoming 'American': The Role of Ethnic Leaders – Swedes, Poles, Italians, Jews. *The Ethnic Frontier: Group Survival in Chicago and the Midwest.* Edited by Melvin G. Holli and Peter D'A. Jones, Grand Rapids Mich: Wm. B. Eerdmans Publishing Co. 1977: 143–75.

Greene, Victor. *For God and Country: The Rise of Polish and Lithuanian Ethnic Consciousness in America.* Madison, Wisc: The State Historical Society of Wisconsin 1975.

Gualtieri, D.R. "Italian Methodist Mission in Toronto." *The Missionary Outlook* 42, no. 1 (May 1922): 355.

Gutman, Herbert. "Work, Culture, and Society in Industrializing America." *American Historical Review* 78, no. 3 (June 1973): 531–88.

Hall, D.J. *Clifford Sifton: Vol. I, The Young Napoleon.* Vancouver: University of British Columbia Press 1981.

Handlin, Oscar. *The Uprooted.* Boston: Little, Brown 1951.

Harney, Robert F. "Boarding and Belonging." *Urban History Review* 2 (October 1978): 8–37.

– "Chiaroscuro: Italians in Toronto 1885–1915." *Italian Americana* 1, no. 2 (1975): 142–67.

– "The Commerce of Migration." *Canadian Ethnic Studies* 9, no. 1 (1977): 42–53.

– *Italians in Canada.* Occasional Papers on Ethnic and Immigration Studies, OP 78–1. Toronto: MHSO 1978.

– "Men Without Women" Italian Migrants in Canada, 1885–1930." *Canadian Ethnic Studies*, 1, no. 1 (1979): 57–84.

– "Montreal's King of Italian Labour: A Case Study of Padronism." *Labour-Le Travailleur* 5 (1979): 57–84.

– "The Padrone and the Immigrant." *The Canadian Review of American Studies* 5, no. 2 (1974): 101–18.

– "Toronto's Little Italy, 1885–1945." *Little Italies in North America.* Edited by R.F. Harney and J.V. Scarpaci. Toronto: MHSO 1981: 41–62.

– "Entwined Fortunes: Multiculturalism and Ethnic Studies in Canada." *Siirtulaisuss-Migration* 3(1974–84): 68–94.

Hayes, Carlton J. *Essays on Nationalism.* New York: The Macmillan Co. 1926.

– *Nationalism: A Religion.* New York: The Macmillan Co. 1960.

Higham, John. "Current Trends in the Study of Ethnicity in the United States." *Journal of American Ethnic History* 2, no. 1 (1982): 5–15.

– ed. *Ethnic Leadership in America.* Baltimore: The Johns Hopkins University Press 1978.

Iorizzo, Luciano. "The Padrone and Immigrant Distribution." *The Italian Experience in the United States*. Edited by S.M. Tomasi and M.H. Engel. New York: Center for Migration Studies 1970: 43–76.

Isajiw, Wsevolod W. *Definitions of Ethnicity*. Occasional Papers in Immigration and Ethnicity, OP 79–6. Toronto: MHSO 1979.

"Italia e Canadà." *RC* anno 5, vol. 1, fasc. 4 (10 May 1910): 108–12.

Italian Aid and Protective Society. *Constitution*. Toronto: Italian Aid and Protective Society 1920.

Italian Methodist Mission, Toronto. *Directory of Services*. Toronto: n.p. n.d.

Italian Methodist Mission, Toronto. *The Italan Methodist Mission House of Toronto*. Toronto: n.p. n.d.

James Robertson Memorial Committee. *Our Non-English Speaking Canadians*. N.p. 1917.

Kealey, Gregory S. *Toronto Workers Respond to Industrial Capitalism, 1867–1892*. Toronto: University of Toronto Press 1980.

King, John. *McCaul; Croft; Forneri: Personalities of Early University Days*. Toronto: Macmillan Co. 1914.

King, William Lyon Mackenzie. "Foreigners who Live in Toronto," *Daily Mail and Empire*, 25 Sept. 1897 and 2 Oct. 1897: 10.

Laguerre, Michel S. "Internal Dependency: The Structural Position of the Black Ghetto in American Society." *Journal of Ethnic Studies* 6, no. 4 (1979): 29–44.

Levi, Carlo. *Cristo si è fermato a Eboli*. Turin: Einaudi 1946.

Linkh, Richard M. *American Catholicism and European Immigrants 1900–1924*. New York: Center for Migration Studies 1975.

Lopreato, Joseph. *Peasants No More*. Scranton, Penn.: Chandler Pub. Co., 1967.

Lynch, Kevin. *The Image of the City*. Cambridge, Mass: The MIT Press 1960.

Macdonald, John S. and D. Leatrice. "Chain Migration, Ethnic Neighbourhood Formation and Social Networks." *Millbank Memorial Fund Quarterly* 42 (1964): 82–97.

Manzotti, Fernando. *La Polemica sull'emigrazione nell'Italia unita*. Rome: Soc. Ed. Dante Alighieri 1962.

Masters, D.C. *The Rise of Toronto, 1850–1890*. Toronto: University of Toronto Press 1947.

m.b. Review of *Il Canadà presente e futuro in relazione alla emigrazione italiana*, by Pietro Pisani. *RE* anno III, fasc. 1 (Jan. 1910): 44–45.

McLaren, Duncan, ed. *Ontario Ethno-Cultural Newspapers, 1835–1972*.

Toronto: University of Toronto Press 1973.
McLaughlin, Virginia Yans. *Family and Community: Italian Immigrants in Buffalo, 1880–1930*. Ithaca: Cornell University Press 1977.
The Mercantile Agency Reference Book. New York: R.G. Dun & Co. Sept. 1925.
Methodist Young Men's Association. *The Italians*. Toronto: n.p. 1904.
Might's Greater Toronto City Directory. Toronto, 1867–1940.
Molinaro, Julius. "Giacomo Forneri (1789–1869): From Turin to Toronto." *Mosaico* (Sept. 1975): 14–16.
Morawska, Eva. "The Internal Status Hierarchy in the East European Communities in Johnstown, Pa. 1890–1930s." *Journal of Social History* 16, no. 1 (1982): 75–108.
Moroni, Girolamo. "La provincia dell'Ontario." *Boll. Emig.* (15 April 1915): 69–88.
Moss, Leonard and Stephen C. Cappanari. "Estate and Class in a South Italian Village." *American Anthropologist* LXIV (1962): 287–300.
Mother Mary Teresa of St Joseph. *The Servant of God, Mother Mary Teresa of St Joseph: An Autobiography*. Translated by Berchmans Bittle OFM Cap. Wisconsin: Carmelite Convent n.d.
Mulvaney, C. Pelham. *Toronto Past and Present until 1882*. Toronto: W.E. Caiger 1884.
Napolitano, G.G. *Troppo grano sotto la neve: un inverno al Canadà con una visita a Ford*. Milan: Casa Editrice Ceschina 1936.
Nelli, Humbert S. *Italians in Chicago 1880–1930. A Study in Ethnic Mobility*. New York: Oxford University Press 1970.
"Notiziario," "Di alcune notizie sulla provincia dell'Ontario (Canadà)." *RE* anno 7, fasc. 5 (May 1914): 155.
"Notiziario." "Informazioni sulle condizioni dell'emigrazione italiana nella Provincia di Ontario (Canadà)." *Boll. Emig.* 14 (1913): 73–75.
"O.G.C." "La circoscrizione consolare italiana nell'America del Nord." *La Vita Italiana all'Estero* anno 3, fasc. 5 (Jan. 1915): 48–50.
Park, Robert E. "Succession, an Ecological Concept." *American Sociological Review* 1 (April 1936): 171–9.
Park, Robert E. and Herbert A. Miller. *Old World Traits Transplanted*. Chicago: University of Chicago Press 1921.
Pasteris, Emiliano. "Religione e clero in America." *RISS* anno 16, vol. 47 (1908): 3–42.
Pautasso, Luigi. "Conquantesimo anniversario di fondazione dell'Associazione dei Combattenti di Toronto (1927–1977)." *Quaderni Canadesi* 2, no. 2 (Jan.–Feb. 1978): 9.

Pedrotti, Pietro. *L'emigrazione del Trentino.* Rome: Unione Economica Nazionale per le Nuove Provincie Italiane 1918.

Pertusio, Mario. "L'amor patrio degli emigranti." *RE* anno 7, fasc. 5 (May 1914): 129–33.

"Un Piemontese." "Risorgimento italiano negli Stati Uniti d'America." *Rassegna Nazionale* 154, fasc. 16 (June 1907): 721–43.

Pisani, Pietro. "I problemi dell'emigrazione italiana." *Rassegna Nazionale* part 2, vol. 46, fasc. 184 (April 1908): 508–18.

"L'agricoltura nel Canadà centrale." *RISS* anno 16, vol. 49 (Feb. 1909): 223–9 and (March 1909): 321–41.

– *Il Canadà presente e futuro in relazione all'emigrazione italiana.* Rome: Tip. dell'Unione coop. Editrice 1909.

– "L'emigrazione italiana nell'America del Nord." *RISS* anno 18, vol. 54 (1911): 321–49.

Pitsula, James. "The Emergence of Social Work in Toronto." *Journal of Canadian Studies* 14, no. 1 (Spring 1979): 35–42.

Positano, Maria. "L'emigrazione femminile nella Provincia di Bari." *RE* 7, no. 3 (March 1914): 65–75.

Possentì, Carlo. *Relazione al Sig. Min. Del Lavoro. Pubblici di visite delle opere di ponti e strade e di porte, spiagge e fari nelle provincie siciliane.* Milan: Tip. Internazionale 1875.

Pozzetta, George E. "The Mulburry District of New York City: The Years Before World War I." *Little Italies in North America.* Edited by R.F. Harney and J.V. Scarpaci. Toronto: MHSO 1981: 7–40.

Prato, Giovanni. "L'emigrazione della fame in Basilicata." *Rassegna nazionale* 81 (1903): 28–40.

Preziosi, Giovanni. "Il problema politico-intellectuale dell'emigrazione." *RE* anno 1, fasc. 6 (Aug 1908): 1–20.

Principe, Angelo. "The Italo-Canadian Anti-Fascist Press in Toronto, 1922–40." *NEMLA Italian Studies* 4 (1980): 119–37.

Ramirez, B. "Ethnic Studies and Working Class History." *Labour/Le Travail* 19 (1987): 45–8.

Ramirez, Bruno and Michael Del Balso. *The Italians of Montreal: From Sojourning to Settlement 1900–1921.* Montreal: Les Editions du Courant 1980.

– "Montreal's Italians and the Socioeconomy of Settlement: Some Historical Hypotheses." *Urban History Review* 10, no. 1 (June 1981): 39–48.

Ridolfi, Luigi. *I friulani nell'America del Nord.* Udine: N.p. 1931.

– *Lacrime cristiane.* Udine: Arti Grafiche Friulane 1952.

– *Quadri e cuori*. Udine: Arti Grafiche Friulane 1947.
Roberts, Wayne. "Toronto Metal Worker and the Second Industrial Revolution, 1890–1914." *Labour-Le Travailleur* 6 (1980): 49–72.
Rosoli, Gianfausto, ed. *Un secolo di emigrazione italiana: 1876–1976*. Rome: Centro Studi Emigrazione 1978.
Rossi, Adolfo. "Per la tutela degli italiani negli Stati Uniti." *Boll. Emig.* 16 (1904): 1–136.
– "Vantaggi e danni dell'emigrazione nel mezzogiorno d'Italia." *Boll. Emig.* 13 (1908): 3–99.
Rossi, Egisto. *Del patronato degli emigranti in Italia e all'estero*. Relazioni al Primo Congresso Geografico Italiano Genova 1892. Genova: Tip. del R. Istituto Sordo-Muti 1893.
– "Delle condizioni del Canadà rispetto all'emigrazione italiana." *Boll. Emig.* 4 (1903): 3–28.
Rutherford, Paul, ed. *Saving the Canadian City: The First Phase 1880–1920*. Toronto: University of Toronto Press 1974.
Saint Mary of the Angels Roman Catholic Church. *Programma ricordo della chiesa italiana di S. Maria degli Angeli*. Toronto: St Mary of the Angels 1937.
Salvemini, Gaetano. *Italian Fascist Activities in the United States*. Edited by Philip V. Cannistraro. New York: Center for Migration Studies 1977.
Schafer, Boyd C. *Faces of Nationalism*. New York: Harcourt Brace Jovanovich 1972.
Schiro, George. *Americans by Choice: History of the Italians in Utica*. 1940 Reprint. New York: Arno Pres 1975.
Sereni, Emilio. *Il capitalismo nelle campagne (1860–1900)*. Turin: Einaudi 1947.
Shaw, J.E. "Fascismo and the Fascisti." *University of Toronto Monthly* 23, no. 7 (April 1923): 339–40.
Sherwood, W.A. "The Italian Fruit Vendor." *The Canadian Magazine* 6, no. 1 (Nov. 1895): 60.
Smith, Anthony D. *Nationalism in the Twentieth Century*. Oxford: Martin Robertson and Co. 1979.
– "War and Ethnicity: The Role of Warfare in the Formation, Self Images and Cohesion of Ethnic Communities." *Ethnic and Racial Studies* 4, no. 4 (Oct. 1981): 375–97.
Smith, Denis Mack. *Italy: A Modern History*. Ann Arbor: University of Michigan Press 1969.
Smith, Timothy. "Lay initiative in the Religious Life of American

Immigrants, 1880–1950." *Anonymous Americans: Explorations in 19th Century Social History*. Edited by Tamara Hareven. Englewood Cliffs N.J.: Prentice-Hall 1971: 214–49.
– "Religion and Ethnicity in America." *American Historical Review* 83, no. 5 (Dec. 1978): 1155–85.
– "Religious Denominations as Ethnic Communities: A Regional Case Study." *Church History* 35 (1966): 207–26.
Smith, W.G. *Building the Nation: A Study of Some of the Problems Concerning the Church's Relation to the Immigrants*. Toronto: The Canadian Council of the Missionary Education Movement 1922.
– *A Study in Canadian Immigration*. Toronto: Ryerson Press 1920.
Società Italo-Canadese. Constitution. Toronto: Mutual Benefit Society 1919.
Spada, A.V. *The Italians in Canada*. Ottawa and Montreal: Canada Ethnia 1969.
Spani, Cesare. *Pisticci di ieri, Pisticci di oggi*. Ostia: Luigi Spani 1979.
Spear, Allan H. *Black Chicago: The Making of a Negro Ghetto, 1890–1920*. Chicago: University of Chicago Press 1967.
Thistlewaite, Frank. "The Atlantic Migration of the Pottery Industry." *Economic History Review* 2nd series, XI (1958): 264–78.
– Migration from Europe Overseas in the 19th and 20th Centuries." XIe Congrès International des Sciences Historiques. *Rapports V: Histoire Contemporaine*. Goteborg-Stockholm-Uppsala: Almquist and Wiksell 1960: 32–60.
Thompson, John Herd. *Canada 1922–1939: Decades of Discord*. Toronto: McClelland and Stewart 1985.
Timlin, Mabel. "Canada's Immigration Policy." *Canadian Journal of Economics and Political Science* 26, no. 4 (Nov. 1960): 517–32.
Tomasi, Silvano M. *Piety and Power: The Role of the Italian Parishes in the New York Metropolitan Area: 1880–1930*. New York: Center for Migration Studies 1975.
Trow's New York City Directory, 1871–79.
Vangelisti, Guglielmo M. *Gli Italiani in Canada*. Montreal: Chiesa Italiana di N.S. Della Difesa 1958.
Vecoli, Rudolph J. "*Contadini* in Chicago: A Critique of *The Uprooted*." *Journal of American History* (Dec. 1964): 404–19.
– "The Formation of Chicago's 'Little Italies.' " *Journal of American Ethnic History* 2, no. 2 (1983): 5–20.
– "Italian American Workers, 1880–1920: Padrone Slaves or Primitive Rebels?" *Perspectives in Italian Immigration and Ethnicity*. Edited by

S.M. Tomasi. New York: Center for Migration Studies 1977: 25–50.
– "Prelates and Peasants: Italian Immigrants and the Catholic Church." *Journal of Social History* 2 (Spring 1969): 217–68.
Vinci, Adolfo. "Banche e banchieri italiani negli Stati Uniti." *Rivista Coloniale* anno 4, vol. 6, fasc. 12 (Dec. 1909): 1139–56.
Vittorio Emanuele III Mutual Benefit Society. *Constitution*. Toronto 1902.
Ware, Caroline. "Cultural Groups in the United States." *The Cultural Approach to History*. Edited by Caroline Ware. New York: Columbia University Press 1940.
– *Greenwich Village 1920–1930: A Comment on American Civilisation in the Post-War Years*. Boston: Houghton Mifflin Co. 1935.
Warner, Sam Bass and Colin B. Burke. "Cultural Change and the Ghetto." *Journal of Contemporary History* 4 (Oct. 1969): 173–87.
Warner, William Lloyd and Leo Srole. *The Social Systems of American Ethnic Groups*. New Haven: Yale University Press 1945.
Watson, James L. *Emigration and the Chinese Lineage: The 'Mans' in Hong Kong and London* Berkeley: University of California Press 1975.
Weaver, Emily P. "The Italians in Toronto." *Globe Saturday Magazine*, 10 July 1910: 2.
Weaver, John C. "The Modern City Realized: Toronto Civic Affairs, 1880–1915." *The Usable Urban Past: Planning and Politics in the Modern Canadian City*. Edited by Allan F.J. Artibise and Gilbert A. Stelter. Toronto: Macmillan and Co. 1979: 39–72.
Wilson, Kenneth L. and W. Allen Martin. "Ethnic Enclaves: A Comparison of the Cuban and Black Economies in Miami." *American Journal of Sociology* 88, no. 1, 35–60.
Woodsworth, J.S. *Strangers Within Our Gates*. 1909. Reprint. Toronto: University of Toronto Press 1972.
"XXX." "Per l'italianità all'estero." *Nuova Antologia* 83, fasc. 866 (16 Jan. 1908): 337–344.
Zanini, Ludovico. *Friuli migrante*. 1932. Reprint. Udine: G.B. Doretti 1964.
Zucchi, John. *The Immigrants of the St John's Ward: Patterns of Settlement and Neighbourhood Formation*. Occasional papers on Ethnic and Immigration Studies, OP 81–10. Toronto: MHSO 1978.

Index